HOLLYWOOD LIVES

MOVIE STARS *in the* GOLDEN AGE,
their own stories

HOLLYWOOD LIVES

Graham
Bannock

outskirtspress
DENVER, COLORADO

The opinions expressed in this manuscript are solely the opinions of the author and do not represent the opinions or thoughts of the publisher. The author has represented and warranted full ownership and/or legal right to publish all the materials in this book.

Hollywood Lives
Movie Stars in the Golden age, their own stories
All Rights Reserved.
Copyright © 2012 Graham Bannock
v3.0 r1.0
First published in Great Britain in 2011 by © Graham Bannock, 2011

Cover Photo © 2012 JupiterImages Corporation. All rights reserved - used with permission.

This book may not be reproduced, transmitted, or stored in whole or in part by any means, including graphic, electronic, or mechanical without the express written consent of the publisher except in the case of brief quotations embodied in critical articles and reviews.

Outskirts Press, Inc.
http://www.outskirtspress.com

ISBN PB: 978-1-4327-8432-4
ISBN HB: 978-1-4327-8049-4

Outskirts Press and the "OP" logo are trademarks belonging to Outskirts Press, Inc.

PRINTED IN THE UNITED STATES OF AMERICA

Contents

Prologue vii
Introduction xv

Chapter 1:   Hollywood As It Was 1
Chapter 2:   Past and Present 31
Chapter 3:   Fact or Fiction? 49
Chapter 4:   Hollywood Exiles 71
Chapter 5:   Fighting the Studios 101
Chapter 6:   Errol Flynn: The Wildest One 125
Chapter 7:   The Dark Side 145
Chapter 8:   Sensitive Tough Guys and the Genres 173
Chapter 9:   Music and Prejudice 191
Chapter 10:   Hollywood Trials 213
Chapter 11:   Actors in Politics 233
Chapter 12:   Sterling Hayden: The Wandering Star 255

Conclusion 275
Acknowledgements 285
References – General 287
References – Books by Actors 297
Index 313

Prologue

An Autograph Hunter Meets Miss Lizabeth Scott

Lizabeth Scott, Finler/Paramount

I CAUGHT THE movie bug in my early teens and it has never left me. The English town we lived in had three cinemas: the Central or 'flea pit' which had wooden benches like church pews for the cheapest seats; the Gaumont and the Odeon. The Odeon is still there, though divided into several smaller cinemas, the big cream-white tiles decorating the exterior apparently untouched by time. The Odeon was my favourite, as I recall. It did not, like the Gaumont, have an electric organ which rose out of the front apron, but it did have layers of rich curtains, very deep carpets, and variable lighting which could illuminate the dimpled interior walls in an infinite variety of shades.

I particularly remember one summer afternoon in the late 1940s going to see *Desert Fury* (1947), which billed Lizabeth Scott, Wendell Corey, Burt Lancaster and John Hodiak, all studio-nurtured young stars on the way up. Mary Astor was also in it but she was nearing the end of a career that had started in the silent movies of the 1920s. I was not aware of these finer points at the time, nor did I know that the film had been panned by the critics. Halliwell (2006) says that it is a confused melodrama with 'unconvincing characters mouthing unspeakable lines in an airless tedium'.[1] I loved it, but could remember only a few scenes including one in which Burt Lancaster, whom I believe was the sheriff, was belting along a road across the Nevada desert with siren howling and red light flashing on his way to rescue Lizabeth Scott from a murderer's grasp. I do remember coming out of the cinema into the sunshine, past the bicycle racks and into reality (always a let-down). I was thinking that the fascinating larger-than-life-sized characters on the big screen were as remote, and would remain as remote, from my life as the Greek gods I was reading about at school.

꩜

Over fifty years – and thousands of films – later, I was fortunate enough to attend an award ceremony in London at

---

[1] Halliwell's judgements are often not to my taste, especially where they concern films notable for their entertainment and production values, rather than artistic merit or moral purpose. Desert Fury, not having been screened for sixty-five years or so, was reissued on DVD in 2008. A second viewing confirmed my youthful judgement, though in my innocence I had not noticed the homosexual sub-theme in the plot.

which a lot of movie stars were present in person.[2] As on all great Hollywood occasions – for that is what it was, despite the location and the presence of several famous British stars and television personalities – cars disgorged the glittering famous onto a red carpet before crowds of fans. Unlike today, security was minimal; in fact, the London usherettes were so busy gawking at the stars we were not even asked to show our tickets. The theatre on that winter's night was cold, a cold mitigated only a little by the human warmth of a packed house. This was because all the doors were left wide open, presumably whoever was responsible for that was also star-gazing.[3]

The Master of Ceremonies, Robert Wagner, introduced a number of acts. The one I liked best was Ann Miller, who vigorously tap-danced in a skirt slashed to the thigh, showing off her undiminished legs and looking much as she did in *On the Town* (1949). The actual award-winners included Diana Rigg and Anthony Quinn. Quinn and Alan Bates did their *Zorba the Greek* (1964) dance. In his acceptance speech Quinn said something, undoubtedly true but somewhat undiplomatic I thought in a theatre packed with fans, to the effect that fans were important but it was the esteem of one's colleagues that mattered most. Douglas Fairbanks Jnr, who at eighty-five looked frail, but spoke in a powerful voice, introduced Ginger Rogers; sadly she was in a wheelchair. She said, among other things that she trod on Fred Astaire's feet sometimes but he never trod on hers and that she had had a wonderful life. One of the 200 in the audience who stood up and bowed as

---

2 The International Arts Achievements Awards Ceremony at the Dominion Theatre, London, on 18 December 1994.
3 The programme did list some 200 stars and apart from the ones mentioned below I came close enough to them to recognise the following: June Allyson, Eddie Bracken, Kathryn Grayson, June Haver, Roddy McDowall, Jane Powell, Cliff Robertson, Jane Russell and Esther Williams, as well as two British stars, John Mills (who received an award) and Tommy Steele.

Wagner introduced him, was an upright gentleman who was described as the first boy in the Tarzan series.[4] Shirley Bassey outshone and certainly outshouted a contemporary company of dancers and singers.

The night of 200 stars, 1994, Ginger Rogers, Anthony Quinn, Douglas Fairbanks Jr, Anthony Hopkins on stage: photograph courtesy David Koppel.

At the urinal in the men's room, I found myself sandwiched between Robert Wagner and Alan Bates, but it did not seem appropriate to ask for autographs in there. During

---

4   This was Johnny Sheffield (1931–2010). He died after falling off a ladder while trimming a palm tree at his home in California.

the intermission, the stars mingled with the audience and Quinn, who seemed bad-tempered and tense, merely nodded when I asked for his autograph. Sir Anthony Hopkins was bumped into me by the crowd and also gave me his with little grace, though perhaps he was confused by the crush. Patrick Macnee (*The Avengers*) was standing in a corner on his own and was cheerful and welcoming, as was Van Johnson (*The Caine Mutiny*, 1954). I knew that Johnson had been a dancer in vaudeville early on and I asked him if he was still a 'hoofer'. He took my pen (none of them had a pen), replied 'Sure!' with his wry smile, and pumped my hand vigorously. He seemed pleased but did not prolong the conversation. I waited while Petula Clark talked to an acquaintance but she turned towards me with that familiar way some celebrities have of talking to you as if they know you well. She was exceptionally warm and friendly and was most concerned not to write over someone else's signature.

Then I saw Lizabeth Scott, her bright eyes and blonde hair across her cheekbones instantly recognisable. She was embracing a lady who said that Scott was her favourite star. I could not in all honesty say the same, but I murmured something about *Desert Fury* and how I would never forget her in it and we chatted about that for a moment. When I asked for her autograph, she grasped my pen with the fingers in unexpected places, her hand stiff, I supposed, with arthritis. She leaned against me in the crowd, small and lightness itself, and wrote her name with extreme care. That done, she gave me a peck on the cheek. Surprised, I thanked her and began to turn shyly away. To my further astonishment I heard her calling out 'Goodbye' in that unmistakable husky, lisping voice. I turned and we exchanged smiles and the crowd closed around her. That was enough, you could not beat that:

a three-minute emotional relationship with a Hollywood Great.[5] It was easy, really, autograph-hunting, until you met screen goddess Lizabeth Scott and realised she was a warm, vulnerable person, like you and me.

It was about the time of the 200-star show that I first turned to reading movie autobiographies. Most of these books were very readable and a few were arrestingly well written. This is not really surprising since actors are, after all, story-tellers, even if usually of other people's stories. Some, of course, were boring or egotistic or both, but the books run the gamut of human experience. Some actors, such as Charles Chaplin or Anthony Quinn, started off in acute poverty, others in well-to-do families (Raymond Massey, Robert Stack); and some ended in relative, if contented, deprivation (Veronica Lake). Some of these books are lively and amusing and grippingly readable (Evelyn Keyes); some almost continuously funny (Peter Ustinov); others rather serious and informative (Charlton Heston). Some deal with discrimination (Ricardo Montalbán, Sidney Poitier); some are sad, even tragic (Eva Bartok, Frances Farmer). Some stars, like Alan Ladd and Gail Russell, were completely destroyed by Hollywood. Others were given not only wealth but real creative opportunities, and a few, even in writing their

---

5   Lizabeth (also Lisabeth) Scott was born of Slovakian immigrant parents in 1922 and therefore must have been about seventy-two when I met her. She made only twenty-three films, mostly from the mid-1940s to the mid-1950s. Originally a stage actress, her film debut was in 1945 in You Came Along with Robert Cummings. Her beauty and acting ability led to immediate popular success. She was not at all overshadowed by Barbara Stanwyck and Kirk Douglas (which is saying something) in The Strange Love of Martha Ivers (1946), although she had a much smaller part, and appeared with Humphrey Bogart as a femme fatale in Dead Reckoning (1947). Other leading men she appeared with in mostly noirish films, including Charlton Heston, Edmond O'Brien, Dick Powell, Robert Ryan, Robert Mitchum and, in a Western, Alan Ladd. She virtually retired after the 1950s and never married. Her valedictory appearance was in Pulp (1972) with Michael Caine and Mickey Rooney.

books, contributed to literature and history. I hope that this celebration of movie autobiographies will encourage new generations to read these books, which, despite the unending flow of stuff on Hollywood, remain a neglected genre.

Introduction

THIS BOOK IS about Hollywood in the Golden Age (1930–50), the people who made the movies and those who starred in them. That period was golden because it was the time when the big studios ruled film-making, prospered (with ups and downs), and produced many memorable films. The best of these films have stood the test of time and fortunately more and more of them are now available on DVD for anyone to see. There is a perennial fascination with the Golden Age. In 1970, MGM sold off many thousands of items of memorabilia which now change hands at high prices. It was recently reported that the ruby-red shoes worn by Judy Garland in *The Wizard of Oz* (1939) are now valued at over $5 million. The appearance of more and more biographies of their parents by sons and daughters of Golden Age stars is further evidence of the enduring interest in the period. Fairly recent examples are from the families of Humphrey Bogart, Errol Flynn, Cary Grant, Glenn Ford, Lana Turner, Johnny Weissmuller and Loretta Young, many of whose parents did not write autobiographies of their own. These books are all affectionate and sympathetic, though there are also biographies by sons and daughters which denigrate their parents (for example, those about Joan Crawford, Bing Crosby and Bette Davis).

There have, of course, been many books about the stars and studios of that time. This one is unique because it is largely based on the autobiographies of the stars themselves, on their own stories. Perhaps half of the bigger stars of the period have written their personal record of the time and these books seem to be a somewhat neglected resource. Certainly no one has ever written at length about screen autobiographies as a genre and they have received little or no academic attention. Mostly available for a few pounds or dollars in the used book trade, the autobiographies of the movie stars of the past are now rarely read.

Screen actors do not see all aspects of film-making, of course, because, though insiders, as they certainly were, they worked only near the front end of the production process. There is not much in the books about the anti-trust suits, finance and organisation which concerned the actor's bosses. I have tried to fill in these gaps from other sources, mostly in Chapters 1, 10 and 13. The autobiographers, however, did say a lot about things which impinged directly upon them or their colleagues: the anti-Communist witch-hunt of the 1940s; their essays into politics (where they made any); their relationships with the studio bosses; the nature of acting and film-making; and the high and low points of their personal lives. Their lives, in many cases, included stage experience and jobs in various professions prior to their discovery and, for some, war service – a richer mixture than most film actors of today have had. Quite a number of the actors came from abroad and some experienced racial or other social discrimination. Some found being a Hollywood film star acutely stressful – or at best unsatisfying – while for others it was everything they had dreamed it would be. For only a very few was it just a job of work.

Film-making was, and still is, a business. The people who governed the studios (and indeed most of the actors), however much they loved the movies, were also in it for the large amounts of money that could be made. The stars who wrote the books considered here were enormously important to the studios. Their presence helped the public to choose which films to see and helped to reduce the considerable risks in making them. Nevertheless, overheads were high – actors under contract were paid whether they were used or not – and, their costs, like those of technicians and distribution systems, were fixed. The studios invested heavily in nurturing, training and developing their stars. These considerations were not fully appreciated by our actor-writers who, for example, often deeply resented being loaned out to other studios, often at a profit.

On the whole, the actors, perhaps not surprisingly, did not fully understand the implications of the profit motive from the studio's point of view, for example the discipline that the profit motive exerted and which necessitated the decisions taken on story selection and development, casting, hiring and firing and loan-outs which the actors might not necessarily agree with. One thread that runs through most of the autobiographies is a sense of dissatisfaction with the roles the actors were selected for. These decisions were made by studio heads and producers, often ruthlessly. Of course, the bosses were not always right about what the public would want, but it is pretty clear that their judgements were, on the whole, better than those of the actors and there is ample evidence for that in this book. The studio bosses were often tyrannical, but also rational; loan-outs for example, reduced the costs of maintaining a stable of stars, widened their experience and allowed the industry to share scarce talent.

One of the fascinating features of the movie business is that it is so difficult to predict what will please the public, whose ticket-buying decisions then drive the whole process (today cinema box-office is only a minor part of the total). The wishes of the public had to be followed, however, even if they were sometimes led a little by adventurous producers and directors. A key economic characteristic of film-making is that producers never know for sure whether or not a film will be successful until all the expense in its production has been incurred and the film shown. Another key factor in the economics and organisation of movie production is the fact that, unlike the makers of motor cars or TV sets, for film producers each product is different. Finished films are the result of a collaborative, creative effort and mass production methods cannot be used. The tensions between the executives in New York who looked after distribution and financial matters and the creative producers at the studios on the West Coast are rooted in these conflicts between art and business. William Goldman, the screenwriter, said that, in Hollywood 'No one knows anything'. This does not mean that producers were stupid; their judgement and experience eliminated many potential errors before production. Because the camera sees things on the set that the human eye does not fully perceive, however, even as a film is being made, you cannot be sure exactly how it will look on the screen. This is one reason why, every afternoon, the producers watched 'the dailies', the unedited batches of the takes. But the fact remains that even when the film is edited and put together, it is still not at all easy to judge whether it will succeed with the public. This is why 'sneak previews' were held in suburban cinemas before release to gauge audience reaction. Previews allowed essential changes to be made, though at heavy cost, if necessary. Even then there could be uncertainties: members of the public do not know what they want until they have seen it.

Things were not easy for the actors, either. Often final scripts were only ready on the day shooting began and not infrequently just for the portion that would be shot that day. Long stays on location could turn out to be very uncomfortable and even dangerous. The actors rarely knew what film they would be working on next. Brian Aherne compared being an actor with taxi drivers on the rank: waiting for the next assignment to an unknown destination. Shooting films was also made difficult for the actors by the fact that, for economic reasons, the films are rarely shot in sequence. Unlike live theatre, there is no immediate audience reaction. Acting on the stage is very different from filming, for example, more exaggerated gestures and voice projection are necessary – but where they have had experience of both our actor-writers are virtually unanimous: they prefer working on the stage to the film set.

The neglect of star autobiographies may result from preconceived ideas that movie stars are either untruthful or perhaps simply vacuous. In fact, with a few exceptions, these books seem to be remarkably truthful. Many are very well written, even when professional help or ghost writers have not been employed – after all, actors are essentially story-tellers. The range of the experiences revealed is amazing – who would have expected glamour girl Hedy Lamarr to have patented the basic technology of wifi communications and the mobile telephone, or that Errol Flynn shot a man in New Guinea in self-defence, or that the day Virginia Mayo's thirty-year career ended there were no goodbyes, no party, and she just drove home alone?

The stars had a wide range of interests too, for example, MacDonald Carey was a published poet, George Sanders the chairman of a sausage manufacturing business and John Loder owned a pickle factory in Germany. The social backgrounds of such stars was immensely varied: some (Charlie Chaplin, Anthony Quinn) grew up in acute poverty, while Gene Tierney went to a finishing school in Switzerland and Robert Stack also came from a very wealthy family. Though writers of individual biographies in the past have used a few of these books, no one has looked at them systematically. There is not even a list, or a bibliography, available, something I attempt to rectify, though the reader is warned that the list of references is not complete, especially for books by stars of the 1930s.

At any time in the period there were about 200–300 significant stars at work. At least half that number wrote autobiographies, for which there was a ready market, though most were soon forgotten. The listing at the end of the book includes over 170 books, some of them novels or non-fiction works by the autobiographers, and encompasses mainly the stars who made films in the Golden Age, especially in the period 1935 –50. I have limited my coverage to books by actors in America, not necessarily American-born but whose careers were predominantly with US studios, or, like Maurice Chevalier, whose international reputation was the result of his work in Hollywood. This meant excluding the numerous British performers who divided their time between Europe and the US, such as Laurence Olivier, Peter Ustinov, Stewart Granger and James Mason. Other Britons, such as Brian Aherne, Ray Milland, George Sanders and David Niven, settled in the American industry, even though David Niven in particular was 'terribly British' and some of these performers, including Niven, did not live in America all the time.

But the criteria for inclusion is fairly flexible: for example I have included a book by a child actor who grew up to be a director (Robert Parrish), books by stuntmen and stuntwomen, and others by Robert Vaughan and Leslie Caron whose films fall mostly outside the Golden Age – simply because their books are so good. In the text I have concentrated on the best books – the most readable or the most informative – but most of them get a mention at some point. The focus is mainly on the 1940s and early 1950s because this was a period of technological maturity and also happens to be the time I was growing up. The space devoted to particular actors is also partly as a result of personal preference – but is also because of their popularity and the quality of their books.

Many of the actor-writers have commented that acting, for them, was easier than writing. For that reason many had professional help, mainly to impose some structure on dictated recollections, a process which still allowed the actor's own voice to come through. It is interesting, however, that many of the best books were written without professional assistance. Some of the autobiographers found they had a facility for writing and found it so satisfying that they went on to write other non-fiction books and quite a few wrote novels as well, though with or two exceptions (Errol Flynn, Sterling Hayden), the novels did not endure. David Niven, for example, wrote books about the Hollywood scene that sold in millions while his novels were simply awful.

Of course, not all the stars wrote their autobiographies, for example Humphrey Bogart, Clark Gable, Robert Mitchum, Marilyn Monroe and James Stewart. The reasons were not necessarily lack of literacy: Bogart, for instance, was well educated whereas several who did write had left school early and still produced very good books unaided (Joan Crawford,

Edward Arnold). Some, perhaps, did not have big enough egos to write at length about themselves; for others, sheer indifference was an overriding factor (undoubtedly this was the case with Robert Mitchum). One motive for writing a book was a desire to set the record straight or as an exercise in self-examination in sorting out a past which had been a bewildering mixture of success, failure and guilt (see, for example, the lives of Lena Horne, Kirk Douglas and Anthony Quinn). However, vanity or a desire to make money may have also been fairly common motives, as well as the need for something constructive to do towards the end of a career.

Chapter 1, the longest in the book, attempts to summarise the history of the studio system in America and describes some of the vivid characters of the moguls who drove it – something the autobiographies are quite fluent about. The following eleven chapters concentrate on the lives of one or more of the actor-writers, as portrayed by themselves and supplemented by research. Chapter 3 pauses to enquire about the completeness and truthfulness of the autobiographies, an issue which arises again and again in later chapters. Each of Chapters 2 – 12 focuses on an important theme or a major star – for example, the influx of European actors and others to Hollywood in the 1930s and 1940s, the conflicts which arose between the studios and their actors, and the impact of personal, political and racial issues on two actors who wrote especially fine books. Finally, the last chapter draws some conclusions and explains why the studio system broke down and highlights the differences between Hollywood then and now.

Sources, in addition to autobiographies of stars, include autobiographies of directors and executives, biographies, histories of the studios and reference books. These sources are referenced within parentheses in the text and listed at the back of the book and are acknowledged gratefully here. The author also has viewed or reviewed very many films from the Golden Age: no hardship that.

CHAPTER 1

Hollywood As It Was

THE HISTORY OF American film did not begin in Hollywood, or even in America, but in Europe where many of the early innovations in film-making were made. Experiments in motion pictures were being carried out in America, France and England at about the same time in the 1890s. There was no single inventor of cinematography and there was a long pre-history of magic lanterns, peepshows and other developments on the way (A. R. Fulton in Balio, 1985). The Lumière Brothers mounted the world's first public screening of a motion picture in Paris in 1895. A year later, Thomas Edison had the first public performance by his Vitascope (a film projector) in April 1896 in New York. In October of that year, Edison's closest competitor, Biograph, had a first showing of its films. These shows were enormously popular and the inventors engaged in many fruitless patent disputes. In 1908, along with other early pioneers in cinematography, including Selig, Essanay and Pathé, Edison formed the Motion Picture Patents Company (MPPC) to pool their patents in an attempt to establish a monopoly, which was soon to extend to film distribution. The Edison Trust, as it came to be called, used the courts and occasionally physical violence to maintain its monopoly but was fought vigorously by a number of pioneer producer-distributors, notably Carl Laemmle and William Fox. These two pioneers were to establish film companies which still exist today (Universal and 20th Century-Fox). The Trust was finally brought down by an anti-trust suit in 1915, as well as by internal dissension.

At first, motion pictures were exhibited in tents and fairgrounds and soon in burlesque and vaudeville houses as part of the programmes. By 1905, nickelodeons – small theatres created in shop fronts and other buildings – exhibited films which at this stage were all short documentaries. Narrative feature films of an hour or more in length, though common at the time in Europe, did not take over from shorts in the eastern United States until 1911. Nickelodeons were so named because admission was five cents; though their life was brief, there were very large numbers of them. By the time purpose-built cinemas appeared in the 1910s, it is estimated that 26 million Americans a week were visiting picture shows. Almost all of the moguls who developed the industry started in film distribution – and ownership of nickelodeons, theatres and the film exchanges allowed the exhibitors to change their films once or more a week. Lengthy feature films telling stories, rather than just showing pictures of places and events, were first imported from Europe. At this time Hollywood was just a market-garden suburb of Los Angeles, a city which already had a population of over 50,000. Film-making was then restricted to the New York area, Chicago and a few other places in the east, but the movement west would soon begin.

Hollywood, some seven miles north of Los Angeles, was, by all accounts, a lovely place around 1911 when the first film studio was established there. Adela Rogers St Johns (1969), who lived there as a journalist and scriptwriter, described it as 'a fragrant, idyllic peaceful country village in the midst of orange groves with trails leading to the ocean or up into the foothills'. There were, she wrote, 'pepper trees that hadn't been touched since the Franciscan fathers walked that way and the Spanish grandees rode through on prancing horses'. This idyllic place in the Cahuenga valley was developed by Harvey Wilcox, who purchased 120 acres of land there in 1896. He called the place 'Hollywood', an attractive name which his wife had heard on a train going east. In reality, Hollywood had neither holly nor woods.[6] People from the east came to live there or to establish summer residences. In 1903, the residents obtained the incorporation of Hollywood as a city but in 1910 asked for it to be annexed to Los Angeles, apparently to assure adequate water supply for its growing population. At a time when films were shot in the open in natural light, the climate of Los Angeles in those pre-smog times was very favourable, with sunshine for much of the year. The varied scenery, including sea, mountains, foothills and scrub and even desert nearby, was ideal. It was a long way from New York but even that carried the perceived advantage that it was out of reach of the Trust.[7]

Cecil B. DeMille (1881–1959), the producer-director, is mentioned often in the autobiographies reviewed in this book.

---

6 Kevin Brownlow in Kobal (1985) provides some valuable information about very early Hollywood and its film-makers. Wilcox, the developer, did plant some English holly trees to give the name some credence, according to Brownlow, but they would not grow. Many of the pepper trees had to be cut down because their fruit messed up cars.
7 It seems that the appeal of Hollywood as a refuge from the Trust may have been exaggerated because, as Scott (2005) points out, some of the earliest producers to establish studios in the area were members of the Trust themselves.

It was DeMille who, in his last film, cast Charlton Heston and Yvonne De Carlo in *The Ten Commandments* (1956) (see Chapters 8 and 12 below). From the autobiographies, we learn that Anthony Quinn married DeMille's adopted daughter Katherine; and, as a strong Republican, DeMille supported the Communist witch-hunt of the 1940s (see Chapter 11). He was an early film-maker in Hollywood, and although not the first by any means, his story tells us quite a lot about this period.[8]

Cecil B. De Mille ('CB', as he was known) was an outspoken egotist: he told his actors and staff, 'You are here to please me. Nothing else matters.' Before becoming a director, CB was an actor and, like his elder brother, William, a playwright. Cecil was ambitious and became very competent at producing and directing enormous epic films. It was William who has been quoted as saying: 'The trouble with Cecil is that he always bites off more than he can chew – and then chews it.' In 1913, at the age of thirty-two, CB was invited by Jesse Lasky, a producer of plays, and Lasky's brother-in-law, Samuel Goldfish (later Goldwyn) and a lawyer to join the three partners in their new company as Director General. The company was called The Jesse L. Lasky Feature Play Company. CB was not the first choice for this job – that was D. W. Griffith who turned the invitation down on the grounds that the company was insufficiently capitalised.[9] At this point CB had never even been in a film studio. It had been decided that the first film for the new venture was to be *The Squaw Man* (1914), based on a successful play about an English military man who takes the blame for his brother's crime and emigrates to the American West to seek a new life. With little delay, CB boarded a train

---

8   DeMille never claimed that he was the first to film in Hollywood and specifically says that the claim is mistaken in his autobiography (DeMille, 1959).
9   D. W. Griffith (1875–1948) was a pioneering producer and director famous for The Birth of a Nation (1915) and Intolerance (1916).

for Flagstaff, Arizona, with some actors and a cameraman, some five people in all. They thought that Arizona would be far enough away from possible interference by the Trust, though CB carried a revolver in his luggage just in case. At Flagstaff, he got off the train but immediately saw that the scenery was not right and got straight back on it, continuing to Los Angeles where he knew films were already being made.[10] He was told of a livery stable to rent in Hollywood and went out and obtained a monthly lease on the building.[11] His company established themselves there, building a stage at the side of the building for filming (in those days before floodlights, films were shot in the open) and started work. Soon, CB found a cottage nearby in the valley where his wife could join him. He travelled to and from the studio cross-country on horseback because the roads were rough and indirect. This presumably explains why he tended to wear leather puttees and long boots (for protection against snakes and brushwood), a jacket, jodhpurs and carried a riding crop. This gear became standard dress for film directors, along with a megaphone for shouting instructions. One day he found that film negatives stored in the barn had been deliberately spoiled by an unknown intruder. At first he took to sleeping there and later arranged for duplicates to be made and stored at home for safe-keeping. Another day on his ride, shots fired from a concealed position whizzed past him. It was clear that someone –perhaps from the Trust – was trying to prevent the film being made. After this incident he took to carrying a large revolver prominently and the incident was not repeated.

10 As a further example of misreporting, many writers to this day, from Adolph Zukor (1954) to Michael Friedland (2009) say that DeMille arrived at Flagstaff in a snowstorm, while DeMille himself states that it was sunny (DeMille, 1959)
11 The building, which is quite elegant for a barn, was declared an historic monument in 1956 and has been moved to a new position in Hollywood where it can be seen today, converted into a museum.

Back in New York, Goldfish was able to sell exhibition rights for the unseen film for cash to pay for a second production. When the film was exhibited to his fellow directors, though, it was found that, through inexperience and the use of second-hand British equipment, the sprocket holes in the celluloid stock has been spaced incorrectly, making the picture unstable when projected on the screen. This blunder, which could have ruined them, was quickly remedied by a kind member of the Trust from whose film laboratory the principals had sought help in desperation.[12] When released, the film was a great success.

DeMille was tough, single-minded and a stern disciplinarian. Like moguls Louis B. Mayer, Harry Cohn and Samuel Goldwyn, his character inspired loyalty, love –hate relationships and many anecdotes. One of these, amply confirmed by eyewitnesses, is that CB always had a man with him on the set whose sole job was to slip a chair under him whenever he chose to sit down. It is said that CB never looked behind him until one day when it was not there and he fell. Another story much polished and lengthened in retelling is that, for an enormous and expensive crowd scene of the Israelites being chased by Egyptians, he had four cameras trained on the spectacle. One by one the cameras failed and at the last the fourth cameraman who was positioned on a distant hill and had not heard the command to begin, waved and called out 'Ready when you are, Mr DeMille'. According to Zierold (1969), it was confirmed that the shot was in fact safely captured on at least one of the cameras, but like many Hollywood stories the polished version is funnier than the truth.

---

12 The makers of The Squaw Man had to pay for the lab work and also needed money to produce additional prints of the film. The financial shortfall was met by Harry Cohn (see below) in return for a share in the company. Cohn sold his share later on at a considerable profit and used the money to set up his own studio (Eyman, 2010).

In another anecdote, CB called an extra in a crowd scene to come up and speak to him. The extra had been talking to someone on the set after a call for silence. In front of everybody CB asked her (a red-headed girl in a long green dress) to repeat what she had said that was so important. Apparently, and CB had some difficulty in getting her to admit this, it was: 'I wonder when that old bald-headed son of a bitch is going to let us go to lunch?' CB gave a glimmer of a smile and shouted 'Lunch!' This is the version of the story told by Henry Wilcoxon in his autobiography (1991). Robert Parrish (1976), a child actor, who later became a director and was also present at the time, gives a more polite version of the extra's remarks, identifying him as a man, not a girl – though Parrish was very young at the time and could be mistaken. Such contradictions between eye-witnesses illustrate the difficulties of distinguishing legend from fact, a topic we go into in more depth in Chapter 3.

At the time DeMille was making *The Squaw Man*, there were already various film studios scattered about the Los Angeles area, including several at Edendale, another suburb, 10 miles east of Hollywood. Edendale was where Mack Sennett of Keystone made Charlie Chaplin's first film in 1914.[13] Hollywood proper had several studios, the first being the Nestor Film Company, which was established in a former roadhouse, and was driven out of business by the restrictions on alcohol imposed by the local residents (who did not welcome actors either). Nestor, formerly the Centaur Film Company, was founded in New York in 1908 by an Englishman, David Horsley, who designed his own camera simply because he could not wait for one to be sent over

---

13   Edendale's availability of land was limited by the canyon in which it was situated. But for this, Edendale rather than Hollywood might have become the centre of the industry.

from England. Horsley did not get a licence from the Trust and decided to move west to Hollywood in 1911, long before DeMille got there.[14] Actually, only three of the major studios ever had a studio in Hollywood itself (and of these only Paramount remains today). Nonetheless Hollywood has become the label for the American film industry so that it is no longer simply a geographical location but more of a symbol, or a metaphor.

At the time, film-stars were not identified by name and it was another pioneer, Carl Laemmle (see below), who broke with the convention of actor anonymity and began the star system.[15] It soon became a competitive advantage to have a company of well-known actors but the salaries of the most popular ones escalated rapidly. Charlie Chaplin, who started with Sennett at the then high salary of $150 per week, moved first to Essanay and then to the Mutual Film Corporation for $10,000 a week plus a large bonus. Later he went to First National to do eight films for $1 million over eighteen months. At the same time, Mary Pickford was earning just under $1 million a year (Knight, 1957). In 1918 Chaplin had his own studios in central Hollywood. The public wanted to know more and more about the stars they liked, so the MPPC published the first 'fan' magazine, the *Motion Picture Story Magazine* in 1911 (Slide,1998) and there were soon many others.

---

14 William Selig, a former travelling magician and minstrel show operator, also developed his own camera and projector in Chicago and did gain admission to the Trust. Selig claimed to be the first to shoot a narrative film in Los Angeles in 1908 and soon afterwards established studios at Edendale and Glendale (Watson, 2001). Other early American film pioneers in the West included Thomas Ince, D. W. Griffith, who originally was an actor and stayed with Biograph for many years, and Mack Sennett.

15 It was said of Carl Laemmle that he had a very large family. This was because of his many relations with jobs in the company. Laemmle established his large studio at Universal in Universal City to the north of Hollywood. Later, MGM were at Culver City to the south and Warner's at Burbank, some way out of town to the northeast.

But it was in Europe that some of the technology was first developed, as well as the techniques of camera work and such innovations as feature films and newsreels. Méliès and others from Europe have had a lasting impact upon movie-making.[16] By 1908 Pathé Frères were the world's largest film production company.[17] Berlin opened a giant picture palace in 1911, well before the great cinemas of New York were opened between 1914 and 1917. According to Gerben Bakker in Sedgwick and Pokorny (2005), European producers actually had between 30 and 40 per cent of the US market from 1907 to 1910. Shortly before the 1914–18 war, the European share fell and was not to recover much as the American market expanded. The European decline was the result of reduced competitiveness rather than any falling off in their domestic markets – after all, films were encouraged as good propaganda and production was generally maintained. The European producers, however, could not match the escalating cost and quality of American producers who were able to take advantage of an expanding market. In 1909, the average cost of making films in the US was somewhere between $550 and $1100. By 1929 Fox films cost some $308,000 each to produce and this cost escalation continued. In 1939, MGM, always a high-cost producer, was spending almost $1 million per film on average. Convers to sound from 1927 had pushed up costs faster still. Sou movies were three times as expensive as silent pictu

---

16 Georges Méliès, a former magician like Selig, was a French pioneer who may have been the first to use dissolves, double exposures and other tricks. Another pioneer in America was Edwin S. Porter, a precursor of Griffith and in England G. A. Smith and James Williamson of the so-called Brighton School (1900–1910). G. A. Smith preceded Griffith in the use of some film techniques such as close-ups and moving camera shots. Smith patented a two-colour film-making process in 1908 (Sklar, 2000)
17 Films were produced in many countries both in and outside Europe. The Nordisk Company of Denmark was the world's second largest film producer before 1914.

(see Gerben Bakker and Andrew Haussen in Sedgwick and Pokorny, 2005). The US industry was able to cherry-pick the best directors, stars and literary properties from Europe, while governments there from the early 1920s reacted to the industry decline with quotas, tariffs, exchange controls and other devices which further weakened the industry. By 1918 the US dominated the international film market.

Rising costs and an expanding market in America were accompanied by increasing concentration and vertical integration as the bigger companies bought up cinema chains and distributors. By 1930, five companies dominated the industry: Warner Brothers, Loews-MGM, Paramount, RKO and 20th Century-Fox. Together with the little three (Universal, Columbia and United Artists), the eight companies collected 95 per cent of film rentals paid to national distributors. The big five owned or controlled 3,000 of the 18,000 cinema theatres in the US in 1945 (a result which helped to keep out foreign competition) but since they were also the larger first-run theatres in metropolitan areas they accounted for nearly 70 per cent of national box office receipts (Balio, 1985). In terms of their percentage of total rental income in 1939, MGM was the largest studio with 22 per cent, 20th Century-Fox had 17 per cent, Paramount and Warner's were level-pegging at 14 per cent each, and RKO had 9 per cent. These figures were not vastly altered in 1956, except that MGM's share had shrunk to 17 per cent, along with RKO down to 4 per cent, while Fox and Warner's had increased their share. Among the smaller studios, Columbia had 7 per cent of rental income in 1939 and 9 per cent in 1956, United Artists and Universal had also increased their share (Finler, 2003).

Expansion was not continuous in the inter-war period and the industry was hit by the Depression which began in 1929.

HOLLYWOOD AS IT WAS

For a while the innovation of sound kept up audience numbers but average weekly attendance fell from 80 million in 1929 to 60 million in 1932 and 1933. By 1933 Paramount, Fox, RKO and Universal were all in receivership or being reorganised, though all were to recover. When the companies failed, financiers, including investment bankers, put what they regarded as sound businessmen in charge, some of whom tried to run the studios like utility companies. The studios were burdened with more and more detailed cost accounts, personnel managers and other trappings of 'scientific management'. The results were disastrous. The bankers called on J. P. Kennedy, father of John F. Kennedy, later President and a former film executive, to report on the situation. His advice was to get rid of the 'sound businessmen' and to put in charge film-makers who knew how to run a creative business.[18] Significantly, Warner's and Columbia, still run by their original founders, survived as did MGM whose studios were run by the experienced mogul Louis B. Mayer. Adolph Zukor, the creator of Paramount, who had been kicked upstairs, was put in sole charge of the studios, while Barney Balaban, the founding partner of a theatre chain, headed up the business. In six months they had turned Paramount around and the company entered a new era of prosperity (Balio, 1993).

It became accepted that financing and distribution, always the province of the New York offices, should become

---

18 J. P. Kennedy was a wealthy banker and financier who came to Hollywood in 1926 and later, during the Second World War, was President Roosevelt's ambassador to London. In the 1920s and 1930s, by various means, some of them questionable, he acquired interests in a number of studios and at one point was managing four companies simultaneously: FBO, Pathé, Robertson-Cole and Keith-Albee-Orpheum (KAO, a theatre chain). These companies were to be among the components of RKO assembled by the Radio Corporation of America (RCA). Kennedy derided the other moguls as 'pants-pressers' in a reference to their former occupations, but they had more feeling for movies than he did. In her biography of J. P. Kennedy, Cari Beauchamp (2009) says that he 'shifted the gears of an entire industry from one that took the creative long view to one whose guiding doctrine was the next quarter's balance sheet'.

clearly distinct from production, now almost entirely located on the West Coast. The physical distance reinforced the cultural dichotomy between the two ends of the business and led to frequent antagonism between them. The head offices in New York raised the money to meet increasing capital requirements, set the Hollywood operations budgets for total expenditure, the number of films to be produced by category, a release schedule and organised distribution. By 1931 double features became the norm, with an A picture coupled with a B. The B features were shorter, had lesser known stars and cost less to make, but they were enormously important for industry economics. They accounted (including films made by the small 'poverty row' producers) for 75 per cent of the total number of films made. Since, on average, the major studios did not make more than a film a week, the Bs were essential to keep the whole system operating efficiently throughout the year. B films also provided the means for trying out and training new actors, as well as keeping actors under contract occupied.

The studios in Hollywood had a chief, or vice president, who negotiated star contracts, dealt with labour issues and in some cases functioned as head of production. One of the important changes in the inter-war period was that the first generation of moguls (Fox, Laemmle, Zukor) were being gradually supplanted by a second generation of paid creative managers who did not necessarily own the business (Irving Thalberg, Darryl Zanuck and Hal Wallis, for example). There was no clear break or indeed clear division between the generations. Louis B. Mayer lasted a long time as head of MGM (from 1924 to 1951). His son-in-law, David O. Selznick, straddled the first and second generations in terms of role, if not in chronology, because he started as an employee and ended up as an independent mogul. Accompanying the generational shift were changes in management structure. There was a trend to decentralisation as the single central producer system gave way to multiple unit producers reporting to a production chief. Under the older, central producer system, one person, Jack Warner for example, supervised story development, decided on lead casting (the functions of the producer) and appointed a director to film it. In some cases, the producer and director were the same person, as in the case of DeMille at Paramount, John Ford at Fox and Frank Capra and Howard Hawks at Columbia, their status and autonomy being determined by the production chief. The role of directors tended to change and to decline in importance in the 1930s – one of the reasons for the formation of the Screen Directors Guild in 1938 (see Chapter 10) Apart from the exceptions of the producer-directors, the growing complexity of film-making and the push towards greater efficiency in the Depression, which encouraged the shift to the unit production system, meant that increasingly directors tended to be given a script and a cast and were expected to get on with it.[19] Studios were organised by department, for example: central administration; story development; art (which covered set design and costumes and make-up); still photography; cinematography; editing and publicity. At its peak, MGM employed 6,000 people in twenty-seven departments and was producing forty pictures a year.

An essential part of the system, right from the beginning, was of course distribution. At first, the shorts for nickelodeons were sold at a cost per foot to exchanges (either independent

---

19 The reader may wonder about the auteur theory (creative authorship) which holds that it is the director who gives a film its essential qualities. It is true that some producer-directors do put their recognisable stamp upon a film, Joseph von Sternberg and Alfred Hitchcock are cases in point, but essentially film-making is a collaborative venture involving top management, writers, designers, cameramen and many others.

or owned by the studios), which provided the means to distribute film prints and to change them weekly or more often as needed. As feature films emerged, films were rented out on the basis of a percentage of the box office revenue obtained by each theatre, though B films might be charged on a flat fee basis. Elaborate arrangements were necessary for films to be allocated to 'runs' so that the large, first-run houses, in city centres got the A pictures first for a limited period before they were released to local theatres. There were special arrangements for 'Super As', like *Gone with the Wind* (1939), for which higher than usual seat prices were charged. A system of 'block-booking' arose in which output was sold in packages of As and Bs. This simplified matters and gave both the theatres and the studios a guaranteed outlet and supply. However, the practice meant that theatres were committed to buy films, often unseen whether they wanted them or not, although some flexibility was allowed. Block-booking was one of the practices attacked in the anti-trust actions from 1938 onwards (see Chapter 13). The film exchanges sent staff to attend previews and circulated publicity material such as the front-of-house cards and posters now sought after by collectors. Exchange staff also had to travel around theatres to sell the product and in some cases to verify box office takings. For major productions, the stars themselves were expected to travel around the country to promote their films to the general public.

※※※

By 1930, the movie industry was a very big business; although it was only forty-fourth in rank order of all industries in the US, it was the greater part (75 per cent of revenue) of the entertainment business as a whole, including sports, gambling, vaudeville and so on (Marc D. Huettig in Balio,

1985). From 1900 to 1930 what were to become the big five, and for that matter the little three, grew by both acquisition and internal expansion. Some of the original pioneers led the growth, some of their companies were acquired and many smaller ones went out of business. Metro Goldwyn Mayer (MGM), the best known, did not come into existence until 1924. Marcus Loew's theatre chain acquired Metro Pictures Corporation, a film producing and distributing company in 1919.[20] Metro had absorbed Goldwyn Pictures Corporation (after Sam Goldwyn had left it) and Loew merged Metro with Goldwyn and Louis B. Mayer Productions to form MGM. The new company's brand of the roaring lion with the Latin motto *Ars Gratia Artis* (art for art's sake – actually it was more art for money's sake) was taken over from the one devised for Goldwyn earlier, as was the Goldwyn studio in Culver City.

These were the ways in which Goldwyn, who had already moved on to form Samuel Goldwyn Inc., left his permanent mark on the movie business. Louis B. Mayer (LB) became head of the new studio with his boss Marcus Loew in New York and his head of production Irving Thalberg, whom LB had hired away from Universal in 1923. From the 1920s until the early 1930s, MGM's central producer was Irving Thalberg. LB took over that role, aided by unit producers, after Thalberg's death and continued MGM's commercial, if not artistic, success. MGM's films reflected LB's strong sense of family values and have been criticised for their lack of social bite. The company's A films had high production values, indeed Mayer

---

20 Marcus Loew, who was born in 1870, was as important in the evolution of the industry as the other moguls but because he was a theatre man not directly involved in movie production he has attracted less interest than the others. Loew realized, however, the importance of good pictures hence the creation of MGM. Loew's conservative but far-sighted policies resulted in a sound business which survived the Depression, policies which were continued after his death by his long-time employee, Nicholas Schenck (Balio, 1985).

boasted that the firm did not make B pictures at all. MGM had a roster of about forty well-known stars, many of whom, including Greta Garbo and Greer Garson, were discovered and signed up by LB himself. The business was consistently profitable throughout the Depression and did not make a loss in any year until 1957.[21] Unlike his fellow moguls, LB never had a significant ownership stake in MGM, though with profit sharing divided between himself and Thalberg, he was the highest paid executive in the industry and indeed in the United States.

Louis B. Mayer (1884–1957)[22] was one of the great Hollywood moguls who dominated their studios in the Golden Age and have featured frequently in the subsequent literature on the subject. Like the others, LB had been a poor immigrant from Europe (Russia in his case); he had little education, and in fact dropped out of school aged twelve to work in his father's scrap-metal business in New Brunswick, Canada, where the family initially settled. Eventually LB left home and, apparently alone, travelled to various cities in the US, including Boston, where he married, aged about nineteen and worked as a scrap dealer, the trade he knew. His business did not thrive and after briefly working in a theatre selling tickets, he came to appreciate the potential for movies. In 1907 he was able to rent a theatre of his own, combining movies with vaudeville, acquiring a second one in 1911 and a third in 1913. By this time LB had moved into distribution. He made a substantial amount of money from the acquisition of the New England distribution rights for D.W. Griffith's *The*

---

21 I have made use of Joel W. Finler's (2003) invaluable book on Hollywood in this section on the studios, in addition to the other sources cited.
22 LB claimed to have lost his birth certificate and his dates are uncertain. He said, patriotically that he was born on 4 July, but this was probably his own invention.

Birth of a Nation (1915). He was then able to move into production, first by helping to set up Metro Pictures, an important distributor/producer, and second, in 1918 by founding his own company. With his great affection for his mother and two daughters Edie and Irene, he wanted all his films to embody strong moral values,[23] saying 'I will only make pictures I won't be ashamed to have my children see' (Zierold, 1969; Marx, 1975). His motto was 'Get the best' and 'when they're good they make me look good'. At MGM he formed a good relationship with the media magnate William Randolph Hearst and helped to finance films starring Hearst's mistress, Marion Davies (LB's moral values here had to be compromised by business imperatives). In return, MGM got favourable nationwide publicity from Hearst media.

Mayer himself does not seem to have been deeply interested in the detail of the movies MGM made, as distinct from their business aspects. Among the exceptions were the Andy Hardy series of stories with Mickey Rooney, which ran from the 1930s to the 1950s, films which enshrined LB's family values. He was very interested in his stars and the power his position at the studio gave him. He regarded himself as a father figure for his actors. There is a story told by Robert Taylor who went to LB to ask for a raise in salary. The boss put his arm around him and sobbed that he regarded Taylor as his own son. When asked if he got his raise, Taylor said, 'No, but I gained a father'. Mayer was an emotional person and there are many stories of his putting on fits and tears to get his own way.[24] But MGM did seem to be a happy studio and many

23 Irene married David O. Selznick; LB was against this but respected him as film executive. Irene's sister Edith married William Goetz, also in the business, but LB did not approve of Goetz at all and excluded Edith and anyone from the Goetz family from his will.
24 LB was also known to go beyond histrionics and deliver knock-out punches, mostly to people who insulted motherhood in some way. The victims of this

actors and executives spent most of their working lives there. LB himself never got on with Nicholas Schenck who became head of the Loew empire after Marcus Loew died in 1927. LB often quarrelled with Schenck, another Russian-born Jew, and resigned following a dispute in which Schenck refused to support him over a difference of opinion with Dore Schary, who had been brought in as head of production. Perhaps to his surprise, the resignation was accepted and LB suddenly went into an unhappy retirement, living only six more years in which he had hoped to make films as an independent but never did.[25]

All of the big five studios were vertically integrated, and in addition to theatres had large numbers of subsidiaries, including distribution companies, film laboratories and equipment suppliers. Paramount had more theatres than the others. Adolph Zukor, who quietly dominated the company for fifty years, joined forces with Jesse Lasky and took over Paramount, a distribution company which gave its name to the whole enterprise.[26] The result was the biggest movie company in America at the time and it continued to expand until the Depression when it was revealed to have over-stretched

violence included John Gilbert, Von Stroheim and Charlie Chaplin. Apparently his days of humping scrap metal had given him a powerful build. Though short at 5′3″, LB was squarely built and, a good dancer, light on his feet.

25 LB was earlier depicted as a tyrant and a satyr, but in recent years a more balanced view has emerged, as later chapters illustrate from actor-autobiographies. He was not a womaniser, the first of his two marriages lasted forty years. He did, however, have a vindictive streak and used his power to blackball several people.

26 Adolph Zukor (1873–1976) was one of the earliest moguls and outlived all of them. He started in the fur business and then followed the classic route from exhibition to production. He founded the Famous Players Film Company in 1912 and later merged it with Jesse L. Lasky's Feature Play Company, which Lasky had founded in 1913. Together they developed Paramount with Zukor in New York and Lasky in Hollywood. Zukor had had Mary Pickford under contract for five and a half years (the happiest of her life, she said) but lost her when he refused to match an offer from First National (Pickford, 1956). With Laemmle, Zukor was among the first to import longer feature films from Europe.

itself. Despite its chequered record, Paramount was the only studio to rival MGM for its roster of stars.

Like Laemmle, Lasky, Loew and Zukor, William Fox was a pioneer of the very early period, beginning with the ownership of a nickelodeon in New York in 1904 and commencing film production in 1914. He employed the early sex-bomb, Theda Bara, and director Raoul Walsh and others, forming the Fox Film Corporation in 1916. In the 1920s, Fox acquired a major chain of theatres and was one of the pioneers of sound. Fox lost control of the business in the early 1930s and in 1935 it was merged with the youthful but brilliantly successful 20th Century Pictures run by Darryl Zanuck and Joseph Schenck (brother of Nicholas) to form 20th Century-Fox. Fox soon became one of the leading companies. At first it was its stars, Shirley Temple and Will Rogers, who were most prominent. Rogers was killed in 1935 but Zanuck soon built a galaxy of talent, including among the actor-autobiographers reviewed here, Henry Fonda, Loretta Young, George Sanders, Maureen O'Hara and Gene Tierney.[27]

Warner Brothers was a family firm built by four brothers, Albert, Harry, Sam and Jack, the youngest who was to bring the studio to international prominence. Jack Warner ran the studio in Hollywood with Sam, Harry ran the New York Office, and Albert, who had an eye for economy, was the Treasurer. Born of Polish-Jewish immigrants, after trying

---

[27] Darryl F. Zanuck (1902–79) was younger than the earlier generation of moguls who mostly had ownership in their businesses. He differed from them in not being Jewish and although originally coming from the Midwest he also spent much of his youth in Southern California, whereas most of the others came from the East. (Custen, 1997). Given his background as a screenwriter, he emphasised the importance of original stories based on recent events. Zanuck was very much a 'hands-on' producer in terms of casting and story development; see the collection of his memos in Zanuck (1993).

various occupations, the four brothers joined together in 1904 to start a nickelodeon. They then had a small cinema and later film exchanges, produced some pictures in the East where they ran foul of the MPPC. The brothers opened a small studio in Hollywood. Warner Brothers Inc. was incorporated in 1923. In the 1920s the business survived on the unlikely combination of leads: John Barrymore, the great stage actor and alcoholic, and Rin Tin Tin, a performing dog (though not in the same pictures). It was Warner's that gave a start to Darryl Zanuck by hiring him as a scriptwriter who ended up as production chief. Hal Wallis replaced Zanuck as production head when he left in 1933. Warner's then took over Vitagraph in 1925, an early film producer competing with Edison and which had been formed in 1897. In 1925, Warner's went public with a share issue and was one of the first to utilise the new sound technology with a new company, Vitaphone Corporation, a joint venture with Western Electric. Although not Warner's' first film with sound and not even a full talkie, *The Jazz Singer* (1927) was a tremendous success. In 1928 Warner's bought one of the largest cinema chains.

Sam, who had driven the transition to sound, died in 1927 of a cerebral haemorrage. First National, initially a distribution company which had moved into film-making, including six Charlie Chaplin features between 1918 and 1922, was absorbed in 1928. First National's studios in Burbank became the centre of Warner's production. By 1930, Warner's, which had been struggling in the 1920s, had become one of the largest integrated studio groups. Like its competitors, Warner's were hit badly by the Depression but avoided receivership and recovered slowly to boom during the Second World War and afterwards. Warner's had a good roster of stars including, among those actor-writers reviewed here, James Cagney, Bette Davis, Edward G. Robinson and Ronald Reagan. It made all kinds of films, including 'women's pictures', gangster films, musicals and social problem films.

Jack, the youngest and best known of the four brothers, was a vulgarian and something of a wit – he had appeared in vaudeville in his youth. At a studio dinner for Madame Chiang Kai-shek, he surveyed a row of inscrutable Chinese faces and said out loud 'Holy Cow, I forgot to pick up my laundry.' To Albert Einstein, famous for his relativity theory, he said 'Well Professor, I have proved a theory of relatives –don't hire em' (quoted in Zierold, 1969).

Radio-Keith-Orpheum Pictures (RKO) was created by the giant Radio Corporation of America (RCA). RCA had valuable patents and expertise in the new technology of sound and decided to build a major film studio to exploit it. RCA first purchased a small studio, Film Booking Offices of America, in 1928, in the following year merging it into the Keith-Albee-Orpheum theatre chain. In 1930, RKO took over the American Pathé studio and distribution organisation. David O.Selznick was appointed Head of Production and fully integrated Pathé into the business and signed up Fred Astaire and Katharine Hepburn. Management changes led to the departure of Selznick in 1933 to join his father-in-law, Louis B. Mayer at MGM. In that year RKO went into receivership. The company was to recover slowly but it took seven years and very many management changes to do it. Despite its problems, RKO produced a number of distinctive films in the period of recovery: 1933 saw *Flying Down to Rio*, which introduced the successful Astaire –Rogers dancing team and *King Kong*; *The Hunchback of Notre Dame* (1939) and *Kitty Foyle* (1940) which marked Ginger Rogers transition as a dramatic actress by gaining an Oscar. Howard Hughes, an enthusiastic and wealthy film-maker, bought RKO in 1948. Hughes' films were made with great enthusiasm and at enormous cost, but except for *Scarface* (1932), which was directed by Howard Hawks, Hughes' films were never really distinguished. *The Outlaw* (1943) caused a furore with the American censors because of Jane Russell's décolleté (but was nevertheless given a U certificate in the UK as suitable for children). RKO lost money throughout Hughes' reign: he basically ran the company into the ground. It was to recover during the Second World War boom but did not survive the TV era, in fact its studio properties were sold in 1958 to Desilu Productions. TV film producer Desilu made its fortune initially from Desi Arnaz and Lucille Ball's *I Love Lucy* series who owned them (see Chapter 9). Throughout its history RKO was the least profitable of all the major studios, but in the 1940s it was a leader in the vogue for film *noir*.[28] RKO's success in producing good movies reflected the skills of some of its producers, including independents and its permanent technical staff, who remained with the company through its ownership and management changes.

Of the little three, Universal was the oldest, founded in

---

28   Film noir ('black' films) is a term first introduced by French critics to refer to a genre of movies in America in the 1940s and 1950s (though some were made in Britain also). Noirs were economically produced and typically dealt with corruption, betrayal, cynicism and disillusionment. They were filmed in black and white to match the mood of the stories and often used 'odd angles, oppressive compositions . . .dimly lit rooms. . .and outdoor scenes inevitably shot at night, often in rain-drenched streets' (Siegel and Siegel, 2004). Many influences affected the film noir, including German Expressionism, post-war realism and novelists, notably Dashiell Hammett and Raymond Chandler (Kerr in Kerr,1986) but they were also relatively cheap to make. Citizen Kane (1941) set the trend and popular noirs starring our actor-autobiographers include: The Maltese Falcon (1941; Mary Astor); (Double Indemnity (1944; Edward G. Robinson) and The Woman in the Window (1944; Edward G. Robinson and Joan Bennett) and Out of the Past (1947; Kirk Douglas). All of these films were successful and highly regarded but the autobiographers were not particularly prominent among noirs (see Chapter 8).

1912 by Carl Laemmle, one of the first moguls. It had an even more chequered history than Paramount. It did not succumb to the Depression, though it was forced to sell its small chain of some sixty theatres to avoid it. Universal lost money in most years of the 1930s. In 1935 Laemmle, who had been at the helm for twenty-four years, was forced out. Universal had been late to convert to sound but was one of the first to combine film and TV production, a process enhanced by its long tradition of economical operation established by its founder. In the 1930s and 1940s, Universal was successful with horror films, Deanna Durbin musicals and Abbott and Costello comedies. The company was absorbed into the MCA group in 1957. Its former studios are still in production and Universal City is a much-visited theme park.

United Artists was founded in 1919 by Douglas Fairbanks, Mary Pickford, Charlie Chaplin and D. W. Griffith. It was a star-producer cooperative without a theatre chain, intended to distribute the productions of its founders rather than allowing one of the big studios to capture the profits from distribution. The idea was not their own but was put to them by Benjamin Percival Schulberg, then a young man with literary ambitions who was later to become general manager of Paramount when Zukor gained control.[29] He had hoped for a similar position at UA but was shut out. At the time the project was greeted with scepticism and the President of Metro said: 'So the lunatics have taken charge of the asylum'. In fact, UA retained its independence much longer than Metro and the basic idea was a sound one. From the outset UA experienced difficulties

---

29 B. P. Schulberg (1892–1950) is not to be confused with his son, Budd Schulberg (1914–2009), who did achieve his father's literary ambitions. Budd wrote the script for On the Waterfront (1954), a novel about Hollywood, What Makes Sammy Run? and much else. He was a friendly witness for the HUAC (see Chapter 10).

because only Griffith was able to make his quota of productions (which made little or no money) and the others had prior commitments which delayed their full participation. Charlie Chaplin, in particular, was very slow to produce his films and the only way they could come up with enough product to keep the distribution system busy was to turn to other independents like Mack Sennett and this became the norm. Griffith left in 1924, but a new administrative partner, Joseph Schenck, joined. Schenck revitalised the business and brought in Darryl Zanuck. He also involved Samuel Goldwyn and Gloria Swanson and later Walt Disney on distribution deals, and Alexander Korda, who became a shareholder. In 1933, Schenck and Zanuck, as we have seen, left to found 20th Century Pictures.

There were many disputes between the partners, especially between Charlie Chaplin and Mary Pickford. Goldwyn left amid a lawsuit in 1939 and Douglas Fairbanks died that year. UA had become something of a revolving door as famous stars and producers were bound in with deals and then left again. Pickford and Chaplin were bought out respectively in 1956 and 1957. Shares were then sold to the public and a new management team introduced which, from 1950, adopted a new policy of participating fully in the financing of pictures. The founders' method of operation was to let the stars, who all had their own studios, finance and produce the films. After considerable successes and vicissitudes, UA was brought down by the failure of, and uncontrolled expenditure on, a Western blockbuster, *Heaven's Gate* (1980), and the company was soon after bought by MGM (Bach, 1985).

Columbia, the youngest of the little three – and the best managed – was founded in 1920 by two brothers, Harry and Jack Cohn. They had worked together as office boys in an advertising agency, but started the business with a friend, Joe

Brandt, and initially called it CBC after the initial letters of their names. In 1924, the company changed its name to Columbia Pictures Corporation and in 1929 went public, though the voting stock remained controlled by the three founders. In 1932, Harry bought out Brandt after an abortive coup attempt by his brother, Jack (relations between them were rarely cordial). Harry became President of the Corporation and remained head of production, a unique situation in the industry. A. P. Giannini, a banker and founder of the Bank of Italy, which became the Bank of America, was at this time one of the three controlling shareholders and had supported Harry (Thomas, 1967). Giannini was a populist and was unsympathetic to the Wall Street banking establishment. Edward Buscombe in Kerr (1986) suggests that Giannini may have been the inspiration for the idealistic small-town banker in *American Madness* (1932), a film directed for Columbia by Frank Capra.[30]

Columbia's studio on Poverty Row in Hollywood was managed by Harry Cohn with his brother Jack in the New York office. Harry was a streetwise New Yorker of mixed German Russian parentage. The brothers had little education and Harry in particular was aggressive, outspoken and vulgar in his speech, but he had an uncanny sense of what made a good picture. A former streetcar attendant and song plugger, Harry bullied his staff but respected those who stood up to him. One of these was his brilliant director Frank Capra, who insisted that he would leave if he could not make his films without interference. The studio produced films cheaply and on time. Employees had to clock in and out and at one time Harry had the sound stages wired so that he could eavesdrop

---

30 The film, set in the Depression, is the story of a banker who is threatened with failure because he supports local businesses and does not foreclose on them. He is saved by the local people who increase their deposits. Walter Huston starred.

on what was going on. Hedda Hopper, one of Hollywood's prime gossip columnists, wrote that you had to stand in line to hate him. Harry Cohn, however, never went back on his word and could be kind-hearted. A former leading silent actress, down on her luck, advertised for work, any work, and Cohn was the only one who called and gave her some (Zierold, 1969; Capra, 1971).

Harry had no interest in politics, only in his studio for which he knew talent was essential – he often said 'I kiss the feet of talent'.[31] Not able to afford a roster of big stars, Columbia borrowed actors and directors and managed to make one or two really good A films a year, with a very regular output of Bs. The studio borrowed sets as well as people from other studios and did everything it could to reduce costs, for example by arranging shooting so that expensive stars could appear in all their scenes before leaving the lot. Columbia made some of the best films of the period, including *It Happened One Night* (1934), Capra's comedy, which won the studio its first Oscar and many others. In the 1940s Columbia made a number of Technicolor musicals with Rita Hayworth, one of its big stars (*Cover Girl*, 1944). Alas, Cohn alienated his sensitive and vulnerable star with his bullying and she left the studio only to return sporadically.

Columbia made money throughout the Depression years and in fact did not make its first loss until 1957, the year Cohn died from a heart attack. One of the strains on him at the end was that he discovered that Kim Novak, whom he thought of as a replacement for Rita Hayworth, was having a romance with black Sammy Davis Jr, also on the payroll, which he

---

31 Buscombe calculates that exactly half of the Hollywood Ten (See Chapter 10) the directors and writers who were imprisoned during the Communist Witch Hunt were employed at Columbia during the 1930s but this seemed to reflect its openness to talent and not any political leaning.

contrived to terminate because he feared it would ruin the studio. Harry Cohn was a major figure in Hollywood and two thousand people went to his funeral. Glenn Ford, actor, said of him, 'He could be cruel, kind, giving, taking, despicable, benevolent, compassionate and malevolent, all at the same time' (quoted in Thomas, 1967).

In addition to the big five and little three, there were also many smaller studios in the Golden Age, including a third tier of studios of which the most notable was Republic Pictures Corporation, founded in 1935 and which ceased as an independent producer in 1959. Republic made many B pictures, especially Westerns and an occasional A film, for example *Rio Grande* (1950) and *The Quiet Man* (1952), both with John Wayne, who was under contract there for many years. Monogram Pictures was another third-tier studio which briefly merged with Republic but regained its independence, later metamorphosing into Allied Artists Pictures Corporation (not UA). Republic and Monogram had film exchanges but the others rarely did. Below them was a fourth tier in what was called Poverty Row, a specific geographical area of Hollywood. The lower tiers thrived when the demand for Bs exceeded supply, but most of these companies proved to be short-lived – though an exception, as noted, was Columbia, which started there.

Beyond the fourth tier were a few very important independents which mainly worked through bigger studios for studio premises and distribution, often for stars and directors as well. These independents are not easily characterised because they slipped in and out of the big studio net in origin and ownership and sometimes lost independence and then regained it. They were invariably run by producer-directors of outstanding talent, and in fact carried with them the seeds of the Hollywood of today in which the big studios rely heavily on independents for their creative output. Disney, with its animated cartoon, falls into this category. Two of the prestigious independents in the Golden Age achieved the status of much bigger studios: David O. Selznick, who worked at RKO and MGM and married the boss's daughter, reappears several times in this book and Samuel Goldwyn deserves a special mention because he played a major role in building three studios: United Artists, Paramount and MGM, as well as his own independent company.[32] Like Selznick, Goldwyn had a strong drive to independence, saying once, 'I was always independent even when I had partners'; Selznick, having achieved independence with tremendous energy and success, burned himself out long before Goldwyn, who had one of the longest careers in Hollywood.

Samuel Goldwyn, a poor immigrant to New York via London, got a job making gloves, persuaded the boss that he could sell them and made enough money with the help of friends and relations to make a small start in distribution. As we have seen, he formed a company to make feature films with Jesse Lasky, a successful theatrical impresario, partnered by DeMille. Goldwyn left his partners, having helped to provide a major impetus and then formed Goldwyn Pictures Corporation in 1916 with a number of outside shareholders. These stockholders ousted him as President of the company which merged with Metro and Louis B. Mayer Productions to form MGM. Free of that entanglement, Goldwyn founded a third venture, Samuel Goldwyn Inc., which he controlled absolutely. He parted company with United Artists, which he had joined to supply product and was eventually able to buy

---

32   Selznick's methods and values are copiously illustrated in Rudy Behlmer's collection of his memoranda (Selznick, 1973).

the UA studio facilities in 1955. Goldwyn created many stars, including pop-eyed comedian Eddie Cantor, Danny Kaye, Lucille Ball, Susan Hayward and others – although, as he said, only two, Gary Cooper and David Niven, acknowledged their gratitude in public, or indeed at all. Goldwyn had a strong sense for quality, and, like Louis B. Mayer, he wanted to produce films for the whole family and prided himself on using the best writers he could get. There was a story about George Bernard Shaw, who was unable to agree with Goldwyn because, as he said, 'You Goldwyn are only interested in art whereas I am interested in money.'

Goldwyn is remembered not only for the films he made and the organisations he contributed to but for the sayings, mostly malapropisms, attributed to him. For example, when his colleagues tried to steer him away from a literary property which they described as 'too caustic', he replied, 'To hell with the cost, if it is a sound story we'll make a picture out of it.' Goldwyn was also advised against plans to film a successful Broadway play on the grounds that the leading character was a lesbian. 'We'll get around that,' he said, 'we'll make her an American.' His most famous malapropism was 'include me out', which he said to members of the Motion Picture Producers of America when he disagreed with the prevailing viewpoint about the need to introduce blacklisting. There is controversy about whether Goldwyn's reported sayings were all accidents or not. In any event, malapropisms were not unusual in Hollywood at the time when many people came from Europe and had only an imperfect command of English.[33]

Goldwyn's pictures as an independent included *Wuthering*

---

[33] According to his biographer, Goldwyn did deliver many of his reported sayings spontaneously. Eventually, he got tired of his clownish image and, concerned about his son being ribbed at school, he hired a publicist in 1943 to clean up his act. This did not work apparently (Scott Berg, 1989).

Heights (1939), *The Westerner* (1940) and *The Best Years of Our Lives* (1946). Goldwyn, obviously highly intelligent, had had negligible education, like his fellow immigrant moguls, but was one of the very few independent producers to survive after the studio era. His active career in fact lasted almost sixty years (Siegel and Siegel, 2004).[34] He had come a long way from the days when, as a boy of twelve, he 'wandered for a whole week through the streets of London with no more ardent guaranty [sic] of the future than a loaf of bread' (Goldwyn, 1923).

---

34 Goldwyn's own autobiography, written very early in his career, does reveal something of his origins and early doings, but is mainly devoted to the stars he promoted (Goldwyn, 1923).

CHAPTER 2

Past and Present

A FEW ACTOR-AUTOBIOGRAPHERS spanned the last decade of silent films and survived into the Golden Age, that is from the late 1920s to the 1950s or later. What is striking about these durable screen stars is the sheer number of films they made. The silents on average were shorter than the talkies and they were produced in great numbers and in simpler ways, many of them without scripts or even elaborate sets. Moviemaking changed enormously between its beginnings in the 1890s and the 1930s. It is an indication of the scale of the change that, with a few exceptions, such as the comedy shorts of Charlie Chaplin, silent films are almost unwatchable today whereas the better films of the 1930s can still be seen with enjoyment now. The differences are not simply attributable to the addition of sound but to the greater sophistication of the production process (and its cost) as well as the elaboration of story that dialogue permitted. Many cinephiles would disagree with this and claim that towards the end silent pictures were a very advanced art form with a comparative impact very much greater than that between, say, black and white and colour films later on. None of our early actor- authors, however, expressed such thoughts or regretted the advent of sound. Mary Pickford, who retired in 1933 only a few years after the coming of sound, had no problems with her voice but seems to have felt that she had simply done enough. Regret for the silents arose for her only from the fact that in the silent days movie actors 'were citizens of every country' because language was not a barrier. She gave no indication in her autobiography of concern about the sound revolution and her book ends: 'While I would not have missed that Yesterday I have no desire to go back and live it over. For me now there is only the great Today and the promise of Tomorrow.'

Mary Pickford, Charles Chaplin and Douglas Fairbanks Snr: Dr Macro/ United Artists.

In fact, none of the books by people who acted before and after the sound revolution say much about it at all, the change was largely taken for granted, even though for a while it caused chaos. Adolphe Menjou does have a chapter in his 1948 book, entitled 'Came the Revolution', which recounts his concern that he might fail to make the transition, though it turned out not to be a problem for him. Actually Menjou benefited from sound because his ability to speak other languages meant that his studio could produce foreign language versions of his films at low cost. His chapter is mostly devoted to this and to the technical problems that sound created in the short run. A few actors, of course, did not make the transition. Menjou mentions the German actor, Emil Jannings (1882–1950)[35] and Tommy Meighan (1879–1936; who in silents Menjou said had been the highest paid star in the business) whose careers ended abruptly. Another case was John Gilbert (1895–1936), the romantic star whose voice turned out to be not romantic at all. (There are, in fact, reasons to suppose that all of these stars would have gone into decline anyway even if sound had not come). Brian Aherne (1969), who always had something interesting to say about most events, explains in his book that whilst the sets of silent films were actually very noisy, with carpenters banging, furniture or equipment being dragged around and shouting directors, paradoxically for talkies there had to be silence and actors could hear themselves speak without distraction. Both Menjou and Aherne say that for a while the sound technicians became all-powerful but this did not last as soundproof cameras and booms to carry microphones came into use. Sound did not interrupt Joan Crawford's upward trajectory and she wrote, 'I did not

---

35   Jannings was in The Blue Angel (1930) with Marlene Dietrich, made in Germany, and thereafter in some silent films in the US. See Chapter 4.

panic because I didn't have enough sense. I'd been talking all my life; it seemed perfectly natural.'

When John Barrymore (1882–1942) published his autobiography in 1926, he was, he anticipated, at the mid-point in his career. His book is entirely about his time in the theatre. All he said about movies, at the very end of the book, was that he liked to 'interlard them' with the theatre. In fact he was to shift almost entirely into film-making. His first film was in 1913 and despite his heavy drinking, which increasingly impaired his performances, he went on making movies until the year of his death. This was probably because he got bored after the first performance of a play. He also says that he never wanted to be an actor but a painter in which he showed some talent. Movies suited him and a rich offer from Warner's was enough to get him to leave the stage. Most satisfying and accessible today are his performances in *Grand Hotel* (1932) and *Twentieth Century* (1934). On the stage he had been famous for his 'Hamlet', but he never appeared in that role in a film.[36]

Mary Astor (1906–87) was for a short while Barrymore's mistress. She made several silent films including *Don Q, Son of Zorro* (1925) with Douglas Fairbanks Snr. Astor had a long career running from 1921 to 1964 when she was in *Hush . . . Hush Sweet Charlotte* (1964) with Bette Davis. Her best remembered performance is with Humphrey Bogart in *The Maltese Falcon* (1941) as the hard-hearted Brigid O'Shaughnessy that Bogart reluctantly despatches to her just deserts. Astor's autobiography (1971) is very interesting and curiously distant with her wide-eyed attitude to the film business. It is notable for the clear detail she goes into about lighting and camera technique. Like Tallulah Bankhead (1902–68), Astor was

---

36   Barrymore was the brother of Ethel and Lionel Barrymore. An odd thing about his book is that the pages are not numbered.

a teenage beauty queen, a not uncommon entry point into films. However, Bankhead was primarily a stage actress and she and Bankhead had little else in common.[37]

Edward Arnold (1890–1956), whose parents were German and very poor, was an overweight character actor who remained consistently popular and in work for a very long time. At the point at which he wrote his autobiography (1940), only seven of his forty-four years were in pictures, but he continued in movies right up to his death sixteen years later. He started on the stage at the age of fifteen and only went to Hollywood in1932. Arnold made quite a few silent films at Essanay in Chicago and combined this with stage acting.

Adolphe Menjou (1890–1963) started as an extra at the Vitagraph studios in New York. His father was French and Menjou was fluent in six languages. Born in Pittsburgh, he went to Cornell University to study engineering but left before graduating. Menjou played Louis XIII in *The Three Musketeers* (1921), his second film with Douglas Fairbanks Snr. His autobiography (1948) is that of a very funny raconteur and in it he says that he had made 146 films and he was to continue to make them until 1960. Menjou achieved early stardom in the silent period, though later he descended to being a character actor, albeit one in virtually constant demand. After the success of *The Grand Duchess and the Waiter* (1926) he signed a new contract with Jesse Lasky at $5,000 a week. He comments on this in his book: 'I had finally arrived at the top. Of course, I had developed insomnia, a Hollywood Ulcer, my first gray hairs, and my wife was suing me for divorce, but at last I was a real star' (Menjou, 1948).

---

37 According to Halliwell (2001), Bankhead made two films in 1918, one in 1928 and several in the 1930s. She popped up again with a fine performance in Hitchcock's Lifeboat (1944). Her breathless autobiography (1952) barely mentions her film appearances.

◄ HOLLYWOOD LIVES

Menjou was a natty dresser and was described by Clark Gable as 'a Hollywood Intellectual' but his reputation for intellect probably owed more to his prodigious memory and wit than to any powers of analysis – though he did cleverly sell out of Wall Street before the 1929 crash. A kindly and friendly person, he spoiled his reputation by being a friendly witness at the 1947 House Un-American Activities Committee (HUAC) hearings (see Chapter 10) and named people he thought were Communists. Menjou appeared in almost every kind of film, from Westerns to romantic comedies. He is especially memorable in the Deanna Durbin vehicle, *One Hundred Men and a Girl* (1937), and in the much grimmer *Paths of Glory* (1957).

Menjou was full of admiration for Charles Chaplin (1889–1977) whom he described in his book as a genius. You would expect Chaplin himself to produce a good autobiography and he did, in 1964[38]. Chaplin's long life was full of success and suffering and incident but although it had a happy ending the whole book is rather gloomy and was coloured by the shabby treatment he received in the United States, later rectified to some extent. Anyone who has seen Richard Attenborough's biopic, *Chaplin* (1992), with its astonishing performance by the American actor, Robert Downey (1965–) in the title role, knows the outline of Chaplin's life. He was born into poverty and was only fourteen when his mother was placed in a mental asylum, his father already dead from dropsy. He wrote of that time: 'As I walked from the hospital towards home, I could feel only a numbing sadness. Yet I was relieved, for I knew that Mother would be better off in the hospital than sitting alone

---

[38] Ten years later Chaplin published *My Life in Pictures*, which has fifty-five illustrations. Two other autobiographical works of his appeared in the interwar period.

◄ 36

in that dark room with nothing to eat. But that heart breaking look as they led her away I shall never forget.'

His mother remained in the asylum until 1921 when Chaplin was able to bring her to California. In the meantime, determined to succeed in England, he managed on his own, taking various odd jobs and pursuing his dream of a theatrical career. He registered with an agency which got him a job in a play at £2.10s a week and eventually a place in Fred Karno's vaudeville company. The company went on tour in the US in 1910 and Chaplin went with it. He was successfully auditioned for Mack Sennett's Keystone Studio and in turn filmed with the Essanay, Mutual and First National Studios, each time racking up his earnings on the back of the growing public success of his films. By 1917, astonishing as it is, he could afford to build his own studio on the basis of a contract to supply a certain number of films. It had been at Keystone that Chaplin had invented the character of the little tramp with Derby hat, baggy trousers, moustache and cane. Although this character was enormously successful, Sennett would not meet Chaplin's contractual demands, saying, wrongly, that 'without the support of our organisation you would be lost'. During the First World War Chaplin was rejected for service in the British Army on the grounds that he was too small and underweight. Later, he became close to Douglas Fairbanks Sr, whom he described as 'the only real friend I have ever had' and these two, with D.W. Griffith and Mary Pickford, set up United Artists in 1919 (as described in Chapter 1).

The rest of Chaplin's life was less hectic but equally dramatic. In 1943 in America he was the subject of a paternity suit. A blood test which proved that he was not responsible was not acceptable at the time and he lost the case. The HUAC subpoenaed him but he was never called to the hearings, perhaps because he sent a cable to assert that he was not a Communist. In 1952, however, after a visit to London and Paris where he had been greeted by enormous crowds, he was denied re-entry into the United States and was barred until he had faced an Immigration Committee to answer 'charges of a political nature and of moral turpitude'. Chaplin decided that he did not want to go back to 'that unhappy country' and from 1953 made his home in Switzerland. He did not return to the US until 1972 – when all seemed to have been forgiven – to be presented with an Academy Award (his third). Britain was even slower than America to recognise Chaplin's achievements and his knighthood did not come until 1975. Chaplin married Paulette Goddard, the actress, who became his third wife in 1936.[39] They were divorced in 1942 and a year later he married eighteen-year-old Oona O'Neill, daughter of the playwright Eugene O'Neill, who bore him eight children. Oona survived Chaplin's death to die at the age of eighty-eight.

The comedy shorts that Chaplin made are his greatest achievements. He was reluctant to adopt sound and his feature films after the 1920s, which included *Modern Times* (1936) and *The Great Dictator* (1940), are, in some cases, heavy-going, particularly *Monsieur Verdoux* (1947). Like all his partners in United Artists, Chaplin did not really survive the adoption of sound.[40]

39 Paulette Goddard (1910–90) was a light comedienne who started off as a chorine. She appeared in Modern Times and The Great Dictator. Her many other films included The Cat and the Canary (1939), Reap the Wild Wind (1942) and The Diary of a Chambermaid (1946). Her third husband, after Chaplin, was Burgess Meredith.
40 Claire Bloom (1931–) played with Chaplin in Limelight (1952), her second film. She admired him very much and in her own words was a 'surrogate daughter'. Very much a British stage actress, she did not settle in Hollywood, despite her ten-year marriage to Rod Steiger. One of her later memorable Hollywood roles was as the estranged wife of George C. Scott, who played Hemingway in Islands in the Stream (1977). She wrote two autobiographies (1982, 1996) the second being very much about her personal life.

PAST AND PRESENT

Douglas Fairbanks Snr (1883-1939), the first of the mega-stars, did have a rather high-pitched voice but it was probably not that which held him back from continuing stardom after the adoption of sound so much as an inevitable diminution in his athleticism and the bewildering consequences of this for a man who had built his life on dramatic physical activity. Fairbanks had always been physically restless. At the age of three he climbed a vine- covered lattice to the roof of a barn at home and jumped off, attempting to show his elder brother Robert that he could fly. He was not seriously injured but the incident illustrates his need from an early age to show off (Hancock and Fairbanks, 1953). As an adult, he published a book, *Laugh and Live* in 1917, the title of which embodies his philosophical approach to the millions of fans who looked up to him for guidance. This was another aspect of his character which, along with athleticism and showmanship, defined his persona (Cooke, 1940). He also published other books in the same vein, but never wrote an autobiography.

Fairbanks started on the New York stage in 1900. He had a brief sojourn at Harvard University where, reportedly, he spent most of his time in the gym. After that he took a trip to Europe, worked in Wall Street, then went back to the theatre. By 1910 he was a well-established star on Broadway and that led to Hollywood in 1915 with an association with the Triangle Corporation. His initial contract there was for $2,000 a week, which was a lot at the time. It took Fairbanks a while to establish his screen character and in this he was assisted by screenwriter Anita Loos and her director-husband, John Emerson. In 1916 he made eleven films, which Cooke (1940) describes as 'comedy melodramas decorated with acrobatics'. At the end of 1916, he formed his own production company and in 1919, as already mentioned, became a founder of United Artists. His earlier films were essentially satires on what could now be described as 'political correctness' and his later ones, from the 1920s, were costume pictures: *The Mark of Zorro* (1920) and *The Three Musketeers* (1921). These were immensely popular and were followed by others, for example, *Robin Hood* (1921), *The Thief of Bagdad* (1923) and what is often cited as his best, *The Black Pirate* (1926). In *The Taming of the Shrew* (1929) Fairbanks co-starred with his then wife, Mary Pickford and this film marked the beginning of his decline. From 1933 to 1936 he lived in England and France. In 1935 he was divorced from Pickford and in the following year married Sylvia, Lady Ashley, announcing that he was 'through with acting'. He died only four years later.

Mary Pickford (1893–1979) was born in Canada. Her father died when she was very young and her mother put her on the stage when she was only five years old. By 1909 she was making films with D.W. Griffith. Empowered by her great popularity with the public, Pickford moved from studio to studio, as Chaplin had done, increasing her salary until with Adolph Zukor she was making $10,000 a week. She left Players Lasky, though, to go to First National, who were willing to give her a measure of independence. Earlier, against her mother's wishes, she had married Owen Moore, an actor. She became the business brain of United Artists (Chaplin proved to be a difficult partner and would often not even answer the telephone to her). Her marriage to Moore lasted a long time but was not a happy one and Pickford finally divorced him to marry Fairbanks.

Both of them were worried about the effects of their divorces on their cinema public but it worked out all right and they were very happy. Pickford wrote: 'Despite my success I had been a very lonely person. More than anything else I had wanted desperately to be approved of and that approval Douglas gave me.' Pickford's autobiography (1956) has a photograph taken during their honeymoon in Europe of Fairbanks standing on his hands

PAST AND PRESENT

on top of a building in London with his still girlish wife looking on. Wherever they went, crowds appeared. One of the great advantages of silent films was, as she put it, 'through our voiceless images we were citizens of every country in the world'. Like Mickey Rooney, Pickford continued to dress like a child long after she was an adult. But she knew when to stop and made her last film in 1933. Sadly, in 1936, she and Fairbanks divorced and he drifted away to Europe. Neither of them wanted this outcome, it seems, which Pickford said was driven by the media. Forlornly, she wrote that Fairbanks had loved her more than she him and they only split up when he felt his youth slipping away. She quickly remarried, to Buddy Rogers, another actor, and went on to outlive Fairbanks by forty years.

The Pickford autobiography is beautifully written and manages to convey both her sweet demure character as well as the steely ambition that lay behind it. Cecil B. DeMille praised Pickford's character, acting ability and public-spiritedness in a Foreword to the book. It was entirely appropriate that the Fairbanks in their house, Pickfair, were called the royalty of Hollywood.

Douglas Fairbanks Snr was the son of a Charles Ullman, a lawyer. In his autobiography, Fairbanks Jnr explains why it was that his father's born name was not Fairbanks. What happened was that Fairbanks Snr's mother, his grandmother, on divorce from Ullman, reverted to the name of Fairbanks which she had gained by a previous marriage and this name was legally adopted by her children. Fairbanks Jnr (1909–2000) was the only son of Douglas Fairbanks and Mary Pickford was to become his stepmother. Junior was only nine years old when his parents divorced. He was brought up by his mother and wrote in the first volume of his autobiography (1988) that his father 'was perfectly tender and nice' but was somewhat distant and lacked parental feeling for him. Perhaps Senior felt that his own youthful, bouncy and cheerful persona on screen and off was not really appropriate for fatherhood. He insisted that Junior called him 'Pete' and he called his son 'Jayar'. There may also have been an element of jealousy in his feelings for his son and he was very much against Junior taking up a career in films. If so, he would have been upset when Jesse Lasky, worried about competition from United Artists, gave Junior a film role at the age of only thirteen. The boy did try to avoid roles that would be competitive, often to little avail because that was what the public seemed to want. Meanwhile, his father, having made a very generous divorce settlement, was not aware that his former wife and son were very short of money, a fact carefully concealed from him.

Douglas Fairbanks Jr with Rita Hayworth in *Angels Over Broadway* (1940): Dr Macro/Columbia.

Junior's screen debut was not a great success, and although he did later establish himself as a well-known actor, he never achieved megastar status. It was John Barrymore who showed him the ropes. Fairbanks Jnr's best-known appearances were in *Dawn Patrol* (1930), *The Prisoner of Zenda* (1937) and *Gunga Din* (1939). Less well known is the British thriller, *State Secret (*1950), in which he played an American surgeon who is asked to operate on a Ruritanian dictator and is chased by Nazi-like characters in Hitchcock fashion across the country and over the mountains. Junior was more intelligent, less athletic and more conventionally handsome than his father. He could have achieved more on the screen than he did but his heart was not in the movies: he made them for the money. This may have been a factor in the ending of his first marriage to Joan Crawford, who wrote that Junior was not as ambitious as she was and yet he 'had a dozen talents for my one'. He also needed more stimulation than she did and wanted the house full of people every evening. In fact, as his later career demonstrated, Fairbanks Jnr was ambitious in a different way; he wanted to play a part, however small, in the big events of his time. He was to succeed in this.

Fairbanks Jnr, like his father, was an Anglophile.[41] He played a part in getting FDR's gift of second-hand destroyers to Britain before the US entered the war and he also worked for the repeal of the US Neutrality Act which had kept America out. During the war, as a US naval officer, Fairbanks worked on the staff of Louis Mountbatten helping to plan and participating in the disastrous Dieppe Raid in 1942 that David Niven was also a part of. Junior served in naval operational

---

41 Connell (1955), Fairbanks Jnr's biographer, tells us that his subject had a facsimile of a British pub, the Rose and Crown, in his Spanish colonial-style house at Pacific Palisades.

units supporting Tito in the Adriatic (like Sterling Hayden)[42] and also secretly financed RAF hospitals. Many of his wartime activities are described in the second volume of his autobiography, *A Hell of a War* (1995).[43] He became friends with many people in the international diplomatic community and Connell (1955) describes how in 1952 he had Queen Elizabeth II and the Duke of Edinburgh for dinner at his house in the prestigious district of the Boltons in London.

Fairbanks Jnr's divorce from Joan Crawford (1905–77) took place three years before his father's divorce from Mary Pickford in 1935. Fairbanks Snr's own last throw at marriage came in 1936, only three years before his death. Father and son had a fairly distant relationship but after Snr remarried they became closer and even discussed forming a movie company together. In the Prologue to Jnr's first autobiography he describes a visit to what turned out to be his father's deathbed. His father loved the classics and Jnr read him bits of Shakespeare and Byron. Quite unexpectedly, Snr died that night (he had only been ill for a couple of days) and Fairbanks Jnr wrote that when his father died he became 'more of his own man...but I had lost the one I always wished most to please'.

An enormous amount has been written about Joan Crawford and her autobiography, *A Portrait of Joan* (1962) is very good and, despite some omissions, apparently very honest. She was born Lucille LeSueur in San Antonio, Texas. Her father 'vanished' and she became a dancer at a very young age, playing in nightclubs as Billie Cassin (taking the surname of her stepfather, Henry Cassin). Discovered by an agent for MGM, she made her first film in 1921 but her real debut was

---

42   Lord Mountbatten (1900–79) was Chief of Combined Operations and later Supreme Allied Commander of the South-East Asia theatre. He was assassinated by the Irish Republican Army in 1979.
43   A third volume was promised but never appeared.

in *Pretty Ladies* (1925). Many, if not most, of her films can be seen as autobiographical, especially *Queen Bee* (1955). *Dancing Lady* (1933) has a scene in which a youngster, desperate for a job, pushes her way into the manager's office (Clark Gable). In her book she says that this scene was criticised as unrealistic and her performance overdone, but it was actually something from of her own experience.

Much later, after she moved to Warner's, she plays a determined woman driven to succeed in *Mildred Pierce* (1945). This performance won her an Oscar and it was again exactly as she was. Joan Crawford was undeniably a great star but she had some blips in her career and each time successfully reinvented herself.[44] She was supposed to have had a long feud with her rival, Bette Davis, and there is a book about that (Considine, 1989). Far worse was a book by one of Crawford's adopted daughters, Christina, entitled *Mommie Dearest* (1978), which portrayed her as a monster who beat her children with wire coat-hangers. Mercifully, the book did not appear until immediately after her death. It would have been very hurtful to Crawford who was proud of her ability to combine a working life with motherhood. *Mommie Dearest* was very popular and was made into a much less popular film of the same name, starring Faye Dunaway. It is doubtful if there was much truth in the allegations of savage ill-treatment, though one can believe that Crawford would have been a strict and demanding parent. Another of her daughters said

---

[44] Crawford had a long career (forty-nine years), a little more than Menjou (forty-four years) but somewhat less than Melvyn Douglas (1901–81), who worked in films or on the stage for over fifty years, though he started later than the other two, after sound was introduced. Douglas actually had a gap in film-making from the early 1950s to the 1960s, and in his later period, when he reinvented himself as a character actor, he won two Oscars for best supporting actor (for Hud (1963) and for Being There (1979)). His disappointing autobiography (1986) devotes space to his theatrical interests and his politics as a member of the Democratic party.

that there was little truth in the book and Douglas Fairbanks Jnr commented convincingly that Crawford would never have used wire coat-hangers as being too harmful to her impeccable wardrobe! Of course, attacking famous parents in print could be very profitable and Bette Davis and Bing Crosby were to receive similar treatment at the hands of their respective offspring.[45]

In addition to her autobiography, Crawford wrote another book towards the end of her life, *My Way of Life* (1971), which offered health and beauty tips, hints on how to be a good hostess, how to combine a career with motherhood, and so on. It was really all just a question of organisation: 'I organise myself right down to the second because I'm greedy. Greedy to fill every minute of my days with all the things I want to accomplish . . . with a little organisation a woman can excel as wife, homeworker, mother, career woman and gracious hostess, be lovely to look at and to be with.'

Michael Korda (1999), a member of the Korda film-making family and therefore familiar with the issues in movie stardom, happened to be the editor of Crawford's second book. He felt that 'Joan's how-to-do book was, in fact, a kind of autobiography, not of the life she had lived but of life as she would *like* to have lived.' Korda is very amusing about Crawford and her fastidious and compulsive ways (which no doubt could be very irritating) and finally thought that the object of writing the book was to give her an opportunity for a publicity tour to get her back into the limelight. He clearly did not take to Crawford personally and is a little unkind about a

---

45 See B. D. Hyman, My Mother's Keeper, William Morrow (1985), on Bette Davis. The book appeared when Davis was recovering from a stroke and an operation. Gary Merrill (1915–90), in his autobiography, gives an affectionate, if exasperated account of his marriage to Davis and heavily criticises her daughter's book. For Bing Crosby, see Chapter 9.

lonely woman used to adoration by millions of fans but now feeling her age and at the end of her career. Crawford's book offers fascinating evidence, if any be needed, of the drive and steely determination that made her such a very big star for a long time.[46]

---

46   Crawford gave no acknowledgment to her editors of her book, or indeed to anyone else. Korda also worked on Ronald Reagan's second autobiography and is very amusing about that, this time in a more kindly way.

CHAPTER **3**

Fact or Fiction?

DAVID NIVEN (1910–1983) was an actor who improved many otherwise mediocre films but never became a superstar. He had a long career and made some ninety-one feature films. With his erect carriage, gentlemanly air and trademark moustache, he looked the military man he was. In a bathing costume or without a shirt, Niven was revealed as surprisingly muscular. Somehow his head did not fit the rest of the body – the impression was rather like those seaside photographer's stages where you stick you head into a hole over the incongruous image of a circus strong man or a fat lady. He was a womaniser and, in his early years especially, something of a con-artist, but these characteristics were an integral part of his personality. His greatest achievement may have been the book he wrote about his life, *The Moon's a Balloon* (1971) and its sequel, *Bring on the Empty Horses* (1975), which together sold a total of over 9 million copies – certainly much more than all the other autobiographies in this book taken together.

Niven, or Niv, as he was affectionately called, is an interesting actor to start with in attempting to answer the question whether screen actors' autobiographies were true and complete representations of the facts? The answer, in his case, is definitely not. This is not in itself a criticism of the books. It is well understood that as art the novel may get nearer to the truth than non-fiction and what Niven wrote were really only novels broadly based on fact. Detailed and comprehensive accounts of reality are often boring and even misleading in this sense. Graham Lord (2003), Niven's official biographer, attempts to disentangle accuracy from falsehood in Niven's books and quotes Peter Ustinov, a great raconteur himself, as saying: 'all great storytelling needs a degree of fictional embellishment . . . you're not really telling a lie, you're just concentrating something into a nugget'. Niven claimed that all the stories in *Balloon* were true but the book is not subtitled 'an autobiography' or even 'memoirs', but 'reminiscences', which carries with it the sense of recovered knowledge, not a researched and verified account. Several of his friends commented that with continuing retelling and successive improvements, Niven could not tell the difference between truth and invention. Some of his stories were constructed by studio publicists from things he told them and then repeated so often that even Niven himself believed them.

There is nonetheless evidence that in his autobiography Niven made some effort to leave out some of these fabrications. One was that while in Cuba he had joined Castro's army of rebels. This story reappears, no doubt recounted by Niven, in Fred Astaire's autobiography, cited below, but not in Niven's own book. The fact is that Niven did spend a week in Havana waiting for a connecting liner on his way from New York to Los Angeles, but there was no question of joining an army. A similar story, also omitted from *Balloon*, is that while in Mexico, where he went when his US visa expired and while waiting to re enter the US, Niven instructed Mexican rebels in the use of firearms. The truth as told in *Balloon* was that he had merely cleaned guns for visiting American tourists who were on hunting expeditions.

David Niven with Merle Oberon in *Beloved Enemy* (1936): Dr Macro/Samuel Goldwyn.

Niven was born in London of a military family – and not in Scotland as he led people to believe.[47] Lord suspected, and Munn (2009) confirms, that Niven's real father was not

---

47   His birthplace is not given in Balloon, although he is careful to mention that his 'father' owned a house in Argyllshire. Niven applied to join the Argyll and Sutherland Highlanders when he came to first join the army. His second choice was the Black Watch and his third, 'Anything but the Highland Light Infantry', which is where they placed him.

William Niven, as stated in *Balloon*. William was a rich man's son with a large family who fell upon hard times and was killed in the Dardenelles when David was seven years old. David's real father was Sir Thomas Comyn-Platt, a diplomat. Platt, later Niven's stepfather after he married his mother after William's death, paid for David's education at a series of expensive private establishments, including a prep school in Worthing and at Stowe, a new school at the time, which was to become one of the best public schools in the country. David, who always had a poor relationship with Platt, greatly admired the headmaster at Stowe, J. F. Roxburgh, who became his role model, and it was attendance at Stowe that was to turn the young Niven, a rascally boy, into the polished gentleman he was to become. Though even at Stowe he got into many scrapes and there, among other misdemeanours, he was caught cheating in an examination. While still at school he says he fell in love with a seventeen-year-old prostitute that he met in Bond Street and who initiated him into sex. It was also at Stowe that he discovered his ability to make people laugh with his impressions and stories – to entertain became for Niven a compulsion.

He failed to pass his School Certificate at sixteen (though he did well in English) but finally got through it at eighteen to secure a place at the Royal Military College at Sandhurst, having failed to get into Dartmouth for the Navy. He left Sandhurst in 1929, having quite distinguished himself in their shows and by becoming an 'under-officer', though he came well down in the final rankings. He was posted as a second lieutenant in the Highland Light Infantry and sent to Malta. There his boredom and frustration were relieved only by becoming friends with Michael Trubshaw and plenty of

FACT OR FICTION?

opportunities with girls.[48] After his mother's death in 1932 at the age of only fifty-two, Niven took an extended leave to America, which captivated him, and he decided he wanted to work in Hollywood as soon as possible. He had met Barbara Hutton in London and at her invitation spent that Christmas with Barbara and her family in New York. Having glimpsed the sort of life he really wanted, on return to Britain he resigned from the army, sold his body to a London hospital for £6 10s for eventual use in research and sailed to Canada. (Three years later, his brother Max was to buy him out of this hospital agreement as a present.)

On arrival in Canada in 1933, Niven made his way to New York where he got a job as a liquor salesman; Prohibition having ended after fourteen years. He inherited some money from his mother and went to Hollywood in pursuit of his ambition. There, he met a young woman, Gretchen, who was later to be reincarnated as Loretta Young. He also met and consorted with Douglas Fairbanks Jnr, Ronald Colman, Fred Astaire and Irving Thalberg. All this was achieved by charm and networking. Lord explains that it was not so difficult then, 'Hollywood was just a village, the actors had as yet no reason to hide themselves away behind high walls with security men and dogs. In a grocery or drug store you might well find yourself standing next to Clark Gable or Joan Crawford' (Lord 2003). Niven called in on people on the slightest pretext. In his autobiography, Fred Astaire wrote:

[EXT]
One day Phyllis went to answer the front doorbell. She suddenly returned in a rather frightened state. She said,

---

48 Michael Trubshaw (1905–88), British stage and cinema character actor, usually of military types. Trubshaw's trademark was a large handlebar moustache.

'There's a dwedful man at the front door without a shirt on who says he knows your sister and that he's just been playing tennis at Don and Bee Stewarts house. He wants to see you.'

When I came face-to face with this individual I detected immediately a rather military-looking Britisher of unquestionably fascinating personality.

We had a drink or two and heard all about his stint in the Cuban army since getting out of the Scots Guards, his racing mules in Florida and I don't know what all, and that he was thinking about going into the movies but so far he had no chance to do anything but think about it. To us he certainly seemed to qualify with that personality. He had us in stitches the entire time. His name was Niven . . . How glad we were that he stopped by that day. We gained one of the closest of lifetime friends. (Astaire, 1959)[49]
[EXT ends]

At this stage, Niven's new friends were not able to help in getting screen work and after returning from the visit to Mexico to renew his visa, he registered with Central Casting and was given roles as an extra in a number of Westerns. Edmund Goulding, one of the first British directors to settle in Hollywood, introduced Niven to Samuel Goldwyn and only six weeks after his return from Mexico he was signed to a seven-year contract. His first film for Goldwyn was *Barbary Coast* (1935), in which he received no billing, but it was a start. At this time Merle Oberon, with whom David had been intimate

---

49 Phyllis was Mrs Astaire; note the references to the Cuban Army and the Scots Guards.

FACT OR FICTION?

in London, was also signed by Goldwyn and the two began a long-term 'secret' affair.[50] Merle coached David in acting and was helpful in his relationship with Goldwyn. She is referred to in *Balloon* as 'the Great Big Star'. Niven's first leading role came in *Thank You, Jeeves!* (1936), though it was only a 'B' picture. In *The Charge of the Light Brigade* (1936), however, he had a significant supporting role to Errol Flynn and Olivia de Havilland, although he dies halfway through the picture. The film was very successful and Niven was well on his way to an established career, consolidated in *Dodsworth* (1936) and *The Dawn Patrol* (1938) in which he plays a cheerful, death-defying flyer in the First World War. Niven and Flynn became friends after *Light Brigade* and during one of Flynn's separations from his wife, shared not only their common interest in girls and drinking but also a house, rented jointly from Rosalind Russell who dubbed it 'Cirrhosis By the Sea'. However, Flynn and Niven drew apart later as the former's antics became too much, even for Niven.

In 1939, when war was declared, Niven felt it was his duty to return to Britain and join up. He had some difficulty in securing a release from his contract with Goldwyn, who became aware that the official advice to expatriate British actors was to stay put (see next chapter). On getting back, to Niven's surprise and disappointment, he was turned down both by the RAF and the Scots Guards. He finally joined the Rifle Brigade, the 'Green Jackets', an elite light infantry regiment. He was able to do this because of a chance meeting

---

50 Merle Oberon (1911–79), an exotic beauty, was born in India of mixed parentage. Her mother was Indian, a fact she kept secret, not allowing her mother to live with her for fear of revealing the truth. Her screen career began in Britain with Alexander Korda and she later married him. Munn (2009) says that Niven told him that Merle made him into an actor and that he regretted not marrying her. Michael Korda, Alexander's brother's son wrote a roman-à-clef (1985) about Oberon's life.

with one of their battalion commanders at the Café de Paris, where he also caught a glimpse of the woman he was later to marry.[51] Soon he was to meet her – Primula Rollo, a cipher officer in the Women's Auxiliary Air Force (WAAF) – and they married shortly afterwards in September 1940. After training, Niven volunteered for service in a new Commando regiment called Phantom. He participated in a raid on Guernsey in the Channel Islands, on which the official line (which Niven dutifully follows in *Balloon*) was that it was successful – later revealing to Munn that it was actually a fiasco. He also helped to plan, and participated in, the disastrous raid on Dieppe in 1942 in which over 1,000 men lost their lives and many more were injured or captured. Douglas Fairbanks Jr was also in this action, carrying out diversionary attacks. While still in the army, Niven was released to make two films: *The First of the Few* (1941) and *The Way Ahead* (1944).[52]

By 1942 and after Primmie had left the WAAF so that she could make a home for David, she bore the second of their two sons. Niven, however, admitted to Munn that he had continued

---

51 There are various accounts of this meeting. In Balloon, Niven says he met his future wife at the National Gallery, having previously glimpsed her at the Café de Paris. In another version, told to Munn, he said that he jumped into a slit trench at Biggin Hill RAF station during an air raid and found he was sharing it with her (Munn, 2009).

52 In the first of these films Niven plays a test pilot who helps in the development of the Spitfire fighter aircraft, in the second he is an army officer who turns an assorted group of recruits into fighting men and finally leads them into battle. Of The Way Ahead, Lord (2003) writes that 'the film leaves a residue of deep regret that the characters of Britain and the British have changed so drastically since then'. For this film, Peter Ustinov, in reality a private in the army at the time, had to be appointed Niven's batman (servant) so that he could consort with officers. The preparatory work was done at the Ritz Hotel, and in his very funny autobiography, Ustinov says that in order to keep up with the cost of ordering rounds of drinks for his colleagues at the hotel he was obliged to sell the only valuable asset he had, a nude by Derain, for which a dealer gave him £60. Many years after the war, Ustinov was to notice the Derain on the wall of Niven's home. He had bought it soon after for £65, a fraction of its value (Ustinov, 1977).

FACT OR FICTION?

with his philandering. In 1944 he was promoted to Lieutenant Colonel and in an Anglo-American liaison role attached to SHAEF, his rank enabled him to sit in on meetings with Generals Eisenhower and Montgomery. Niven was one of several famous people, including Dirk Bogarde and Ernest Hemingway, to claim that he was the first Allied soldier to enter Paris after the liberation. Although he outlines his work for Phantom and SHAEF, he did not go into detail, except in amusing anecdotes. Niven rarely spoke of his wartime experiences, which included experience of battle and death in the Phantom raids and the D-Day landings, and even the concentration camps he visited in Germany. He told Munn, 'My mental scars are more than I can handle. I leave them alone when I can . . . I was a bighead in Hollywood but not in the war.'

In 1945, home from the war, Niven signed a new contract with Goldwyn and was shocked to find himself thumped for back-taxes from the British Inland Revenue, who claimed that he had been a British resident since 1939. For *A Matter of Life and Death* (1946) Niven was loaned out to Michael Powell and Emeric Pressburger. This colour film is about an airman shot down, falling in love with a radio operator (Kim Hunter) as the plane goes down. Later, undergoing a life-saving operation, he has to fight before a court in heaven to be allowed to live, his survival being a mistake by one of the other world's minions (Marius Goring). It is one of Niven's best films even though it was not commercially very successful and slightly controversial because of some anti-British sentiments expressed by the prosecution (Raymond Massey). Soon after he was back in America with Primmie, feeling happy to be in what he now considered home. (Niven was fiercely patriotic as we have seen and did not become an American national but he was to spend much of the rest of his life outside both Britain and America.)

In 1946, Primmie died in a tragic accident at the home of Tyrone Power. The party was playing 'Sardines' or 'hide and seek' and in the dark she fell down a long flight of steps into a cellar after opening a door that she presumably expected to be a cupboard. Cesar Romero, whose idea it was to play the game, and Oleg Cassini (see Chapter 7) carried her upstairs but against medical expectations, she died in hospital the next day.[53] Niven was distraught; it was undoubtedly the biggest tragedy of his life and he never really recovered from it. He distracted himself with work and increased his womanising.[54] His films after 1946 included *The Bishop's Wife* (1947) with Loretta Young and Cary Grant, which was good, and *Bonnie Prince Charlie* (1947), a film for Korda of which he was ashamed and cross with Goldwyn about. In Britain, he met and very soon married Hjördis (pronounced 'yerdiss') Tersmeden, aged twenty-eight, a Swedish divorcée and a very beautiful model. One advantage in Niven's eyes was that, like Primmie, she was not an actress, although there were strains when Hjördis received offers from studios. Happy at first, in the long run this second marriage was not successful. Despite this Niven, who said he always loved her, stuck it out to the end. The couple adopted a two-week-old Swedish baby, Kristina. Incredibly, both Munn and Lord say that the child was actually David's through an affair and Lord says that

---

53 Cesar Romero (1907–94) had a long career starting on stage as a dancer, 'The Latin from Manhattan'. The tall versatile character actor was of Cuban parentage. He appeared in Westerns, romantic comedies and musicals and film noir. One of his later appearances was as a shady figure trying to force his way into the action in Ocean's Eleven (1960). Romero was like Anthony Quinn in his roles, another multi-purpose foreigner.

54 It would be tedious to recount all Niven's reported affairs, but top stars he was intimate with included Rita Hayworth and Grace Kelly, according to reliable accounts. Evelyn Keyes refers to a one night-stand she had with him: he 'was darling, a marvellous sense of humour, a delightful story-teller, delicious as French pastry' (Keyes, 1978).

FACT OR FICTION?

Kristina herself believed he was her real father, though he was unable to find proof of this.

Niven had made a series of poor films, culminating with *The Elusive Pimpernel* (1949), which had a delayed release to become, despite everything, a box office success. The year 1948, in which Niven had married Hjördis, was fateful in another respect, as, out of frustration (and out of character), he provoked Goldwyn into releasing him from his contract. Niven soon found he was in trouble and received no other offers. He spent time writing a novel, did some television work and made another film in Britain.[55] The studios did not approve of their stars appearing on television but Niven, now free of contractual constraints, was one of the first to do so. He invested in a new company, Four Star Television, alongside Dick Powell, Charles Boyer and Ida Lupino. The idea was that the actor-founders would contribute performances on a regular basis and in some cases, as in Dick Powell's Zane Grey Theater, present them as well. The venture was to prove very profitable and though Ida Lupino dropped out, the others continued and prospered. Founded in 1952, Four Star fell into decline later in the decade and Powell died in 1963.[56]

The Moon's a Balloon gets sketchy after 1948 even though

---

[55] The book, Round the Rugged Rocks was published in 1951 by Cresset. Niven became ashamed of it later and tried to buy up all the copies. The contract he signed gave the publisher an option on his next book which was to cause difficulties when he came to sign with Hamish Hamilton for The Moon's a Balloon.

[56] Dick Powell (1904–63) started as a juvenile singer but later transformed himself into a screen tough guy in Murder, My Sweet (1944). He also became a good businessman, director and producer. His second and third wives were Joan Blondell and June Allyson. He died of cancer, possibly caused by filming near a nuclear test site. It is a pity that Powell, an underrated actor, never wrote an autobiography, as he had a very interesting life. Charles Boyer (1899–1978) made films in France and Hollywood. With a heavy accent, he was equally good in dramatic, romantic and comic roles, an example of which is Cluny Brown (1946) with Jennifer Jones, not to be missed. Though billed as 'The Great Lover', he was married for forty-four years and committed suicide after the death of his wife.

there were to be many important events in Niven's life and some of his best films were still to come. In fact, about 85 per cent of the text of his book covers the period up to 1948 when Niven was still only thirty-nine years old, so that the remaining 15 per cent had to cover the twenty-two years up to its completion and he was to live another twenty years after that, working right up to the end. His later work included notably: *Carrington V.C.* (1955), *Around the World in Eighty Days* (1956), his own favourite, and *Separate Tables* (1958). *Separate Tables* won him an Oscar for his role as a British retired Major in a small hotel who tells stories about his war experiences but turns out to be a phoney. Ironically Niven's phoney major was the exact opposite of Niven's own character, though the story-telling was common to both. Other films worth mentioning are *The Guns of Navarone* (1961) and the less commercially successful *55 Days at Peking* (1963). Niven's last film, *The Curse of the Pink Panther* (1983),was a sad continuation of the original hilarious, *The Pink Panther* (1964) in which he had starred with Peter Sellers.

In 1960 Niven sold his house near Hollywood in Pacific Palisades and acquired a large wooden chalet in French-speaking Switzerland at Chateau d'Oex. In 1962 he also bought a villa near Cap Ferrat on the Côte d'Azur. Niven started to write *The Moon's a Balloon* in 1966, although it was not until 1969 that he embarked on a serious attempt to complete his reminiscences. The publisher, Jamie Hamilton, had a large influence on the book –Niven had wanted to write another novel but was persuaded not to and needed a lot of pushing to get it done. Writing *Balloon* was not easy – Niven found that writing was very much harder than acting. It took almost five years in all and a great deal of editing was needed, something Hamish Hamilton was pleased to do because they knew they had a success on their hands. It did so well that Niven, always feeling short of money, signed a contract for a sequel in 1971, the year *Balloon* was first published. The title of the sequel, *Bring on the Empty Horses*, came from a command shouted by director Michael Curtiz during the making of *The Charge of the Light Brigade*. The book was published in 1975 and was an immediate success, selling 1.5 million copies in the USA in two weeks, according to Munn. *Bring on the Empty Horses* is mainly about Hollywood characters, but largely avoids duplicating the earlier book and includes one of the best short descriptions of Hollywood in print.[57] Robert Wagner (2008) wrote that everyone loved David, except his second wife, and that troubled marriage must have made his last years difficult. In 1977 he had been devastated by his daughter Kristina's terrible car accident, which nearly killed her. Her injuries necessitated many operations and a long recuperation time. Shortly after this, in 1979, the first signs of the motor neurone disease which was to kill Niven appeared.

Katharine Hepburn (1907–2003) was a startlingly different character from Niven. She was born on the East Coast – and said that the popular image of her was that of the Statue of Liberty: there was a certain resemblance. She had a slim, angular figure and prominent cheekbones, loved sports and in some ways lived the life of a man, even though she was feminine and could be very glamorous. One of Hepburn's lines in *Rooster Cogburn* (1975), in which she appeared with John Wayne, was 'I grew up more forceful and independent than a woman should be'. Like Charlton Heston, she was a cerebral actor who

---

57 After this, Niven was to write a second novel, Go Slowly, Come Back Quickly (1981) but it was a flop and lost money for the publishers who had paid a large advance.

worked hard at her craft and was determined and ambitious: from her earliest days, she said, she wanted to be famous and had a powerful ego. Her ambitions were fully realised and her name today – years after her death – achieves the international recognition accorded to few and is probably only exceeded by that of Marilyn Monroe. There was a tension between her desire for fame and an equally strong urge for personal privacy, though this trait only inflamed prurient interest. Very much an individualist, Hepburn had radical political views and was one of the first women in Hollywood to wear men's clothes in public. She had deep romantic attachments to both women and men, though the most passionate were with men.

Hepburn started on the stage and returned to it a few times, but her true medium was the movies. In films she had an early success, followed by some ups and downs – though mostly ups, which finally brought her the accolade as the 'screen's first lady'. She won an Oscar for her third film, *Morning Glory* (1933) when only twenty-six years old. Her remaining three Oscars did not come until she was sixty and the last at the age of seventy-four[58] and these were for: *Guess Who's Coming to Dinner* (1967), *The Lion in Winter* (1968), and her penultimate movie, *On Golden Pond* (1981), a lyrical depiction of a mature marriage. Other much-loved films with Hepburn were *The Philadelphia Story* (1940),[59] and *The African Queen* (1951), as well as most of the nine films she made with Spencer Tracy.[60] Anyone as versatile and unconventional

---

58 The annual awards of the American Academy of Motion Picture Arts and Sciences have, since 1927, been measures of esteem by fellow professionals and not necessarily an index of quality or box office success. Some excellent pictures have not received awards, especially in years when there were many contenders.

59 Howard Hughes bought the film rights for this stage play for Hepburn and she let MGM have them on condition that she was in the movie.

60 Spencer Tracy (1900–1967) started on the stage but was exclusively in films from 1930, according to Halliwell. Tracy won his first Oscar for Captains

FACT OR FICTION?

as Hepburn was bound to make some failures ('clinkers' in American parlance) and it is plain from her autobiography that her most traumatic failure was on the Broadway stage in 1939 in *The Lake* as she devotes a whole chapter to it. On screen, it was *Sylvia Scarlett* (1935), in which she plays a girl masquerading as a boy. She dismissed *Scarlet* 'a real disaster', as it was also for its director, George Cukor. She played a budding stage actress in *Stage Door* (1937) a film with Ginger Rogers and Constance Collier, in which Hepburn seems to portray her real character. At that time she was included in the list of actors who were 'box office poison' (see Chapter 4), another trauma for her, but bounced back with *Bringing Up Baby* (1938), a Howard Hawks comedy with Cary Grant.

Hepburn wrote two books: *The Making of the African Queen* (1987) and *Me: Stories of My Life* (1991). The content of both is well described by their titles. Like her autobiography, *The Making of the African Queen* is written in her own distinctive voice, which, if you are familiar with her films, can be heard in every sentence. Both books are in biggish print with lots of fine pictures. The autobiography has been much criticised for what it leaves out. By this the critics mean that it does not go into detail about her personal life, though she does devote chapters to her marriage and to her long relationship with Spencer Tracy. In an exhaustive biography, William J. Mann (2006) focuses on her personal life, suggesting that Hepburn was bisexual (though he does not use that label).[61] Moreover, he argues that the men with whom

---

Courageous (1937) and another for Boys Town (1938) and nominations for several others, including his last, Guess Who's Coming to Dinner (1967). He was an actor's actor and many of our autobiographers pay tribute to his talent.

61 There are several biographies of Hepburn, including one by her friend Scott Berg (2003) which gives a very human portrait. The screenwriter and director Garson Kanin wrote a book Tracy and Hepburn (1971), which upset her so much she did not speak to him for two decades.

she had long-term relationships were similarly sexually ambivalent. He speculates that Tracy's drinking was a sign of an internal struggle with his homosexuality, but produces no real evidence for this. Certainly there is no evidence at all hat Hepburn's husband, Ludlow Ogden Smith, 'Luddy', was sexually conflicted and her autobiography explicitly says that they slept together, at the outset at least. Nor has there ever been any evidence that Howard Hughes, another person with whom she had a relationship, was homosexual and certainly, he spent a lot of time and money pursuing women. Hepburn herself may have been bisexual; she certainly had long-term living-in female companions, but it is quite probable that sex was not an important factor in her life and she is entitled to some privacy in these matters. Mann's accuracy is equally doubtful on other issues on which he tries to undermine her truthfulness. He argues that Hepburn paints an over-idealistic picture of her parents, but she does not conceal the fact that her mother was promoting the Suffragette movement and birth control while her father was a specialist in sexual disease. Hepburn mentions the liberal politics which she inherited from her parents but does not dwell on this nor upon her feminism, which Mann correctly says was not of the fervent kind.[62] She devotes a chapter to her husband Luddy, to whom she was married from 1928 to 1934

---

62 There is a chapter in the book in which she recounts how Louis B. Mayer, whom she liked and respected, sent for her to ask why she had made a speech at a Screen Actors' Guild meeting in support of the strike by the CSU (described below in Chapter 10). Reagan (1965) thought Katharine's action sufficiently noteworthy to say in his first autobiography that her speech was lifted verbatim from a CSU strike bulletin and that she was speaking in a sincere effort to end the mess. Hepburn also made a speech before an audience of 30,000 at a Henry Wallace political function. Wallace was formerly Vice President under Roosevelt and the function was in support of his unsuccessful Progressive Party candidacy for the 1948 presidential election. Hepburn chose to wear a red dress at this event and her speech condemned the HUAC for its infringements of freedom.

and whom she describes affectionately as 'a friend' – but he gets no more space than Leland Hayward, her agent, with whom she had a romance, and others in her life such as Howard Hughes and George Cukor. Also mentioned – all with affection and respect – are her many long-term female friends. Do her omissions matter? Of course not. The book does not, as she makes clear, follow a particular path and there are some well-written episodes on a range of matters, including her younger brother's suicide and two hospital admissions of her own – one for an eye operation and another following a nasty car accident – but it is never boring.

The thing which attracted most attention in Hepburn's autobiography was that she 'came out into the open' about her past relationship with Spencer Tracy which, although well known, she had not hitherto publicly acknowledged. Mann argues fairly convincingly that, although she loved Tracy, their relationship may not have been a physical one and certainly not as continuous as she asserted. In her book, *Me: Stories of My Life* (1991), Hepburn says that 'we just passed twenty-seven years together in what for me was absolute bliss'. Mann shows that they were not together and hardly even saw one another for long periods, particularly in the 1950s and early 1960s (Tracy died in 1967). Hepburn never lived permanently with Tracy in the cottage in the grounds of George Cukor's house, and had another cottage of her own, though she did stay with him when he was ill and was there the day he died. All this is quite consistent with the carefully phrased recollections in *Me*, even if the impression given is misleading. Louise, Tracy's wife, did not know about her husband's relationship with Katharine, and told Hepburn that she thought it was 'only a rumour'. (Louise was dead by the time *Me* appeared.)

It can be seen that assessing whether the recollections in star autobiographies are faithful reflections of reality or not is difficult, especially as far as intimate personal matters are concerned. There is no evidence, for example, for the persistent rumours that Randolph Scott and Cary Grant, who shared a house for a while, were bisexual; certainly Flynn and Niven, who did the same thing, were not. In a few cases, however, actors were willing to write about these things. Rock Hudson (1986), near the end of his life, 'outed' his own homosexuality and revealed the problems it had caused him. Farley Granger (2007), who lived much longer than Hudson, was frank in revealing his bisexuality in his autobiography, written late in his career, by which time standards had changed somewhat. Marlene Dietrich and Katharine Hepburn were careful to write about their lives in a way that was consistent with the image of themselves they wanted to project to the public. Some wrote books which revealed so much pain and, in their own eyes, so much discredit upon themselves that the reader is compelled to believe in their veracity – Gene Tierney, who wrote about her mental problems, and Mercedes McCambridge and Macdonald Carey about their alcoholism, for example.[63]

63 Gene Tierney did not mention in her book the widely reported affair she had with Spencer Tracy during the making of Plymouth Adventure (1952), but on purely personal matters like this, few of the books can be, or should be, completely truthful. As another example, Eva Bartok (1926–98) did not reveal in her autobiography (1959) that Frank Sinatra was the father of her child, though she did admit it later. Macdonald Carey (1913–94) was good in Shadow of Doubt (1943) and in a few Westerns, but he gave up films for the long-running series Days of our Lives, in which he played a doctor. Carey published three books of poetry as well as his autobiography (1991). Mercedes McCambridge (1916–2004), a character actress who studied the classics and was very successful on radio, had a very tough life. She did not get the sort of roles she wanted later, but won an Oscar for her very first film, All the King's Men (1949). She was nominated for her role in Giant (1956) and had a gunfight with Joan Crawford in the

Others included fabrications or omitted things which had nothing to do with their personal lives. We encounter several examples of these omissions and fabrications in this and subsequent chapters. Errol Flynn certainly, and David Niven probably, made things up, or at least embroidered reality to the point of falsehood.[64] Ronald Reagan almost airbrushed his famous first wife, Jane Wyman, out of his second autobiography. Charlton Heston left out entirely any account of his activities over many years in the National Rifle Association (which were politically highly controversial), while Henry Fonda said nothing about his period of being blacklisted. Most surprising of all, Hedy Lamarr failed to mention the astonishing fact that she had patented a pioneering development in electronics. It is not surprising that George Sanders did not discuss his apparently shady business activities in his book, though in fact these did not mature until after his book was published (see Chapter 4).

It might be thought that over-selectivity or untruthfulness would be more likely among those with inflated egos, yet Kirk Douglas and Tony Curtis – who were both reputed to have giant egos (and possibly justifiably so) – wrote books which, as far as one can tell, are very open and accurate. This is so even in the cases of Paul Henreid, Mickey Rooney, Maureen O'Hara and Janet Leigh, who did not seem to have an inflated

---

strange Western, Johnny Guitar (1954), all roles for which her rather plain appearance and strident voice made her suitable. She overcame alcoholism, but in 1987 her only son killed himself and his family. She had published a book about a European trip she made with her son as a little boy and dedicated it to him (1960). Like her later autobiography (1981), the book was highly literate but bitter-sweet. It reveals that she too made a suicide attempt in 1963 and had two failed marriages.

64 Niven also got some facts wrong. Lord (2003) shows that he gave the wrong date for the death of his wife, Primmie, and that there were many other errors in his chronology. But this hardly matters: his book The Moon's a Balloon was not intended to be a faithful autobiography but an entertainment.

view of themselves, did not seem to dissimulate, and their books seem to be as truthful as any. On the whole, therefore, star autobiographies do not appear to be packed with lies as many have contended. Their sins are more likely to be ones of omission rather than commission. As Brian Aherne wrote: 'there are too many living people involved, too many will get their feelings hurt – and perhaps run to their lawyers – if one tells the truth, and if one doesn't one is a bore . . .'

This chapter ends with a look at a practical joke which characteristically was mentioned in Errol Flynn's autobiography (1959), with him as the supposed victim, and was then repeated by the supposed perpetrator, Director Raoul Walsh (Walsh 1975) and in an interview with Schickel (1975), repeated again by David Niven (1975), recounted again at third hand but with innocent belief by Henreid (1984) and was finally quashed by Flynn's friend, the stuntman Buster Wiles (1988) and by McNulty (2004). The tale concerns Flynn's friend John (Jack) Barrymore. Immediately after Barrymore's death there was a wake, with Flynn, Walsh and others all drinking heavily. Flynn was called away and Walsh says he left to carry out the macabre practical joke. With friends, Walsh bribed the undertaker to allow them to borrow the corpse and set it up with a drink in Flynn's living room.[65] The story goes that on returning home, Flynn, well oiled, saw Jack sitting there, gave a scream and ran out of the house, only to be stopped by his friends and told 'it's only a gag'. There are some differences between the various accounts. Henreid's

---

65 Raoul Walsh (1887–1981) was a tough director of action films and directed Flynn in They Died with Their Boots On, Desperate Journey, Gentleman Jim and others. He was once an actor and began in the silent days. A man after Flynn's own heart, Walsh wore an eye-patch to cover the loss of an eye when a jack-rabbit smashed through the windscreen of his car. Halliwell (2001) quotes Jack Warner as saying: 'To Raoul Walsh a tender love scene is burning down a whorehouse'.

version is that the stunt was Peter Lorre's idea and Lorre asked him and Humphrey Bogart to participate but he declined, though 'the others' went ahead. (Lorre, Henreid says was a notorious practical joker, though in this case his victim may have been Henreid, not Flynn.) Walsh says that the undertaker had been one of his character actors and had agreed to lend him the body. As Niven pointed out, this would have been highly illegal and moreover it would not have been possible to arrange Barrymore's corpse in a chair because rigor mortis would have set in. Buster Wiles says that he, Walsh and others were at a dinner party when a call came through announcing Barrymore's death. During a toast to Barrymore, Wiles suggested that it would be funny if someone stole his body and sat him at a table in a nightclub. The suggestion was taken seriously, but Wiles pointed out that the perpetrators would still be in jail had they done it, and also reminded them of the fact that rigor mortis would have made it impossible. According to Wiles, Flynn would never have screamed or run away, even if there had been forty stiffs in his living room. Finally, McNulty (2004) established that a friend of Barrymore's, the writer Gene Fowler and his son, close friends of Barrymore, had actually spent the whole night with the body in the mortuary, thus ruling out any attempt to move it. A pity – it was a good story that has clearly entertained a lot of people, but it does illustrate the power of Hollywood myths.

CHAPTER 4

Hollywood Exiles

HOLLYWOOD GREW BY importing people and ideas from the East Coast of the United States and from Europe. As Baxter (1976) points out, even the palm trees were not indigenous.[66] It is true that the early film-makers, such as D. W. Griffith, Mack Sennett and Cecil B. DeMille were American-born, but the First World War saw a trickle of imported talent, notably Stan Laurel and Charlie Chaplin from England, which, in the 1920s and 1930s, fuelled by the weakness of British cinema, the strength of the London stage and the shared language, became a steady stream. Well before this, though, in the early 1900s, poor immigrants from Eastern and Central Europe landed in New York and later fortified by experience in film distribution found their way to Hollywood to become the moguls who ran the studios. Examples, already mentioned in Chapter 1, included Samuel Goldwyn (Poland), Carl Laemmle (Germany), Louis B. Mayer (Russia) and Adolf Zukor (Hungary). The future

---
66 The same was true of the French Riviera which, in its early days, was inhospitable and mosquito-ridden but was to become another home of cinema, though not on the same scale as Hollywood, and for the same reasons: spectacular scenery, good light and, initially, low costs.

◄ **HOLLYWOOD LIVES**

moguls fanned out and adopted a range of occupations in various places – Goldwyn as a glove-maker in Gloversville, 200 miles from Manhattan; Laemmle a clothier in Oshkosh; the Warner's opened a bicycle shop in Youngstown, Ohio; Mayer did scrap-dealing in New Brunswick; Zukor became a furrier in Chicago; Lewis Selznick a jeweller in Pittsburgh; and William Fox temporarily stayed in New York as a tailor (Scott Berg, 1989). In the 1920s and 1930s more immigrants came from continental Europe, where film-making was already established, and they possessed the specialised skills that were in demand. From the middle to late 1930s there were still more actors, writers and musicians emigrating to America to get away from the rise of fascism, and from the 1930s especially, immigrants to Hollywood were sought by talent-fishing expeditions, including those by the now established moguls themselves. Some of the earlier immigrants were made redundant by the coming of sound in the late 1920s. In the sound era, for those able to acquire fluency, European accents were regarded as attractive and gave an impression of culture and sophistication. Of course, even some English-speaking actors who were successful in the silents did not survive the transition to sound.

Paul Henreid (1908–1992) was an established European actor, forced to leave his home country by the Nazi encroachment. He came to Hollywood from Austria, via Britain. Henreid's father was a banker, ennobled by Emperor Franz Joseph for his services. Henreid had a brief early career on the stage in Vienna, a minor part in a film made in Nice and two more in 1935 and 1936 in his home town. By then the Nazi shadow was being cast over the future and although he was offered a good contract with the large German film-maker, UFA, he turned it down because it would have required him to join the National Socialist Actors Guild, binding him to uphold Nazi ideology. Instead, he continued to act in the Vienna theatre and also appeared on the London stage and in cabaret there. His rejection of a contract with UFA soon led to his exclusion from a film he wanted to do in Vienna because he had been blacklisted by Goebbels, who was then responsible for UFA. Henreid's autobiography (1976) offers many incidents which echo his later film career. At one point he was being typecast for Nazi roles, but then as a romantic lover, before having a variety of roles as a pirate, a gangster and others in which he could display his versatility. Finally he became a director. He had a facility for languages and learned to speak French and English fluently.

At one cabaret performance in London, Henreid was passed a note from Baron von Ribbentrop, then German ambassador, requesting Henreid to dance with his wife. The reader can imagine the ensuing scene in a film with Conrad Veidt in the role of Ribbentrop.[67] Henreid refused the request, saying that he was an actor not a gigolo and adding that he did not care for Nazis.

> *[EXT]*
> *Ribbentrop never moved a muscle. His face grew white, but he just sat there staring at me with his cold blue eyes. I walked away feeling quite good about it. Even now I think it was one of the high points of my life. But it was also a*

---

67 Conrad Veidt (1893–1943) was a wonderful German character actor who was in the famous Cabinet of Dr. Caligari (1919) and who also soon fell out with the Nazis. He appeared in several British films, including The Spy in Black (1939) with Valerie Hobson and, later in Hollywood as Gestapo Major Strasser in Casablanca (1942). Joachim von Ribbentrop a former champagne salesman was Ambassador to Britain (1936–8) and thereafter German Foreign Minister. While in Britain he gained the nickname 'Von Brickendrop' for the number of diplomatic gaffes he made. He was close to Hitler and was hanged after the Nuremberg Trials.

reminder that even in London I was not completely free of Germany's reach. (Henreid,1976)[68]
[EXT ends]

A year or so after this incident, in 1938, the Germans invaded Austria and some 79,000 persons were arrested. Lisl (Elizabeth Gluck), a divorcée and successful couturière, later Henreid's wife until his death, went to take her parents to England, returning via Germany and France. She was also carrying some jewellery out of Germany for some Jewish friends and en route had a puncture, which some German soldiers cheerfully repaired for her but fortunately they did not search the car. After arrival in Paris on her way back, French officials from the Deuxième Bureau came to her hotel and asked her to accompany them, blindfolded in a car, to a château outside Paris. They wanted her to become a French agent because of her known loyalty and entrée into Viennese society. Flattered at being asked to be a Mata Hari, as she thought, she said she would let them know. On Paul's horrified advice she did not become a spy and in fact on a subsequent visit to Vienna, where she had left her business, she was arrested by the Gestapo but narrowly escaped, thanks to the intervention of a high-up German official that she had been introduced to.

There was now no question of returning to Austria as the couple had hoped. Paul got the role of the German master in *Goodbye, Mr Chips* (1939), followed by two films with Edmund Gwenn, and *Night Train to Munich* (1939), in which he again played a Nazi.[69] The last of these films was very suc-

---
68   When Henreid reached Hollywood he agreed, reluctantly, to change his name from von Hernried to Henreid.
69   Edmund Gwenn (1875–1959) was an English stage actor who later became a distinguished character actor in Hollywood. His American films included

HOLLYWOOD EXILES

cessful and led to an offer from RKO in Hollywood. At the time there was a threat of Henreid's internment in Britain and other difficulties. Under the exchange control laws he could not take more than £25 with him and he could not get an immigration visa for the US because the Austrian quota was full up. These problems were all overcome. Someone, believed to be Conrad Veidt, vouched for him to the British authorities and he simply smuggled £2,500 in cash out of England, concealing the money behind the mirror in his toilet case. The visa difficulty was removed when a US official decided that he could be included in the Italian quota. (Henreid's place of birth was given in his passport as Trieste, then in Austro-Hungary, because his parents had a summer villa there, but as part of the First World War settlement Trieste had become part of Italy.)

Henreid's first American film was *Joan of Paris* (1941), with Michèle Morgan and the young Alan Ladd.[70] Henreid reached the peak of his Hollywood career with his next two films, *Now, Voyager* and *Casablanca*, both released in 1942. It was in *Now, Voyager* that he used the trick of lighting two cigarettes in his mouth and passing one in a romantic gesture to his leading lady. The dust-jacket of his book bears a picture of his performing this – now politically incorrect – gesture.[71] Demonstrating

---

Hitchcock's Foreign Correspondent (1940), Miracle on 34th Street (1947) and The Trouble with Harry (1955) which he made at the age of eighty.
70 Henreid wrote that this was Ladd's debut in an 'A' picture, but in fact Alan Ladd had already made some thirty films, including a small part in Citizen Kane (1941). Henreid was not impressed with Ladd's performance but Ladd was to become a very big star with his next two films, This Gun for Hire (1942) and The Glass Key (1942). Compared with Henreid, who was over 6'3" in height, Ladd was small at 5'5". A swimming champion high-diver, Ladd was very conscious of his diminutive stature and sometimes his leading ladies had to stand in a trench for their scenes together. Ladd's most famous role was in the Western, Shane (1953). Ladd (1913–64) died of a drugs overdose shortly after The Carpetbaggers (1964), a film in which he looked weak and tired.
71 The basic idea of the cigarette trick came from the author of the script. Henreid changed it to make it more effective by lighting both cigarettes at the same time, instead of one by one as the author intended. Even Bette Davis thought it attractive

once again that actors do not always know where their best interests lie, Henreid did not want to do *Casablanca* until the story was changed so that his character, Victor Laszlo, rather than Bogart, got the girl, even though he was not her real love. Laszlo's wife (played by Ingrid Bergman) had married him when she thought Bogart was dead. Meeting him again by chance in Rick's Café therefore – with the earlier affair unknown to Laszlo – creates a problem. Bogart heroically gives up his love to allow Laszlo to escape, and at the end of the film goes off with Claude Rains, the Vichy police chief, to join the Free French.

Practically everyone over fifty today seems to have seen and loved *Casablanca* which, even then, was an enormous success and continues to gain new fans. The film, brilliantly directed by Michael Curtiz, was started without a finished script and with much of the casting falling into place at the last minute. The ultimately magical casting was achieved partly by chance, as Ronald Reagan and Ann Sheridan were initially announced to be playing the leads.[72] Henreid was the first choice for the role of the Resistance leader, but was otherwise engaged. The producer Hal Wallis decided to wait for him because he had 'the dignity and integrity the role demanded' (Wallis, 1980). Bogart was also not keen to take a role and had to be talked into it. *Casablanca*, with its assembly of Europeans anxiously waiting for letters of transit signed by General de Gaulle to go to America and escape the Nazis, may be Hollywood nonsense, as Robertson (1993) points out, but it still bewitches audiences

---

and female fans of Henreid's, of which there were enormous numbers, got their boyfriends to do the same.

72 Hollywood mythology contends that George Raft turned down the lead in Casablanca as he had for many films and Wallis (1980), the producer, seems to confirm this. However, Rudy Behlmer (1982) produces documentary evidence that in fact it was Wallis who turned Raft down in favour of Bogart, even though Jack Warner had suggested Raft for the role. Behlmer also reveals that Dooley Wilson, who was Sam, the black piano player in Casablanca, could not actually play the piano and had to be dubbed by a staff musician.

HOLLYWOOD EXILES

long after the political background of the time has been forgotten.[73] All the main characters, except Bogart and Dooley Wilson, his piano player, were European-born. Bergman, on loan from Selznick, was Swedish; John Qualen, who played the Norwegian resistance worker, was Canadian with Norwegian origins; Peter Lorre, the racketeer who gets shot and S. Z. Sakall, the head waiter, were Hungarian; Marcel Dalio, the croupier, and the girl singer were French; Leonid Kinskey, the barman, was Russian; Claude Rains and Sydney Greenstreet were British; Conrad Veidt was German; and Helmut Dantine and Henreid were Austrian.[74]

Most émigrés were to become US citizens, as in the case of Henreid, who was naturalised in 1946. A few, notably Charlie Chaplin, who remained British all his life, did not. Charles Laughton, born in Scarborough in England, became a US citizen in 1950 and died there.[75] Ronald Coleman stayed in Hollywood and never returned professionally to England and died in Hollywood. There were some successful European artists who could not make it in Hollywood but they did not stay. Among the British, Ivor Novello did not achieve American success, while a few, though not exactly failures, did not stay in Hollywood – Leslie Howard and Laurence Olivier being the most prominent.

---

73 Robertson says that no uniformed Germans were ever in Casablanca during the Second World War, while there was no such thing as letters of transit signed by the Free French leader.
74 The 1953 autobiography of S. Z. Sakall (1884–1955) has the distinction among the star autobiographies of being the most difficult to find in the second-hand book trade and consequently is the most costly to buy. Sakall had a very successful film and stage career in Europe before he arrived in the US in 1939 with a contract with Universal. He is, of course, known as 'Cuddles' for his jowls, portly figure and amiable Hungarian sense of humour.
75 Charles Laughton (1899–1962) was a great, if eccentric, actor on stage and screen. His wife from 1929 to his death, Elsa Lanchester, a considerable actress herself, wrote a book about their early life together, which seems not to have suffered from the fact that Laughton was gay (Lanchester, 1938).

◄ HOLLYWOOD LIVES

Paul Henreid and Humphrey Bogart in *Casablanca* (1942): GB/Warner Bros.

Brian Aherne with S.Z. Sakall, 1940s: Finler.

Others still, such as Cary Grant, George Brent, Brian Aherne, Bob Hope and Ray Milland, adopted mid-Atlantic accents, settled in and became American stars.[76] Ray Milland (1905–86) was born in Wales and his unique nasal twang and clear diction was gradually overlain but never eradicated by an American accent. His anecdotal autobiography (1974) is one of the best of its kind. Milland made some 200 films, starting in Britain in 1929 and continuing until two years before his death. He had an interesting early life in which a few years in the Household Cavalry made him a good horseman and a crack shot. These qualities stood him in good stead in a film career which led from light comedy to significant acting achievements, as in *The Lost Weekend* (1945), for which he gained an Oscar, and Hitchcock's *Dial M for Murder* (1954). While preparing for *Lost Weekend*, Milland entered Bellevue Hospital in New York for a night, but found it so terrible that he sneaked out before dawn in his nightshirt, only to be captured by a policeman outside and forcibly returned to the asylum where, after some difficulty, he persuaded them that he had been there of his own free will.

Clive Brook (1887–1974), another durable British actor whose first film was in 1919, has been quoted as saying in 1933, 'Hollywood is a chain gang and we lose the will to escape. The links of the chain are forged not with cruelties but with luxuries.' The Second World War presented a new problem for the members of the British colony: some were too old to return to Britain, some were not medically up to it,

---

[76] There were also many female British actors in Hollywood. Madeleine Carroll (1906–87) made about the same number of films in Britain as in America (including the 1935 version of The 39 Steps), but from 1943 gave up her film career to join the military Red Cross (Chamberlain, 2010). She married, among others, Sterling Hayden (see Chapter 12). Ida Lupino (1918–95) eventually became a distinguished film director. Her father was the English stage comedian who also made films.

for example Errol Flynn, but some of those of the new generation did not hesitate and went home to join up (David Niven, a trained soldier, for example). Others, for example Brian Aherne, who were too young to fight in the First World War, wondered what to do.

Sir Cedric Hardwicke and Cary Grant flew to Washington to represent the others and ask for advice from the British ambassador, Lord Lothian. They were told that actors up to the military age of thirty-one should go back but that older actors should stay because:

> . . . the maintenance of a powerful nucleus of older British actors in Hollywood is of great importance to our own interests, partly because they are continually championing the British cause in a very volatile community which would otherwise be left to the mercies of German propaganda and because the production of films with a strong British tone is one of the best and subtlest forms of British propaganda . . . (quoted by Aherne, 1969, from a cable by Lothian)

A problem for those that followed the instructions and remained in Hollywood was the criticism levied by the British media that they were deserters. One article was entitled 'Gone With the Wind Up'.[77] The Hollywood British busied

---

77 Leslie Howard (1893–1943) did appear in Gone With the Wind (1939) but returned to Britain. He performed propaganda work for his country and the civilian airline on which he was returning from Lisbon from such an assignment was shot down by German fighter-bombers. There were suggestions that this attack was deliberate and aimed at killing not principally Howard but several others on the plane, including the supposed head of British intelligence in Lisbon and the head of the London branch of an organisation evacuating Jews

themselves with selling war bonds and raising money for ambulances. Where they could, which was not always, they made patriotic films like *That Hamilton Woman* (1941) about Lord Nelson and Emma Hamilton and directed by Sir Alexander Korda. Korda was actually asked to return to the Hollywood he disliked by Winston Churchill so that he could do things for MI6; this was the reason why he was later knighted (Morley, 1983; Korda, 1979). *That Hamilton Woman* included a diatribe against Napoleon (Hitler in contemporary terms). *Mrs Miniver* (1942) was about an English housewife (another exile, Greer Garson) surviving the war, and Hitchcock's *Foreign Correspondent* (1940) about an American journalist (Joel McCrea) in Europe. In a radio broadcast, McCrea was urging America, amid the sounds of bombs falling and as the lights go off, 'Hang on to your lights, they're the only lights left on in the world!'.

Paul Henreid, who had successfully played Nazis and romantic lovers, was never to rise to the popular heights of *Casablanca* again. He did appear in *The Spanish Main* (1945) with Maureen O'Hara, which was popular and based on a synopsis he wrote himself and a series of other swashbucklers. In her autobiography, O'Hara (1997) wrote that Henreid was 'too charming and not tough enough' for the role of a pirate. She adds that 'some in Hollywood called him "Crackerbutt Hemorrhoid" because he had no behind at all'. Henreid, though tall, *was* lightly built and it is all too obvious in one shot in *Now, Voyager* that he is wearing a shirt with heavily padded shoulders. His film career was brought to a virtual

---

from Europe. However, recently published records of interrogations of German pilots have revealed that the rumours were untrue and that the passengers were the victims of an indiscriminate attack. Howard, a stage and screen actor, was born in London, though his father was Hungarian. He was a veteran of the First World War.

halt for five years from 1950 when he was blacklisted. This seems to have arisen from his participation in the trip by a number of stars to Washington to protest at the activities of the House Un-American Activities Committee (see Chapter 10). The studios, on the whole, managed to protect their big stars on contract from blacklisting, including Bogart (who anyway publicly disassociated himself from the protest after the event), but Henreid, wanting more varied roles, and against the strong advice of his agent Wasserman, had refused to sign a seven-year contract offered to him by MGM.

Henreid did a few films for independents both in the US and abroad and moved in the direction of movies and serials for television which occupied most of the rest of his career. He recalled that he had directed some 300 TV pictures or segments, including eighty for Hitchcock. He had always preferred the stage, which he called 'a purer form of art', and was ambivalent about his screen career. He was frustrated by his struggles with studio heads, producers and directors to get the roles he sought and play them in the way he wanted. These battles are recounted in his lucid and very readable autobiography, written with Julian Fast (Henreid, 1984).[78] His book does not hold back from admitting the several occasions when his judgement was seriously at fault, and as a result gives the impression of being frank and honest. He was clearly a strong-willed and sometimes testy actor who tried to fight the system and sometimes lost out because of it. He is very cutting about the limitations of some of his co-stars and directors, including Maria Schell, Lee Strasberg, Ricardo Montalbán, Katharine Hepburn and John Houseman – and also of Hedy Lamarr and Ingrid Bergman, both of whom he

---

78 There has never been a biography of Henreid and his autobiography was not reprinted. As a result it is one of the few rarities in the genre in the book trade.

HOLLYWOOD EXILES

liked personally very much.[79] But he greatly admired Bette Davis, Anthony Quinn, Michael Curtiz and Peter Lorre. Lorre, he wrote, was 'a short man with a round face and bulging eyes, was always cast as the whining psychotic, the ultimate slimy, slinky villain, yet in real life he was a cultured attractive man'. Of Errol Flynn (on whom much more in Chapter 6), he wrote, 'in spite of the bad press he has recently received [he] was a warm and generous man'. Although the quality of Henreid's autobiography, which is written in chronological sequence, falls off as his film career declined, it is admirably lucid and enthralling. One cannot help thinking that Henreid's life as a whole was considerably more interesting than most of his films. Fortunately, and fairly unusually in Hollywood, he had a very happy and enduring marriage with Lisl and their two adopted children.

The film people in Hollywood, native and emigré alike, used to be referred to as members of a colony in the early days. This was partly because the community was inward-looking and partly because the various nationalities, especially the French and German speakers, tended to socialise together. At the time there was little cultural activity in Los Angeles and people tended to entertain at home. Morley (1983)[80] quotes

---

79 Maria Schell (1926–2005), the sister of the better known Maximilian Schell, was an Austrian actress who appeared in a number of films in Hollywood in the 1950s and up to the 1970s. She was slated to appear with Henreid in a film made in Germany in the 1950s during Henreid's blacklisted period, but dropped out, to his relief. Lee Strasberg (1901–82) was an acting coach, one of the founders of the Actors Studio and who influenced Marlon Brando and others. Of Strasberg, Henreid wrote: 'I never felt Lee Strasberg could act, and I fail to see how someone who can't act can teach acting.'

80 Sheridan Morley (1941–2007) was an author, critic and broadcaster. He was the son of Robert Morley, the British actor, and the grandson of Gladys Cooper, the actress, so he had the entrée to the profession and lived in California when young.

some figures from Central Casting on the nationalities of people given work in 1935: of 25,000 actors and extras that year, some 3,000 were Chinese, 2,500 English and 2,300 French. The British were, however, more heavily represented among the stars.

Originally, the British stars (there were a few Scots and Welsh), included several veterans of the First World War, notably Ronald Colman, Basil Rathbone and Clive Brook. Nigel Bruce (who, with Rathbone, respectively played Sherlock Holmes and Watson) received severe bullet wounds and Herbert Marshall lost a leg, though that did not stop him from becoming a popular romantic lead. Reginald Denny (1891–1967) was a pilot in the Royal Flying Corps and had had a successful career in Hollywood as a character actor, though he was too British for some producers which limited his roles. Illustrating the diversity of the émigrés at the time, Denny became interest in pilotless aircraft and opened a model shop on Hollywood Boulevard. His career lasted from the silents to the 1960s.

Of these six veterans, only Basil Rathbone wrote his memoirs but there was another British actor, John Loder (1898–1988), who also produced an autobiography (Loder, 1977). Loder was educated at Eton and was the son of a British general. He was an officer at Gallipoli and at the battle of the Somme. He was captured and put into a German prisoner of war camp until the Armistice in 1918. Afterwards he stayed on in Germany for a while to run his own factory producing pickles. Loder arrived in Hollywood just before the end of the silent era. He later appeared in *Now, Voyager* with Henreid and in *Gentleman Jim* (1942) with Errol Flynn, among other films. After the early 1950s he spent more of his time on the stage in both London and Broadway and in television than in films. Mostly playing romantic leads, he had a fairly good

HOLLYWOOD EXILES

role in *How Green Was My Valley* (1941) and was still acting in 1958 with a small role as one of police inspector Jack Hawkins's men in *Gideon's Day* (1958), an American film directed by John Ford. Loder's very readable autobiography is tantalisingly short at 176 pages and is a distillation of only some memories of an exceptionally varied career. His book ends with his taking up cattle-ranching in South America. He became a US citizen in 1947 but reassumed UK nationality in 1959 and died in London. On the whole, his film career was unremarkable, except for the fact that one of his five wives was Hedy Lamarr.

Morley says that there were 'respectable' Brits and 'renegades' in the British colony and this is confirmed in several of the biographies. Raymond Massey, a Canadian, says in the second of his autobiographies:

[EXT]
In 1937 the British Colony in Hollywood was at its flourishing peak of professional activity and vehement loyalty to the Crown. Its leader was dear old Aubrey Smith. He controlled his colony with firm dignity, his only problem being the erotic antics of Errol Flynn, who after all was, in the opinion of a stalwart member of the colony, 'not really an Englishman but an Australian, old boy!' Similar activities, conducted with greater discretion on the part of a young actor named David Niven, were viewed with tolerance if not envy by the elder brethren of the colony. (Massey, 1979)
[EXT ends]

Sir C. Aubrey Smith (1863–1948) had played cricket for England and founded the Hollywood Cricket Club in 1932, which survives to this day. Membership was not restricted to the British – Errol Flynn and Douglas Fairbanks Jr were members, though its leading lights were Bruce, Rathbone and Niven. Sir Aubrey had a long career on the London stage before Hollywood where he generally played colonels or generals, retired or active, kindly, grumpy or authoritarian as necessary. In real life, in Hollywood, he read *The Times* daily because he considered that no other paper told the truth. John Loder was certainly considered a renegade and his misdeeds included an affair with Marion Davies, the mistress of the newspaper magnate William Randolph Hearst, the inspiration for *Citizen Kane* (1941).

Another of the renegades and an important figure was George Sanders, though his Hollywood career did not start until 1937. Sanders (1906–72) was probably considered a renegade because of his lack of clubbiness and small talk, his cynicism, biting wit and long absences abroad rather than for any damage he may have caused. He was born in Russia, though he was educated in England. He generally played smooth scoundrels and crooks. Halliwell (1997) described him as 'everybody's favourite swine' but he gave the impression in his very readable autobiography (1960) that his supposed wickedness was reserved for the screen. His book is not very revealing about his true nature and his real self is concealed behind a veil of wit. At the outset he paints a vivid picture of his origins (his well- to- do parents were Russians of Scottish ancestry and lived in St Petersburg): 'I was born into a world that was soon to disappear. It was a world of clinking champagne glasses . . . of heel clicking bemonocled princes in gorgeous uniforms' (Sanders, 1960).

His first films were made in Britain. His first in Hollywood was *Lloyds of London* (1937), followed by *Lancer Spy* in the same year. He was in *Rebecca* (1940), *Foreign Correspondent* (1940), *The Moon and Sixpence* (1942) and *The Picture of Dorian Gray* (1944) and *Death of a Scoundrel* (1956) and very many others. His career peaked with *All About Eve* (1950). Of the Oscar he won as best supporting actor in that film, he felt it was not much help to his career and wrote: 'While Hollywood *admires* people who win Oscars, it *employs* people who make money'(Sanders, 1960). Sanders' working life included selling cigarettes in South America where he wounded the husband of his lover in a duel and was briefly in jail; being an advertising account executive; singing and playing the piano in cabaret; and exercising his superb voice on the BBC. Sanders was versatile. At school in England he had excelled in boxing, swimming and running. He once jumped into the Thames to save a drowning man and was awarded the medal of the British Humane Society for it. Noël Coward said of him: 'he has more talents than any of us but he doesn't do anything with them'. Sanders was also a linguist; on his South American trip he learned to speak Spanish without an accent, so much so that he convinced Anthony Quinn (born in Mexico) that he had been born in Argentina (Vanderbeets, 1991). He did a number of films in *The Saint* series, subsequently *The Falcon* series, for RKO between 1939 and 1941, only to get bored with them. (There was also a later *Saint* series on television starring Roger Moore.) Sanders handed the leading role as the Falcon to his less successful but charming brother, Tom Conway, who played his brother in the series until Sanders conveniently 'died'.

Sanders married four times. His wives included Zsa Zsa Gabor (for five years), whose wit often matched his own, and her sister Magda (a marriage which lasted six weeks) and finally Benita

Hume, the widow of Ronald Colman.[81] Of Benita, he wrote that she was 'the best thing that has happened in my life' and he never really recovered from her death. Of himself, Sanders wrote: 'On the screen, I am usually suave and cynical, cruel to women and immune to their slights and caprices . . . But in reality I am a sentimentalist . . .'with an 'easily wounded and ultra sensitive nature'. In fact, Sanders may have been both his screen and his real characters simultaneously; his autobiography is certainly witty and very cynical about women and many other things. Brian Aherne, his close friend (who claimed to be one of only two friends Sanders ever had), wrote an excellent and little known book about him, entitled *A Dreadful Man* (1979). The book includes many letters from Sanders' and Benita to the Ahernes. Aherne says that in George's character, his Slavic blood predominated and he was often boorish and ill-at-ease with Anglo-Saxons and remarkably indifferent to human relationships. However, in Aherne's view, he was capable of genuine kindness and compassion and, although he had no small talk, he was never boring.

It was Aherne who wrote about Sanders' role in an extraordinary and ill-fated business venture that exploded in his last years, a subject taken up later by W. J. West in his biography of Graham Greene.[82] The story is comical and might well have been written in the same vein of humour as Greene's

81 Zsa Zsa Gabor (1917–) is the most prominent of three sisters from Hungary (Eva and Magda were the others), all of whom were beautiful and appeared in films. Zsa Zsa wrote two autobiographies (1960, 1991) and was famous for her marriages and her wit. She also inspired wit in others. Halliwell (2001) quotes Oscar Levant as saying of Zsa Zsa: 'Her face was inscrutable, but I can't vouch for the rest of her.' Levant (1906–72) was an actor, composer, songwriter, pianist and wit and wrote three inscrutable autobiographies himself.
82 Graham Greene (1904–91) was a film critic before he became a distinguished novelist and we encounter him again in his former role in Chapter 9. Some of his novels were deliberately written in the hope that they would be filmed and many were, including This Gun for Hire (1942) and The Third Man (1949). He comes into the Sanders story because unwittingly he was an investor in the film actor's business venture described above. W. J. West's book on Greene was published in 1997.

novel *Our Man in Havana* (1958) and filmed with Sanders in a starring role. It seems, from Aherne's and West's accounts, that Sanders, along with several other movie actors, including Charles Chaplin, William Holden and Robert Mitchum, was advised on his offshore tax affairs by a British solicitor, Tom Roe. Roe set up a group of companies into which his client's funds were invested. One of these companies was Cadco Developments, named after Sanders' autobiography, *Memoirs of a Professional Cad*, according to West. This company was one of eleven interlinked firms; another was the Royal Victoria Sausage Company (RVS). Roe's partner, Dennis Lorraine, had bought a butcher's shop in Brighton in which he claimed to have found a letter from King Edward VII praising the butcher's sausages. Based on this, and funded by Roe's client funds, RVS established a factory in the south of England to manufacture the sausages, with a fleet of vans bearing the royal crest to distribute them. Encouraged by initial success, the partners applied for and received a government development grant and a loan from the Royal Bank of Scotland to build another factory in Scotland. Not only did RVS soon collapse but Roe, in a different venture in 1965, was arrested in Switzerland for attempting to smuggle large amounts of counterfeit US dollars with origins, West says, in the Hollywood Mafia. Roe and Lorraine were immediately imprisoned, though the case did not come to trial and sentence until 1967.

The Report of the Board of Trade inquiry into the RVS collapse (1966), which Aherne quotes at length, expressed the view that George Sanders, Roe and Lorraine should be referred for prosecution. But nothing happened and Roe and Lorraine were convicted solely for the currency offences. Sanders had claimed that he was simply a figurehead with no knowledge of the detail. Incredibly, no one was ever charged over the RVS affair. Aherne speculates that the British government suppressed the BoT Report because it revealed misuse of government money, while the investors whose motives were tax avoidance did not wish to get further involved. West says that Graham Greene, who had hitherto been unaware of the use to which his funds were being made, was forced into tax exile in France solely because of this affair.

In 1972, Sanders deliberately took a lethal overdose of vodka and barbiturates, alone in a hotel room near Barcelona. The loss of his beloved Benita and the failure of a business in which he had invested much of his earnings over the years may have been factors in this suicide, which Aherne wrote was 'inevitable'. He left a note, perfectly in keeping with his screen image: 'Dear World. I am leaving because I am bored. I feel I have lived long enough. I am leaving you with your worries in this sweet cesspool. Good luck.' (quoted by Aherne, 1979) Sanders had a horror of old age and dependency – and failing health was another, perhaps the main factor. The extraordinary thing is that he had predicted his own death. David Niven (1975) wrote that as long ago as 1937, Sanders had told him that when he reached the age of sixty-five he would take his own life, and this is just what he did.

Marlene Dietrich (1901–92) was one of the first of the exotic *femme fatales* imported by Hollywood from Europe, though Greta Garbo (1905–90) from Sweden arrived before her (and even before the coming of sound).[83] Ingrid Bergman (1915–82), who was beautiful but not exotic, was also from

---

83 Also from Sweden, but much later than Garbo, was Viveca Lindfors (1920–95). Lindfors' films were mostly routine, but she had considerable success on the stage. Her autobiography Viveka . . . Viveca (1981) has the subtitle on the dust-jacket An Actress . . . A Woman.

Sweden and made a number of excellent films, including *Casablanca* (1942) and *Notorious* (1946) among many others, and a late triumph in *Murder on the Orient Express* (1974) for which she was awarded an Oscar. Earlier, Hollywood at its most hypocritical had not approved of her romance with Italian film-maker Roberto Rossellini. Bergman was forced into exile in Europe in 1948 but was later forgiven (recounted in her autobiography of 1980). In some ways Bergman's treatment in America paralleled that accorded to Charles Chaplin a little later (see Chapter 2).

Ingrid Bergman outside Notre Dame in Paris when she was working on *Anastasia* (1956) GB/20th Century Fox.

Much later, after the Second World War, came Hildegard Knef (1925–2002). Knef wrote two books (1971, 1975), but did not stay long in Hollywood and made only a few films there. Her first book describes the harrowing time she had as the Russians invaded and Berlin was in chaos. She joined the German Army and was captured by the Red Army but got away. Before that she had a contract with UFA as a juvenile. As a displaced person she had been brought to Hollywood by David Selznick but did not sign the contract offered to her because it required her to change her name and pretend to be Austrian. Her first book, like her second, was written in German, became a bestseller and is a considerable literary achievement. Lilli Palmer (1914–86), another German actress, left Germany in 1933. Her first film was in Britain in the following year and she went to Hollywood for *Cloak and Dagger* (1946) with Gary Cooper, whom she portrays vividly in her well-written autobiography of 1975. *Body and Soul* (1947), a boxing picture with John Garfield, followed along with many others. She had married Rex Harrison in 1943 (but divorced in 1957). Beautiful, warm and intelligent, Palmer seemed to succeed at everything: she published a novel which sold well, made films in several European countries, had her own programme on television and acted on Broadway. She got bored with acting eventually and her last film was in 1985.

With Katharine Hepburn, Garbo and Dietrich developed the fashion for wearing trousers and mannish behaviour. Dietrich was the most beautiful of the three. Ernest Hemingway wrote of her: 'Even if she had nothing but her voice, she could break your heart with it. But she also has that beautiful body and the timeless loveliness of her face.'[84] She also had

---

84 Kenneth Tynan wrote that Dietrich 'had sex without gender' and appealed to men and women alike. The Tynan and Hemingway quotations are reproduced approvingly in her own autobiography (Dietrich, 1989).

beautiful legs, which reigned among the best in Hollywood until Betty Grable appeared in the 1940s.[85] Dietrich herself wrote, 'The legs aren't so beautiful, I just know what to do with them.' The androgynous appeal and secretiveness which Dietrich possessed, along with Garbo and Hepburn, was part of a mystique which Dietrich and Hepburn, at least, deliberately cultivated. Garbo was different – it was avoidance of public exposure that aroused mystery ('I vant to be alone'). Garbo retired from the screen and out of public view when only forty-nine, whereas the other two continued with film and stage performances into their seventies.

Dietrich was her real name, but Marlene was a contraction of her two given names, Maria Magdalena. Her father was a cavalry officer turned police lieutenant who died, apparently falling from a horse, when Marlene was only six years old. In her autobiography, she says that her parents were 'well-to-do'. However, according to Marlene's latest biographer (Wood, 2002), Marlene's mother was struggling on her husband's pension and after his death had to take a job as a housekeeper. This apparently turned out well when she married her employer, but he was killed early in the war. Marlene's

---

85   Betty Grable (1916–73) was an important member of the cohort of the girl-next-door domestic stars who emerged in the 1940s and introduced a new if somewhat bland quality to the screen. Grable appeared mostly in musicals but had personal successes in A Yank in the RAF (1941) with Tyrone Power and Reginald Gardner and song and dance numbers and a noir thriller, I Wake Up Screaming (1941), with Victor Mature and a fine performance by Laird Cregar. Grable became a favourite pin-up during the Second World War. A much-reproduced photograph shows her in a one piece bathing suit and high heels, hand on one hip looking backwards over her shoulder, nicely showing off her rump and legs. This image was to appear on the noses of the Flying Fortresses. She married and divorced Jackie Coogan and bandleader-trumpeter Harry James by whom there were two children. Grable, sexy but wholesome onscreen, off it led a very ordinary, scandal-free life by Hollywood standards. Adrienne McLean in Griffin (2011) speculates about the nature of Grable's appeal given that by her own admission, she was not a good actress, dancer or singer – it clearly had to do with her physical attractions and a perceived ordinariness.

mother, Josephine, brought up her daughter very strictly and trained her not to show her feelings, which made acting difficult for her. At school she developed a serious crush on her French schoolteacher, which was at the root of her love of France. When the First World War was declared, the teacher disappeared quickly and it was brought brutally home to Marlene that France and Germany were now enemies.

Marlene grew up in Dessau and Berlin and when she was seventeen, already a very attractive girl, her mother moved to Weimar city while she decided to remain in Berlin on her own. She earned her living doing odd jobs for UFA and later as a chorine and model. She began to get film roles and in 1923 married Rudolf Sieber, a director and actor. The following year, Marlene's only daughter, Maria, was born. Although they stayed together as a family on and off, it was an open marriage. She kept some sort of platonic relationship going with Rudi until his death in 1976 but never married again. She several times got jobs for him, a requirement sometimes written into her own studio contracts.

The Hollywood director Josef von Sternberg was on leave of absence from Paramount in 1929 when he saw Dietrich on stage in a Berlin musical, *Two Bow Ties*.[86] He arranged for UFA to screen-test her for the role of Lola in a film ultimately to be called *The Blue Angel* (1930). This film was the first major production with sound in Germany and was to be shot simultaneously in German and English versions. The story of the film is based on a novel by Heinrich Mann, Thomas Mann's brother, and is a study in hypocrisy and corruption. It is principally about a respectable schoolteacher who becomes infatuated with Lola, a cabaret artist, and is eventually humiliated and ruined

---

86 Josef von Sternberg (1894–1969) was an Austrian who grew up in Vienna and New York, the 'von' was his own addition.

by it. Neither UFA nor Dietrich thought much of the proposed film but Sternberg, who was to direct, forced it through against opposition and made a classic. (Dietrich wrote that as 'a well-bred girl', she thought the story 'vulgar'. In fact, though she was well brought up, she was already promiscuous and intimately familiar with Berlin nightlife.)[87] The male lead was Emil Jannings, a famous German stage and screen actor, who was jealous of Dietrich, whom he rightly suspected would steal the film.[88] In it she sings 'Falling in Love Again', that was to become her signature tune for the rest of her career. Sternberg was to create a lasting image and personality for her, something which her numerous earlier directors had been unable to do. Soon they became lovers and Dietrich freely admitted many times, as well as in her book, that she was Sternberg's 'creation'. Inspired by her director's brilliant camerawork and lighting (he could do everything), she herself became fascinated by the technicalities and with later, generally lesser, directors would sometimes say out loud during shooting, 'Oh Jo, where are you?'

UFA executives disliked the 'immorality' of the film, which they thought 'un-German', and decided not to take up their option on Dietrich's contract. She had already had an offer from Paramount on Sternberg's recommendation before

---

87   In reported conversations, Dietrich acknowledged her bisexuality but merely writes in her autobiography: 'women are better, but you cannot live with a woman'. Most of her later affairs seemed to be with well-known men and included: Adlai Stevenson, President J. F. Kennedy and his father, Joseph P. Kennedy, General Patton; actors Brian Aherne, Yul Brynner, Gary Cooper, Douglas Fairbanks Jr, Kirk Douglas, Jean Gabin, Frank Sinatra, John Wayne and Michael Wilding; and directors Billy Wilder and von Sternberg. How do we know? Some acknowledged the affairs; some were reported in her daughter's memoir (Riva, 1992) and in researches by Wood (2002). See also an article by Cari Beauchamp, 'It happened at the Hotel du Cap' in Vanity Fair, March 2009.
88   Emil Jannings (1884–1950) had already made two films in the United States, for which he won one of the first Oscars awarded. His heavily accented voice was unsuitable for American talking pictures and he returned to Germany where he eventually became head of UFA. After the war he was blacklisted for his Nazi connections.

The Blue Angel was made and was now free to take it up. In 1930 she sailed to the USA and made *Morocco* (1930), again directed by Sternberg. The film, a Foreign Legion romance starring Gary Cooper, was deliberately released before *The Blue Angel*, for which Paramount had the US rights. The studio believed that *Morocco* was a better introduction to American audiences and indeed the film made Dietrich an international star. Sternberg went on to make five more films with Dietrich for Paramount, including: *Dishonoured* (1931), in which she plays a prostitute who spies for Germany; *Shanghai Express* (1932) in which she again appears as a prostitute, with Clive Brook; and *Blonde Venus* (1932), a gloomy tale in which Dietrich supports her scientist husband (Herbert Marshall) by becoming another's mistress. The studio was disappointed at the commercial returns from these studio-bound, visually beautiful productions. The last Sternberg–Dietrich film was *The Devil is a Woman* (1932). With very few exceptions, later films with other directors did not show Dietrich at her best, though Sternberg's style, which underplayed the story in favour of visual impact, is now badly dated. *The Garden of Allah* (1936), directed by another émigré, Richard Boleslawski, is notable for its fine colour but was a rather silly 'come with me to the Casbah' story, despite a fine cast (Charles Boyer and Basil Rathbone). *Knight without Armour* (1937), produced by Alexander Korda, is much better, and probably underrated for its vivid portrayal of the commitment and chaos of the Russian Revolution. In it, gallant Robert Donat rescues a widowed countess played by a beautiful and withdrawn Dietrich, finally displaying emotion as she becomes separated from Donat in the conflict. After this, the best but not very commercial of the pre-war post-Sternberg films, Paramount let Dietrich go.[89]

---

89   In 1938, The Association of Independent Theatre Owners of America placed

Dietrich was rescued by Universal, who starred her with James Stewart in *Destry Rides Again* (1939), which was a tremendous box office success directed by veteran American director George Marshall. This Western film was a departure for Dietrich, with a chance for her to play some comedy and sing 'See what the boys in the back room will have' and have a fight with another lady. Alas, it was only a short-lived blip in her career. In the early 1940s she did a series of forgettable films, some with John Wayne, of which the best was *The Spoilers* (1942), set in the Yukon and with some of the elements of *Destry*. Fellow German-born Fritz Lang, who was good at film *noir*, failed to repeat the success of *Destry* with *Rancho Notorious* (1952), but in a strong role in Billy Wilder's *Witness for the Prosecution* (1957), with Charles Laughton as the barrister and Tyrone Power as the murder suspect, Dietrich played Power's wife upon whom he depends for acquittal. This film is one of her best, and in the opinion of most critics she stole the film. Her last film of any significance was in the star-studded *Judgement at Nuremberg* (1961), in which she is the widow of a German general executed for war crimes. This film has some good performances but was not a commercial success. As her beauty faded, Dietrich was showing signs in the post-war period of becoming a fine actress.

During the Second World War, Dietrich appeared on war bond tours, and performed in war zones for the US Army and United Services Organisation (USO), enduring many kinds of hardship and danger. She was given the rank of major in the

---

adverts in the trade press, labelling a number of actors 'box office poison', including Fred Astaire, Dietrich, Joan Crawford, Greta Garbo and Katharine Hepburn. In the event, with the exception of Garbo, who did not care, all bounced back. Star power to bring in audiences was of vital importance, especially for the exhibitors unaffiliated with studios – they could choose the films they took, though generally they had to have packages of good and bad; the theatres owned by the studios had to take what they were given.

hope that, if captured, she would get better treatment as an officer, though by then she was detested by the Nazi regime. She even made broadcasts in German from London. Before the war, Goebbels and Hitler, aware of her propaganda value, tried several times, without success, to persuade Dietrich to make films in Germany. Her identification with the Allied cause made her unpopular with many Germans and after her death, according to Wood, some travelled to Paris to spit in her grave. The gravestone was defaced frequently, once with the words 'slut in furs' in German. Dietrich sacrificed a lot to do the USO work: she was never good with money (she had given much of it away) and was hard up and had to sell some of her jewellery and other possessions to make up for loss of earnings. She was trying to atone in a small way for the terrible behaviour of her native people; her autobiography makes it clear that she knew that ordinary people in Germany were well aware of the horrors of the Jewish persecution, but turned a blind eye to it, and at the time she could not forgive the Germans for voting the Nazis into power in the first place.

Marlene's USO tours, which were enormously popular with the fighting men, had given her the confidence to make solo performances on stage all over the world and from the 1960s this became her main career. She continued with her performances until about seventy years of age, when she became a recluse in her Paris apartment, rarely leaving it for the last twelve years of her life. Short of money and suffering from a broken hip bone from one of her several falls on stage, Dietrich nonetheless amused herself with telephone conversations with people she knew or could get access to.[90] She also

---

90   Dietrich did make a sortie to a Paris film studio in 1978 to appear in Just a Gigolo (1978), directed by David Hemmings. She also collaborated with Maximilian Schell over a documentary about her life and in which she spoke but refused to appear. She hated the finished film, of course.

consumed large numbers of books and newspapers. Nancy Reagan said that President Reagan's last call from the White House had been to Marlene. One of Marlene's telephone correspondents was a very young man whom she never met and who, after her death, wrote a book about their conversations (Hanut, 1996). Hanut notes that Marlene greatly admired Hepburn and Garbo who, as mentioned at the beginning of this chapter, resembled her in some ways. These similarities had to do with sexual ambiguity and secretiveness as well as conscious or unconscious image-making. Hanut wrote: 'Who was Dietrich? Who really knew her? No one. She made of her life what the Paramount studio photographers made of her photos – she retouched it. She wanted to bequeath to posterity an Ideal Image.'

Others found Dietrich not so much a mystery as a fascinating if complex human being. Brian Aherne, who had appeared with her in *Song of Songs* (1933), a film he deemed 'rubbish', wrote of his 'lifelong friend who is very dear to me': 'A curious mixture of sophistication, complication, and simple domestic virtues, she is exceptionally well educated for a woman, well-read in several languages, innately musical, wayward, humorous, autocratic, self-reliant, and fiercely loyal to those whom she admits to her friendship.' (Aherne, 1969) In Dietrich's own autobiography (1987), naturally nothing is revealed that is inconsistent with the flawless image she wished to project.[91] The book is formless and consists mainly of very selective memories (Dietrich never kept a diary), interspersed with her philosophies of life and love, anecdotes

---

91 According to Wood, the book was originally written in English and typed out by her. The manuscript was rejected by the English and American publishers and published first in French. Various abridged versions of the French version later appeared in German translations, one of which was translated into English and this is the edition cited here.

about people and what some people wrote about her. Nor are most of her many acts of kindness and generosity even mentioned in the book – or anything but passing references to her husband. Her statement – 'I never wanted to be a celebrity' – is reminiscent of Lawrence of Arabia's skill at 'backing into the limelight'.[92] Whether she wanted it or not, Marlene Dietrich was certainly one of the most famous actresses of all time.

---

92 T. E. Lawrence, soldier, archaeologist and writer claimed always that he never sought publicity but was described as having a genius for backing into the limelight.

CHAPTER 5

Fighting the Studios

UNDERNEATH THE GLOSSY surfaces of completed films were some conflicts generated by the unequal powers of the studio moguls and the personnel who produced and exhibited the movies. This imbalance led to the emergence of guilds representing the writers, actors and directors as well as the craft unions (see Chapters 10 and 11) and pressure groups for the independent theatres; in addition there were various political interests concerned with competition and content. Once the moguls lost control, these other interests would overwhelm the Hollywood of the Golden Age (see Chapter 13). On the whole, though, there were not that many conflicts among the actors themselves and the autobiographies are remarkably free of the jealousy and nastiness which characterise many other communities of professionals (such as academics). Of course there were a few rivalries – between Bette Davis and Joan Crawford, for example, and between Joan Fontaine and her sister, Olivia de Havilland – and, as revealed in Chapter 10, Hollywood was quite divided during the Communist witch-hunts from the 1940s onwards – but these are exceptions.[93]

---

93 The Crawford–Davis rivalry is documented in Considine (1989). Both as parents

There were, however, conflicts between the actors and the bosses. It would be wrong to give the impression that the moguls were sitting on the lid of a steaming kettle threatening to blow them up. As far as the stars were concerned, the studio heads were usually able to calm things down with blandishments, more money, a better contract or, as a last resort, edging them out of the business altogether (and discouraging others from hiring them). Many actors – perhaps most – were reasonably happy, especially in the 1930s when they were aware that, compared to the millions of unemployed, their situation was pretty comfortable, even if they had to get to the make-up room by 6.30 a.m., spend much of the day waiting around while lights were adjusted and sets arranged sometimes for films they did not particularly want to do. Some stars loved it all, as Joan Crawford wrote of Louis B. Mayer: 'Mr Mayer wanted only the best. I esteemed all the gifted people with whom we worked and him most of all. In the many years he guided my career I valued his judgement, his patience and the fact he never played games . . . The dolt he's been described since his death by writers nursing old grudges could never have built the star system and administered the studio that during the thirties and forties was without peer.' (Crawford, 1962)

Pat O'Brien, who worked for various moguls for over three decades, took a tougher but still admiring view:

[EXT]
They were almost all uneducated, with a kind of splendid cunning and a feeling that every means could justify every end. They had great skill in weaving together simple

---

were attacked in print by one of their children though these attacks lacked credibility For the rivalry of Joan Fontaine and her sister, see Fontaine (1978).

FIGHTING THE STUDIOS

stories, pretty faces, passions, popular ideas, glamorous clothes, legendary daring deeds into the great dreams that the world wanted . . . The greatest stars were often slaves to unfair contracts. The less pleasant details of the private lives of these celluloid czars, who had come from pedlars' pack to Rolls-Royces in one generation, made often unsavoury reading. Yet their often directionless energies kept the studios open for fifty years. (O'Brien, 1964).
[EXT ends]

Veronica Lake, with her peekaboo hairstyle, commented that, despite her diminutive stature, she was not adored by the studio brass, who were also mostly short. Lake, who at one time had a private plane a ranch and a house, left Hollywood voluntarily at the peak of her career. She understood the primacy of the profit motive, however, and her conclusions on the moguls were similar to O'Brien's:

[EXT]
The men who controlled Hollywood and its vast wealth deserved their positions. As hated as some of them may have been, no one could take away the guts, fortitude and foresight they displayed in building their empires. They came out of eastern ghettos, sweat-shop garment centers and mundane careers to bet their lives on a nation's need for escape. Those who succeeded reacted to their success as might be expected. They over-indulged in everything. They fed their natural egos, drives and insecurities with what their success could buy. (Lake, 1971).
[EXT ends]

Of course, all the stars had complaints of one sort or

another. Ginger Rogers (1911–95) felt strongly about the male-dominated system. Betsy Blair (2003), at MGM in the 1940s, acknowledged that the studio system 'was marvellously productive. The studios took care of everything for their stars. But the studio executives did consider them as properties to be used as long as they were popular . . . with the exception of a few who actively fought for quality and artistry . . . they thought of the stars as a necessary evil, as children to be controlled and the whole system was geared to keep them childish.'

The moguls could be tough or charming to their well-rewarded employees. Louis B. Mayer regarded his stars at MGM as part of his family and stories of his chasing starlets around his desk are probably inventions. Others, by all accounts, did make the casting couch a condition for advancement. What are we to make of Betsy Blair's story that at one of Mayer's birthday parties: 'I saw June Allyson, fast becoming a star at MGM, perched on Arthur Freed's knee saying "Uncle Arthur, do I have to pay income tax?"'[94]

The fact was that Golden Age stars were indentured employees (Balio, 1993). Details of their contracts varied but many had five to seven-year contracts with six-monthly options. The studio could pick up the option or not as it pleased them, but the stars had no reciprocal right to quit until the expiration of the full term. Should the star refuse a role or otherwise fail to obey instructions they could be sued for

---

94 Arthur Freed (1894–1973), a lyricist and producer, contributed to many of the greatest musicals, including Singin' in the Rain (1952). Freed, like Louis B. Mayer, appreciated the importance of stars. Academics have not been able to model the role of stars in the success of films mathematically, probably because many other factors are involved, such as the quality of the script and the ability of the director, but the moguls knew at the very least that the presence of stars in a film helped to reduce the risk of poor box office performance. (Sedgwick and Pokorny, 2005)

damages or placed on suspension without pay and the period of the suspension added to the term of their contract. The actors were not permitted to hire their own press agents and were specifically required to give media interviews and perform promotional activities, which might include travelling all over the country to mark the launch of a film. There was a 'morality clause' in their contracts which prohibited them from behaviour which could bring the studio into disrepute. The studio could thus control the activities of its employees very tightly and only the biggest stars could negotiate terms allowing them to choose the roles they played or the directors they worked with.

The studios spent a lot of money developing stars, often hired as unknowns. They were usually given experience in 'B' pictures and heavily promoted once public reaction was favourable. It took time to establish the right personality for an actor. Bette Davis, for example, began in 1932 as a blonde coquette, and graduated via vamp roles to become a great dramatic actress. Her style of dress in publicity shots developed accordingly from bathing costumes to dark tailored suits (Schatz in Staiger, 1994). The studios in their promotional activities tried to create the illusion that their stars behaved in their private lives as they did on the screen. This fed the public taste for information about stars and facilitated gains in column inches in magazines and newspapers. The autobiographies confirm that appropriate public romances between stars were promoted by studio-arranged 'dates', often far removed from real life, as in the case of June Allyson and Van Johnson and Vera Ellen and Rock Hudson, though sometimes genuine romances were considered 'appropriate', such as that between Janet Leigh and Tony Curtis and were then heavily publicised.

Rock Hudson: Finler.

Stars were also trained and coached in acting, deportment and singing, fencing, and in the gym, as well as in skills needed for specific roles, such as boxing, horse riding and piano playing. MGM had its own Little Red School House on the lot for educating minors in compliance with the law that they should not be allowed to work excessive hours or permit their schooling to be interrupted. Rock Hudson, who strangely for such a big man, studied ballet at the studio, wrote: 'The studio took care of everything. They could get you a house, a car, airline tickets, special shoes. All you had to do was concentrate on your performance. There was no better method of training'(Hudson, 1980).[95] Some actors, especially after the coming of sound, came to the movies from the theatre but even they needed special training to adapt to the different requirements of acting for the screen. Today, with the end of the studio system and its manufactory of stars these actors come from television as well as the theatre. Even in the 1950s, some movie stars started in television and moved to the big screen later, though few became front-rank stars. Jack Webb (1920–82), star of the television series *Dragnet*, graduated to studio movies, while Lucille Ball, who started in movies, did not become a star until she appeared in her television series.

Tony Curtis with Janet Leigh: Dr Macro.

---

95 Hudson's trademark low voice was created by getting the actor to shout as loud as he could, preferably when he had a cold, to damage his vocal cords which, when they healed, would produce a lower voice.

Most of the actor-autobiographers devote some space to the art of acting. Janet Leigh (1984) quotes Miss Lillian Burns, MGM's acting coach for many years, as saying: 'No one can teach someone to act, because you can't teach talent. You can give fundamental guidelines. You can teach diction, and body control. You can steer someone on how to take and give out a living, breathing character. But you can't teach acting.' There was a general consensus that you learned acting by doing and that there was no other way. For some, acting came naturally. Marlon Brando (1994) cites Paul Muni and James Cagney as naturals whose instincts showed in their work. Some, Brando continued, were successful because of their distinctive personalities, citing Gary Cooper, Clark Gable, Humphrey Bogart, Claudette Colbert and Loretta Young as examples. Many people have said that some stars (John Wayne is the usual example) were simply playing themselves and were not acting at all. But few actors believed this. Robert Wagner regarded these 'personality actors' as consummate performers because they were concealing their skill by integrating their screen character within their own personality. He wrote in 2008: 'an actor [is] acting but you could not see him acting. That is hard to do, the highest achievement in the business.' The stuntman Yakima Canutt (1979), who worked a lot with Wayne, wrote: 'He's so natural in his acting that some people think that he isn't acting at all – but for my money that's the sign of a great actor.

Some actor-writers did not try to intellectualise the nature of acting at all. Mickey Rooney (1991) wrote that acting was 'being yourself', but this is ambiguous in the sense that a screen character *becomes* his real self. Rock Hudson (1986) quotes Raoul Walsh as saying: 'Just do it. Remember, up on the screen you're magnified forty times. Be natural, underplay and it will look great.' Hudson, who for decades concealed the fact that he was gay and outed himself in his autobiography, had another essential characteristic of the screen actor – 'the camera loved him'. A friend said, 'He looks ten times better on the screen or in a still photo than he did in person' (cited by Hudson, 1986).[96] After a long apprenticeship, Hudson learned to act well making his performances look natural. He was an underrated performer: for example, in a scene in *Pillow Talk* (1959), the gay Hudson plays a heterosexual pretending to be gay so as to seduce a reluctant Doris Day, a double role reversal.

Acting is an intangible, elusive art.[97] It is not easily defined since it is both an ability to assume another identity and something that gives pleasure to an audience. The views on the subject expressed in the autobiographies, though apparently differing from one another are all ultimately reconcilable. This is true even of Marlon Brando's views; he was supposedly a Method actor and widely acknowledged as one of the acting greats. He wrote:[98] 'Acting is the least mysterious of crafts.

---

96   Tab Hunter (1931–), many years later, also wrote in his autobiography (2005) about the experience of being gay in Hollywood and his detestation of the necessity to conceal it at the time. Hunter's first film was in 1948 and he was one of the last to sign an exclusive contract with a major studio. Among his films are: The Sea Chase (1955) Gunman's Walk (1958) and a musical Damn Yankees (1958), but he made over fifty and later became a producer and TV star. Farley Granger, also gay, wrote another candid autobiography (2007), which, among other things, reveals how Samuel Goldwyn would only release him from his contract if he paid an enormous sum, which he did. Granger compares Goldwyn unfavourably with Harry Cohn.

97   It is sometimes asserted that the film media itself is not an art, but in essence it clearly is, although there can be good and bad art. This has not necessarily anything to do with realism: movies are transforming reality into an experience for viewers and this is the essence of the art (Stephenson and Debrix, 1965). Historians often criticise films for being ahistorical, but to make a good film history often has to be rearranged, otherwise it becomes a documentary – though even documentaries require rearrangement and form and can be art.

98   Brando, 1994. The Method was an acting system codified by Constantin Stanislavski (1863–1938) of the Moscow Arts Theatre and based on his studies of leading actors. In post-war America, the Method was taught by Lee Strasberg

HOLLYWOOD LIVES

Everybody acts, whether it's a toddler who quickly learns how to behave to get its mother's attention, or a husband and wife in the daily rituals of marriage . . . The difference is that most people act unconsciously and automatically, while stage and movie actors do it to tell a story.'

With practice – the studio was an apprenticeship system – actors, despite experiencing stress and nervousness ('stage fright'), would usually reach a point where they were confident in their own abilities. Virtually all the autobiographies complain about a lack of demanding parts. Often, after great success in a role and when producers wanted to repeat that success, actors felt they were being typecast. Edward G. Robinson, after *Little Caesar* (1931), and James Cagney soon got fed up with playing gangsters. Charlton Heston, towards the end of the Golden Age when he had some freedom over the films he made, chose the films he wished to make (Shakespeare, for example) and backed them with his own money, knowing they would not make much of a profit. He could rely on the glamorous studio products he made to pay for them.

Heston was doing this consciously, but most actors seemed to believe that there need not be a conflict between better roles and studio profit and indeed it was not necessarily so. Although sometimes wrong, the producer's judgements on what actors could do best in order to support the bottom line were generally much better than those of the actors themselves. Alfred Hitchcock reportedly said actors should be treated like cattle – by which he presumably meant they needed to be herded. David O. Selznick said: 'I must say that I have known few film actors, even with

---

(1901–82) at the Actors Studio in New York from the 1940s. Among other things, it involves the actor in preparing for his role by drawing on his own emotional memory. Among the movie stars who trained with Strasberg and his colleagues were James Dean, John Garfield, Eli Wallach, Marilyn Monroe, Jane Fonda and Paul Newman.

FIGHTING THE STUDIOS ▶

those with vast experience, who have sound judgement about what they should do.' Schatz (1988), who reproduces this remark, says that Selznick went on to say that Gloria Swanson and others 'drove themselves into obscurity with startling speed and efficiency once they gained control of their careers and were in a position to substitute their own judgement for that of the people who have developed and exploited them.'[99]

Debbie Reynolds in *How The West Was Won* (1962): Dr Macro/MGM.

---

99 Gloria Swanson (1897–1983) had enormous success in silent films, the first of which she made in 1915. She became a big international star in the 1920s and in her autobiography describes the rapturous receptions she received visiting Paris and London. In 1927 she joined United Artists but made little further progress until she came out of retirement to star in Sunset Boulevard (1952) in which she courageously satirises herself, a role repeated in Airport 1975 (1974). Writing her book (Swanson 1980) she says was 'an agonizing experience, a bit like drilling your own teeth'. Reading it is simply tedious and repetitious.

Debbie Reynolds (1988) recounts how, when Louis B. Mayer told her, a nineteen-year-old with little experience of singing or dancing, that she was to perform alongside Gene Kelly and Donald O'Connor in *Singin' in the Rain* (1952) she *knew* she could not do it. Kelly, who did not want her at all in the film he was co-directing, was appalled, but the boss prevailed. In the outcome, after weeks of harrowing rehearsals and being driven hard by Kelly whom, she wrote, never gave her a single word of praise or encouragement, the film – with her in it – was an enormous success. Mayer had been right, but ironically three days into shooting he lost a power struggle with Nicholas Schenck, Chairman of Loew's and left the studio for the last time. Later, Reynolds was to have a similar experience again when Jack Warner cast her in the lead role in *Mary,Mary* (1963). When she told Warner she could not do it he replied: 'Look kid . . . I'm paying you three hundred and fifty thousand dollars. You think maybe Jack Warner doesn't know what he's doing. You were making seventy-five bucks a week when you first came over to my studio. Now it's ten per cent of the gross. You think I'd waste all that dough on you if I didn't think you could do it? I *know* what you can do.'[100]

There were plenty of other instances where an actor had script approval for a part, rejected it and later saw another actor successfully perform the role. Ginger Rogers (1991) wrote that there were several films that 'I stupidly let slip through my fingers'. She turned down the leading role opposite Gary Cooper in *Ball of Fire* (1941), for which Barbara Stanwyck was nominated for an Oscar, and also the lead in *To Each His Own* (1946), for which Olivia de Havilland won an Oscar. Among others, she also rejected the lead in *It's a Wonderful*

---

100 Quoted in Reynolds (1988). She did do it and got some very good reviews, though the film was not the box office winner that Warner had hoped for.

FIGHTING THE STUDIOS

Life (1946), for which James Stewart was nominated for an Oscar and which today still appears in many people's lists of favourite films. George Raft refused the lead roles in *The Maltese Falcon* and *High Sierra*, both released in 1941. Both of these films were big successes for Humphrey Bogart and consolidated his stardom.

Bette Davis in 1904 costume for *The Sisters* (1938): GB/Warner Bros.

Warner's had a number of well-publicised fights with its stars, probably because of Jack Warner's combative character. The lean times the studio went through in the interwar period left a tradition of exceptionally tight star management at the studio.[101] Having in her own eyes established her worth with her Oscar-winning performance in *Dangerous* (1935), Bette Davis in her autobiography (1962) said she was bitterly disappointed to continue to be placed in poor roles and understandably refused outright to play a female lumberjack as her next part. She was promptly placed on three months' suspension without pay. Davis mentions that, at the time (1936), other actors were fighting the studios: her colleague James Cagney at Warner; Katharine Hepburn at RKO; Margaret Sullavan at Universal; Carole Lombard at Paramount; and Eddie Cantor with Samuel Goldwyn. Davis left for England, where she had been offered a part in a film. In retaliation, Warner's issued an injunction to stop her leaving – but it could not be served on a Sunday, the day she left. They brought a case against her for breach of contract in the English courts. Davis lost the case and had to return to Hollywood. There, Jack Warner made peace with her and even paid some of her legal costs, but her fight had its effect. She then appeared in several films, including *Marked Woman* (1937), in which she played a girl who testifies against gangsters. *Jezebel* (1938) was written especially for her and was to result in a second Oscar. There were to be more conflicts and suspensions during her eighteen years with Warner's (1931–8), but although her salary escalated, she never won control of her career. She said in her book, *The Lonely Life* (1962), she was literally born between a clap of thunder and a streak of lightning. She went on to say that 'I suppose I'm larger than life. That is my problem. Created in a fury I'm at home in a tempest.'

101 Bette Davis's hard work was rewarded by two Oscars and numerous nominations. An enormous amount has been written about her already, so we discuss her only briefly here. She was married four times, the longest lasting (ten turbulent years) with Gary Merrill (1915–90), who also had a role in All About Eve (1950). Merrill described himself in his autobiography (1988) rather as George Sanders did, as avoiding all drudgery and tedium.

FIGHTING THE STUDIOS

James Cagney (1899–1986) was somewhat more successful than Bette Davis in his numerous battles with Warner's. Cagney had many complaints about his treatment. Like Edward G. Robinson, he objected to being typecast in what he called 'dez, dem, dose' (gangster) pictures and complained about the general pace of work which, he argued, affected the quality. In his autobiography (1976), he says that he made six pictures during his first forty weeks at the studio. The first time he sued the studio was because, contrary to his contract, they billed another name above his at the Warner theatre in Hollywood. This was settled out of court, but in 1935 he again filed suit 'to rectify the inequities' of his contract. By then his films were making a lot of money for the studio and he was getting only a small percentage of it. The case was also settled out of court and Cagney did get a new contract which gave him some measure of control over his career. He had argued that there were only a limited number of successful pictures in a personality (in fact he was to go on and make very many more successful pictures, though it was the conventional wisdom of the time that stars were a wasting asset).

Cagney's long-term objective was to retire early and live on his own farm – which he did. His last film, *One, Two, Three* (1961), released when he was only sixty-two, was not a good one but it was one he chose to do long after he had left the permanent employ of a studio. In the 1940s he formed his own independent company, Cagney Productions, and he was one of the first actors to do so after the Second World War. However, he had returned to Warner's for *White Heat* (1949), this time as a psychopathic gangster. In this tremendous hit, he famously cries, 'Made it, Ma! Top of the World' before he is engulfed in smoke and flames as an oil refinery on which he is standing explodes. Cagney Productions made some entertaining films but they did not, pace O. Selznick, reach the commercial or artistic levels Cagney achieved at Warner's.

Cagney was not the first to defy his studio. Myrna Loy (1905–93) in her autobiography (1987) claimed that distinction for her dispute with MGM when she left for England in 1935 without studio permission. She was put on suspension and was off the screen for a year, but being MGM, Louis B. Mayer was able to smooth it over.[102]

The worst features of the contract system were not remedied until the 1940s, which marked the beginning of the end of studio power. What prompted this was a lawsuit brought by Olivia de Havilland (1916–) in 1943 under the Californian anti-peonage law. The California Court of Appeal ruled in 1944 that de Havilland was not bound to perform services beyond seven years from the start of her contract, which had repeatedly been extended because of periods of suspension. This judgement was to benefit returning war veterans whose contracts had been suspended during military service, including James Stewart, Glenn Ford, Clark Gable and Henry Fonda. De Havilland suffered a two-year career break while the case went through the courts but soon vindicated herself by afterwards winning an Oscar for her role in *To Each His Own* (1946) and another for *The Heiress* (1949).[103]

102 Myrna Loy had a long career from silents in the 1920s to the 1980s, latterly mostly in TV films. She is best remembered for her role in the Thin Man series as the wife of the urbane detective, William Powell and for The Best Years of Our Lives (1946) again as a wife, this time of returning soldier, Fredric March. Loy managed to combine great dignity with sophistication in many domestic comedies.

103 De Havilland spent her time on suspension entertaining soldiers serving in Europe and the Pacific. She was born in Tokyo of British parents and was a member of the family which founded the De Havilland Aircraft Company that designed and built the Comet, the first jet airliner. Before the war, she was nominated for an Oscar for her performance in Gone With the Wind (1939). She appeared in several films with Errol Flynn, including The Adventures of Robin Hood (1938). Her autobiographical Every Frenchman Has One (1962) –the 'one' is a liver – is about France and the French, where she still lives. The book

FIGHTING THE STUDIOS

The loosening up of the contract system greatly boosted the influence of the talent agents of which there were about 150 in the 1940s. These agents earned 10 per cent commission on their client's earnings. Talent agencies emerged in the 1920s with the development of the star system and were able to get better deals for their clients and sometimes better roles, but their incentive was to pursue big money rather than satisfying acting opportunities. Agents also tended to be 'captured' by the studios and during the Communist witch-hunt, described later in Chapter 10, the studios used the agents to operate the blacklist. As an example, Betty Garrett in her book (1998) complains that her agent William Morris dropped her abruptly when she came under suspicion. Other influential talent agencies included Charlie Feldman, Myron Selznick (David's brother) and Leland Hayward. The largest agency was Music Corporation of America built by Jules Stein and his protégé, Lew Wasserman, who joined later. MCA started by representing big bands and eventually became so powerful that it ran foul of the anti-trust authorities. The company entered TV production, initially avoided by the film studios, but was ultimately forced to choose between representing and employing talent, an obvious conflict of interest. MCA then bought Universal Studios, giving up the agency business completely. By the 1940s the bigger agents were offering complete packages, comprising not only stars but stories and directors, in other words they were acting as producers (Kemper, 2010).

Actors' feelings about agents varied. Those fortunate enough to be represented by Wasserman personally spoke highly of him. Tony Curtis (2008) wrote: 'with Lew Wasserman as my mentor, doors opened at the slightest touch'. When MCA

---

does not say anything about her estrangement from her sister, Joan Fontaine, which is acknowledged in Fontaine's autobiography (1978).

quit the agency business, Curtis wrote that his career entered a downward spiral (this was after his greatest triumph, *Some Like it Hot* 1959). That decline was steepened by Curtis's divorce from Janet Leigh, which was widely disapproved of in Hollywood, and his career never really recovered. Curtis wrote two autobiographies (1993 and 2008) and unusually the second is better than the first, though that was also very good. More recently, he wrote a wonderful little book about the making of *Some Like it Hot* (2009), which recounts how Marilyn Monroe's delays in getting on the set and psyching herself up to perform necessitated large numbers of takes and made the normally resilient Billy Wilder ill with frustration. Wilder persisted because he knew she could produce magic on the screen. Curtis, who in his youth had a relationship with Marilyn, resumed it briefly during the filming, which naturally made her husband, the playwright Arthur Miller, rather hostile. There are insights into the process of scriptwriting, direction and some of the other characters in the story, including George Raft, and the book is well worth reading by anyone interested in movie-making.

Kirk Douglas (1916–) who had his first breakthrough in a boxing picture, *Champion* (1949), took a much more critical view of agents, and indeed of the whole Hollywood scene, and like Cagney was one of the first to become and independent actor-producer. It was Douglas who later broke the blacklist (see Chapter10). At this early stage, Douglas was represented by Charlie Feldman who got him the offer of an eight-year, eight-picture contract with no options. To Feldman's fury, Douglas did not want to take up this offer because he did not want to be tied up that long. He wrote: 'The studios were corrupt. They took advantage of actors, writers and directors. All their deals were unfair. The agents you paid to represent you were very cozy with the Studios' (Douglas, 1988).

FIGHTING THE STUDIOS

Some agents were not very protective of their clients' interests. Esther Williams (1999) wrote that when she decided to leave MGM in the 1950s, after making nineteen movies and after the failure of *Jupiter's Darling* (1954), she was comforted by the thought that she had $3 million in her deferred payment, or retirement account.[104] Williams had been advised by her agents, William Morris, to sign her contract, but it was not made clear to her that these funds could only be withdrawn at the end of the period of her contract. Her departure beforehand would forfeit the funds. Lew Wasserman, a friend and not her agent, had told her this as she was about to leave; naturally MGM were not placing any obstacles to her exit.

Maureen O'Hara: Finler.

---
104 Esther Williams (1923–) was a teenage swimming champion until noticed by MGM. She could swim underwater for long periods and smile broadly as she did it. She was a very popular swimming star by the 1950s but by the middle of that decade the vogue for aquatic musical pictures had passed and TV was cutting into the studios business. Her 1999 autobiography takes the title of one of her pictures Million Dollar Mermaid (1952). The deferred payment account was a retirement nest egg that could be drawn after a star's peak earnings had passed and thus minimise taxation, but it was also a golden chain on the actor in the interest of the studio.

Maureen O'Hara (1920–), like Curtis, was also represented by Wasserman. At the beginning of her career she had been signed up, at the age of seventeen, by a partnership of actor Charles Laughton and Erich Pommer, an actor-producer. Later, against her wishes, the partners, who were in financial difficulty, sold her contract to RKO. The agency contract with O'Hara's London agents, that had introduced her to the partners, was in turn sold to MCA. Being bought and sold in this way and being dumped in Hollywood with RKO when she wanted to stay at home in Britain was a double blow to her. O'Hara does, however, praise Wasserman, who was soon able to double her salary by fixing her up with a new contract with 20th Century-Fox. O'Hara's second husband, whom she married in 1941 and divorced in 1953, appointed a business manager who siphoned off a lot of her money. The case went to court but was settled out of it when it became clear that there was very little left from the bad investments the manager had made on O'Hara's behalf.

Business managers, and sometimes agents when they combined the two roles, in many cases were unable to resist the temptation to purloin some of their client's earnings on top of their commission. As we have seen, Maureen O'Hara was a victim of this with the connivance of her husband, but it also happened to Debbie Reynolds, Mickey Rooney and many others. George Sanders' business agent also lost a lot of his money but did so with Sanders' active participation, as explained in the previous chapter. For Gene Tierney (see Chapter 7), it was her own father that robbed her and the same happened to child star Shirley Temple (1988). The worst case of a star being swindled by their business manager, perhaps, was that of Doris Day, whose husband and a lawyer abused their positions for per-

FIGHTING THE STUDIOS

sonal gain.[105] In 1974, Day brought a suit against her lawyer, Jerome B. Rosenthal, in the Superior Court of California. The case lasted a hundred days with twelve lawyers participating at a cost of $250,000. The Judge awarded total damages of $22 million, the largest amount ever in a civil suit in California. Day had used the same lawyer who had advised and cheated Kirk Douglas. Douglas was more fortunate than Day: thanks to his wife Anne, they were able to expose Rosenthal and Kirk's friend and business manager, who had swindled him, and recover the money. Douglas tried to warn Day but her husband intercepted the message. It was the same lawyer who ruined Dorothy Dandridge (see Chapter 9). In his book, Douglas says 'unfortunately everyone in Hollywood has stories like these'.

Although ruthless in protecting their own interests, the studios looked after their actors very well too when they did what they were told. For example, the studios could usually fix things with the police and the press when stars got into trouble. In his autobiography (2008), Robert Wagner records how someone picked a fight with him outside an electrical supply store and 'I foolishly responded by ramming his head into the grille of my car. Technically a felony assault.' Harry Brand, 20th Century's head of publicity 'took care of it'. Perhaps the most striking and tragic case of a cover-up in the post-war period was that of Loretta Young's daughter by Clark Gable. Young, ostensibly a deeply religious person, concealed the affair and put the baby into a Catholic orphanage, without telling Gable or,

---

[105] Doris Day (1924–) was primarily a singer and, like Brigitte Bardot, in later life she has devoted herself to animal welfare. Day's birth name was Kapelhoff. Sometimes labelled 'Goody Two-Shoes' for her dislike of vulgarity, she banned swearing on her sets and in her films. These films varied from genteel and naive sex comedies such as Pillow Talk (1959) with Rock Hudson, to Hitchcock's The Man Who Knew Too Much (1956), in which she memorably belted out the song 'Que Sera, Sera'. Oscar Levant has been credited with the quip, 'I've been around so long I can remember Doris Day before she was a virgin.'

until many years later, the girl herself, whom she had 'adopted' as her own.[106] The daughter, Judy Lewis, recently published a book about the experience (Lewis, 1994).[107]

When their usefulness to the studio ended, stars were often let go without ceremony: contracts were just not renewed. This happened to Esther Williams and to Virginia Mayo, both of whom wrote that the same thing had happened to Clark Gable, the 'King of Hollywood' himself. Mayo wrote of the sad end of her thirty-five-year career:

Virginia Mayo with Dana Andrews in *The Best Years of Our Lives* (1946): Dr Macro/Samuel Goldwyn.

---

106 Loretta Young (1913–2000) had a long and successful career. She won an Oscar for The Farmer's Daughter (1947), according to her autobiography, her 74th film. That didactic book (Young, 1961) is more a compendium of homely and religious wisdom than anything else and in some ways resembles a book by Joan Crawford, My Way of Life (1971), though she also wrote a fuller autobiography (Crawford,1963).

107 The Hollywood fixers had a long history. The famous case of the death of Jean Harlow's husband, Paul Bern, in 1932, had Louis B. Mayer himself rushing to the scene and taking away the suicide note (on advice he returned it later).

[EXT.]

My contract was up. I felt as if I had been cut adrift at sea and that no one in this business I'd come to love either noticed I was leaving or cared in the least what might happen to me. No one even looked up as I walked out of those doors and walked to my car. No one waved. No one said thank you. No party. No cake. No lunch. No one even said goodbye. I simply got in the car and drove home. (Mayo, 2001)

[EXT ends]

CHAPTER **6**

Errol Flynn: The Wildest One

ANYONE WHO HAS seen *The Adventures of Robin Hood* (1938) will remember the scene in which Robin (Flynn) marches into the wicked Prince John's court with a deer on his shoulders. Not only is Robin an outlaw with a price on his head, but hunting the royal deer was forbidden. This daring and impudence was characteristic of Flynn's swashbuckling films and, indeed, of his life. In his autobiography he wrote: 'I have been in rebellion against God and Government ever since I can remember.' Flynn was a quite amazing figure and more words have probably been written about him than any other Hollywood star – some of them by himself. As he said, he would rather have written a few good books than made all those films. But it was not to be; he succumbed to many of the temptations of stardom (except, apparently, vanity).

There were many distinctive features about Flynn and his short life (1909–59). Flynn was unique and is one of only two stars in this book to get a whole chapter to themselves. He was an outsider, who, despite dazzling physical attributes and talents and public adulation, seemed never to find fulfilment.

Errol Flynn: Finler/Warner Bros.

The general view is that he tried to fill the vacuum with drink, drugs, sex and adventure. These pleasures never seemed to pall, but eventually killed him. He had few if any enemies, except himself. Anthony Quinn wrote, in his own autobiography (1995), 'I loved Flynn and cherished his friendship. He was a sweet, troubled man and a wonderful athlete. (There was such grace in his movement.)'. Men rarely describe a member of their own sex as 'beautiful', but many did use that word about Flynn. Basil Rathbone, who several times played the villain in Flynn's films, wrote that he 'was one of the most beautiful male animals I have ever seen' (1962). Women were captivated by him: Janet Leigh, one of the most stable and affectionate actresses of the time, wrote: 'When I met Errol Flynn, I actually gasped. He was as beautiful as I could possibly have imagined, *and*, as charming and as lovable, and as naughty' (1984). Evelyn Keyes, who was in *Gone With the Wind* (1939), had the same reaction: 'He was so beautiful it stopped my breath' (1977). Hedy Lamarr, an exotic Austrian actress, wrote that like herself, Flynn was 'over-sexed'. As a rule, he did not have affairs with his leading ladies, although he married one of them, Patrice Wymore, his third wife, who co-starred with him in *Rocky Mountain* (1950). His first wife, Lili Damita, was a French actress whom he noticed on the ship when he first went to Hollywood. Flynn's taste was more for young girls and for short relationships. David Niven wrote of Flynn: 'He was not a kind man but in those careless days he was fun to be with.' At one point, Flynn left Damita – whom he called Tiger Lil', and with whom he had a stormy relationship, because she could not accept his womanising – to share bachelor apartments with David Niven. David was obviously very fond of Flynn, but had no illusions about him: 'The great thing about Errol was you always knew precisely where you stood with him because he *always* let you down' (1975).

꩜꩜꩜

Flynn's taste for very young women got him into serious trouble. In the autumn of 1942 he faced three counts of rape soon after he had finished *Gentleman Jim* (1942). In his autobiography, he wrote that conquest by force was abhorrent to him, and not necessary: 'Women banged on the doors of Mulholland House [where he lived] like ice drops in a hailstorm. I had to bolt the doors against them.' However, in this particular case what he was charged with was statutory rape (of girls under eighteen) and he could have been found guilty, whether they had consented or not. A Grand Jury in a preliminary hearing dismissed the case, but the District Attorney decided to go to trial anyway. The trial, which lasted over several weeks in January and February 1943, attracted enormous publicity and was a terrible ordeal for Flynn. It was a turning point in his life, even though he was found *not* guilty on all counts. Jerry Geisler, an expensive lawyer suggested by the studio, was able to discredit the witnesses, and prove that they had lied. According to Thomas McNulty (2004) and others, it seems that the affair was a political frame-up to do with lack of studio support for the DA's election and also, as Flynn asserts in his autobiography, there was attempted extortion. In any event, Flynn suffered from the after effects – he admitted that he considered suicide after a party held to celebrate his acquittal which very few attended. He was socially ostracised for a long time afterwards. Although the trial boosted his box office in the short term, his career, after these events, took a dive, partly because of a change in public tastes, but also because his movies were just not as good as they had been. His womanising continued, and indeed intensified. During the trial he had seduced and brought to Hollywood from Mexico a strikingly beautiful young lady, Linda Christian (her name was Blanca Welter at the time). It was Flynn who thought up her new screen name and started her in a career in movies. She stayed with him until after the trial but then left him, realising he did not love her.[108] Also at about the same time Flynn met his second wife, Nora Eddington, whom he married in 1943.

---

108 Linda Christian (1923–2011) produced a fluent, if emotionally harrowing, autobiography (1962). Her main later claim to fame was that she married and subsequently divorced Tyrone Power. Her own films were not particularly distinguished.

Linda Christian: Dr Macro.

Before we leave Flynn's sexual exploits there are two other aspects worth mentioning. The first is that he was very serious – even methodical – about experiencing as many women as possible. Earl Conrad wrote a memoir of the time he spent in Jamaica and New York with Flynn while working on the autobiography, *My Wicked, Wicked Ways* (1959). He describes how hunting women was a continuous activity for Flynn, and he had procurers to introduce him to prospective lovers. As another aspect of Flynn, both Hedy Lamarr and Janet Leigh, who incidentally were both able to resist his appeal, say in their books that they saw a two-way mirror on the ceiling of his bedroom, as well as mirrors around the walls, as Leigh put it: 'As the wolf said to Little Red Riding Hood, the better to see you with, my dear.'[109] Flynn was not interested in, nor could he maintain, in-depth relationships with his women. He told Conrad (1978) that, speaking for himself: 'I discovered that the only thing you need, want or should have is the absolutely physical . . . the less you know about your partner the better.' His marriages seemed to be motivated solely by the needs of paternity: 'Women married me, I did not marry them.' He never engaged in serial monogamy or fidelity for long, yet he was totally committed to and affectionate towards his children. This attractive side of Flynn has not been written about until recently. His youngest surviving daughter by Nora Eddington, his second wife, Rory Flynn, has now produced a memoir which adds yet another aspect to Flynn's complex character (Flynn, 2006). This book is notable for the large number of intimate family photographs and for an affectionate depiction of Flynn's last days. Rory was only twelve when her father died.[110]

The other palliatives for Flynn, apart from promiscuity, were drink and drugs of which he made increasing use as he got older. According to Conrad, during their work together on the autobiography at the end of his life, Flynn started drinking early in the day – cherry brandy for breakfast, for example – and continued until he went to sleep at night. From the 1940s he had stashed drinks around his film sets, sometimes hidden in make-up or

---

109 In his autobiography, however, Flynn says that the ceiling mirror was his architect's idea and that he never used it.
110 The book also has a lot about Sean, Flynn's son by his first wife, Lili Damita. Sean was captured as a photo-journalist by the Khmer Rouge in Cambodia in 1970 and never seen again. Rory has an elder sister, Deirdre, who is cited at the end of this chapter. Flynn's other daughter, Arnella, by his third wife, Patrice Wymore, died in 1998.

ERROL FLYNN: THE WILDEST ONE

soft-drink bottles. When this practice was banned by the studio boss and Flynn's nemesis, Jack Warner, he injected oranges with vodka and ate them during breaks in filming. On his own admission Flynn also used opium, cocaine and morphine, in conjunction with alcohol, though he denied using heroin, which he said was hopelessly addictive. All this, together with tuberculosis, the malaria he had picked up in New Guinea, and other ailments, were ultimately to destroy his health. At the beginning, Flynn was a very strong man. He was six feet two inches tall and never really fat, though his face became bloated towards the end. In his youth in Hobart, Tasmania, his mother, a champion swimmer, coached him. Later he did a lot of skin-diving, delighting in going down to the 90 feet or so that was regarded as the limit. Flynn was also reputedly the best tennis player in Hollywood at the time and used to play with Don Budge, who was world champion and the first to win the grand slam of all four major tournaments.[111]

Flynn was a seriously good boxer and considered going professional in Australia in his youth. He kept this up with the studio boxing coach, who rated Flynn as good enough to become a professional. Flynn got involved in numerous brawls – he says that Hollywood tough guys were constantly being challenged in nightclubs and restaurants to show how tough they really were. He did not always rise to these challenges, but there is no record that he lost any. Two stories, among many, illustrate his prowess as a boxer. While making The Charge of the Light Brigade (1936), Flynn was relaxing on his horse between takes when the animal was prodded in the rear by an extra with a lance. Flynn, thrown off when the horse reared, picked himself up and asked grimly, 'Who did

---
[111] In the autobiography Flynn says he won the junior Davis Cup during his time in England, but researchers have not found his name in the records.

that?' David Niven, who was present at the time, says that a gorilla-like man replied; 'I did, want to make something of it?' After a short fight, the extra had to be taken to the infirmary. On another occasion, at a party at David O. Selznick's house, Flynn got into a fight with director John Huston, ostensibly over a lady's reputation, but more probably because both were bored with the party.[112] They went outside and fought for the best part of an hour without a break. Huston was no mean boxer himself, having won twenty-three out of twenty-five bouts as a professional in his youth (he had decided against making it his career when he got his nose broken). The fight ended in a draw when fellow guests broke it up. O. Selznick, the host, called Flynn names and offered to fight him himself, but no doubt fortunately for him, Flynn did not take up the offer. Huston (1980) says admiringly that Flynn boxed strictly according to the Queensberry rules, stepping back when his opponent was knocked down.[113]

Born in Hobart, Tasmania, Errol Leslie Flynn (his real names) had an unsettled boyhood. His mother was of English immigrant descent, while his father, a distinguished Professor of Marine Biology, was of Irish extraction. The young Errol was educated in

---

112 David O. Selznick married MGM mogul Louis B. Mayer's daughter, Irene, but eventually left her for Jennifer Jones, whom he discovered and made a star. Selznick, a movie executive later became an independent producer. As a producer he was very much hands-on and responsible for many famous productions. He was notorious for his long memos and from one of these we learn that in 1937 he was considering Errol Flynn for the lead in Gone With the Wind (1939), but was able to get his first choice, Clark Gable, instead (Selznick, 1972).

113 Possibly, the violence was exaggerated, although various accounts say that both the contestants had to go to hospital afterwards. Evelyn Keyes (1977), who met both Huston and Flynn a day or two later, wrote: 'since neither of them had a scratch those few days later, it couldn't have been much of a scrap'. Keyes subsequently married Huston.

ERROL FLYNN: THE WILDEST ONE

Hobart and Sydney (being expelled from school in both places), and in England, which his father regularly visited for long periods. At the age of seventeen Errol was finished with schooling and worked as a clerk in an export firm but was fired for expropriating company funds. He then began his travels to New Guinea and a series of adventures over many years, including a brief period as a government colonial officer; he was also a plantation manager, gold prospector and what amounted to slave trader. In 1932 he had his screen debut as Fletcher Christian (who was supposedly related to Flynn's mother) in *In the Wake of the Bounty* (1933). This experience got him interested in acting, and after further adventures in the Far East, a year later he was back in England. To gain experience he appeared in twenty-two plays for the Northampton repertory company, days which he later said were the happiest of his life. Some time after this, in 1934, he appeared in a Warner Brothers film made at Teddington Studios in England. This led to a contract with Warner's in Hollywood, in which a recommendation by Douglas Fairbanks Jr was instrumental.

Flynn's first film in Hollywood was a Perry Mason detective story, *The Case of the Curious Bride* (1935), in which he played a corpse; this was followed by another minor film. Then an extraordinary thing happened. Jack Warner and his director Michael Curtiz took a chance on casting Flynn in the lead role of the major piratical saga, *Captain Blood* (1935). The film was already in early production when the lead, Robert Donat, withdrew at the last minute.[114] *Captain Blood* is the story of a wrongly convicted physician accused of rebellion

---

114 Robert Donat (1905–58), an English stage-trained actor of delicate health, had just appeared in The Count of Monte Cristo (1934), which was made in the US. In England he played Richard Hannay in Alfred Hitchcock's version of The 39 Steps (1935) with Madeline Carroll. Carroll, many years later, married Sterling Hayden (see Chapter 12). Donat was awarded an Oscar for his moving performance in Goodbye, Mr. Chips (1939), a film in which Paul Henreid also appeared as a congenial German schoolmaster.

and sentenced to slavery in Jamaica. He escapes and becomes a pirate fighting on Britain's side. Olivia de Havilland, who was nineteen, was tested with Flynn and both were selected alongside Basil Rathbone.[115] In the film, Flynn vanquishes Rathbone as he was to do again in *The Adventures of Robin Hood* (1938), which also starred de Havilland. *Captain Blood* was a smash hit and straight after it Flynn starred in *The Charge of the Light Brigade* (1936) in which the hero dies heroically.

Errol Flynn in *The Charge of The Light Brigade* (1936): Finler/Warner Bros.

Warner's were not able to capitalise on the enormous success of these two films, which established Flynn's swashbuckling

---

[115] Olivia de Havilland was to appear in six Flynn movies and later on completed work begun by Bette Davis and others on breaking up the Hollywood star contract system (see Chapter 5).

ERROL FLYNN: THE WILDEST ONE

screen character. He was wasted in his next, *The Green Light* (1937) and also to some extent in *The Prince and the Pauper* of the same year, in which he played a supporting role to two boys – the king's son and a street urchin who trades places with him. In this medieval fable, Flynn does not appear until a third of the way through but does well in his courageous defence of the boys and shows a convincing fraternal tenderness towards them. There were two more unmemorable movies before *Robin Hood*, perhaps because Flynn was trying to avoid typecasting. His reversion to swashbuckling in that film was a triumphant success and he had now evidently replaced Douglas Fairbanks Sr as the all-time leading exponent of this type of role. *Robin Hood* was in colour; the film was the most expensive Warner's had made up to that time and it shows. *Robin Hood* bears repeated viewings and is a great film.

Flynn did get a chance to demonstrate his versatility in a serious picture in *The Dawn Patrol* (1938) about First World War pilots, which was both a critical and box office success. His versatility was again demonstrated, though it was less welcome to him, in his role as a tough sheriff cleaning up *Dodge City* (1939), the first and best of his Westerns. In *The Private Lives of Elizabeth and Essex* (1939), another lavishly produced film, Bette Davis, then thirty but made up to look sixty, played Queen Elizabeth I and rather overpowers the movie, with Flynn as the Earl of Essex, her improbable and tragic lover. Flynn did his best with this, but Davis, who had hoped for Laurence Olivier and made no secret of it, was pretty beastly to him. In *The Sea Hawk* (1940) Warner's successfully retraced similar ground to that in *Captain Blood*.

Skipping to *Gentleman Jim* in 1942, we find Flynn showing off his boxing skills and convincingly defeating Ward Bond for the Heavyweight Championship in San Francisco in the 1890s.

It has been said that by then Flynn was in poor shape and had to do some of the fight scenes in short takes, which were then incorporated with cutting and editing – but this appears to be another of the Hollywood myths discussed in Chapter 3. Flynn was only thirty-three in 1942 and his physical deterioration did not set in until later. Stuntman Yakima Canutt, who was there, wrote that Flynn was very fast on his feet (Canutt, 1979). *Gentleman Jim* is a cheerful film with a good sense of period and a moving scene in which the former champion attends Flynn's victory party. It is one of Flynn's best and reportedly his personal favourite. Despite a good performance in *That Forsyte Woman* (1949) and, in self-caricature in the *Adventures of Don Juan* (1948), Flynn's best films were now in the past. Near the end he did play degenerates much like himself in Hemingway's *The Sun Also Rises* (1957)[116] and, as his late friend, the actor John Barrymore, in *Too Much, Too Soon* (1958).[117]

According to his co-actors, Flynn, at least before drink and drugs overtook him, was always well prepared for his roles and knew his lines. He continually pressed for 'better' roles than the ones he got, especially as time went by, but he was not popular with several directors (Raoul Walsh was a notable exception). The main problem was Michael Curtiz, who was by far the best director for Flynn and responsible

---

116 Ernest Hemingway did not like any of the fifteen films based on his writings and, according to his brother Leicester, quoted in McNulty, thought Flynn was 'a triple phony'. This unfavourable impression was apparently created by the unfortunate episode of Flynn's claim to have raised a million dollars for the Loyalists in the Spanish Civil War (see below). Their paths crossed quite a few times, not only in Spain but in Hollywood and Cuba, but they never became friends, despite their common interests in drink, boxing and writing. Hemingway, who ultimately shot himself, was ten years older than Flynn, but outlived him by two years.
117 Flynn loved Barrymore, the brother of Ethel and Lionel Barrymore, who was a big stage and movie star in the 1920s and later. As a handsome and self-destructive alcoholic, Barrymore resembled Flynn in several ways (Barrymore's autobiography is mentioned in Chapter 2.)

ERROL FLYNN: THE WILDEST ONE

for most of his best films.[118] Flynn's complaint was that Curtiz was rude and dictatorial, whereas it seems the same applied to Flynn. Raoul Walsh was a tough director of action films, including They Died With Their Boots on, Desperate Journey and Gentleman Jim.

⁂

Another characteristic of Flynn was his love of adventure. These started early with his arduous experiences in New Guinea, which included a daring sea voyage along the Great Barrier Reef. Some of Flynn's adventures may be fictitious, for example his claim to have enlisted in the Hong Kong Volunteers in 1932 with Dr Erben has never been verified. Dr Erben, from Austria, was a medical researcher, photographer and physician whom Flynn met and befriended in their early days together in the Pacific. Erben was undoubtedly a bad influence and encouraged Flynn's whoring and drinking. The interesting thing about some of these early exploits, such as his theft of jewels from a married woman lover – which may not be true – is that they are not to his credit. He seemed to want to paint himself as more wicked than he really was, though of course he was wicked enough. Flynn's adventuring continued throughout his life when the opportunity arose. In 1937, much against the wishes of the studio, Flynn went to observe the Spanish Civil War and secured an assignment as a 'war correspondent' from the Hearst Organisation. He subsequently wrote an article for

---

118 Michael Curtiz (1888–1962) was already a very experienced director when he came to America from Europe (Hungary and Austria) in the mid-1920s. As a director, Curtiz was astonishingly versatile. In addition to the Flynn films, including Westerns, Curtiz directed very successful musicals such as: Yankee Doodle Dandy (1942) and White Christmas (1954) and the melodramas Casablanca (1942); Mildred Pierce (1945) and Flamingo Road (1949). He never fully mastered colloquial English, and like Samuel Goldwyn was famous for amusingly confused language. One of his sayings provided the title for David Niven's book, Bring On the Empty Horses (1975).

Photoplay (reproduced in Thomas, 1980). Many were upset by Flynn's cynical use of the Loyalist cause, as they saw it, for his own aggrandisement. Actually, Flynn probably thought he was developing his writing career and certainly did not need the publicity which would have followed him everywhere whether he went to Spain or not.

Matters were made worse by the fabrication of a totally untrue story by Erben that Flynn had raised a million dollars in Hollywood to build a hospital and buy ambulances for the anti-fascists. According to Wicked Ways, it was Erben who suggested going to Spain in the first place, but Flynn was keen to go for two reasons. First, for a break from his volatile and possessive wife, 'Tiger Lili' ('civil war seemed mild after her'), and second, simply to satisfy his curiosity: he always needed change and stimulation. In 1956, at the time of Fidel Castro's Cuban Revolution, Flynn became friendly with Castro, who appealed to his rebellious nature, though Flynn was not really interested in politics. Flynn went to Cuba with a camera crew to make what would be his last feature film, Cuban Rebel Girls (1959). A very young actress, Beverly Aadland, who was with Flynn when he died in Vancouver, was his companion/ 'secretary' and appeared in the film – by all accounts a very poor one but it obviously appealed to Castro as useful publicity.

⁂

Flynn wrote his first novel, *Beam Ends*, shortly after arriving in Hollywood[119] (1937). The book is the story of a voyage

---

119 Beam Ends is a nautical term meaning that a ship is on its side and in danger of capsizing – beams being the cross-members which run transversely across the ship. According to McNulty (2004), Flynn also wrote a screenplay which he sold to Warner Brothers in 1938 for $25,000. Sirocco was Flynn's first yacht; he bought another in Hollywood, which he then renamed Sirocco. This second boat was sold later because of its association with the rape case and replaced with Zaca, a 118-foot schooner, in 1946. The Zaca was used in Orson Welles'

ERROL FLYNN: THE WILDEST ONE

from Sydney to New Guinea, a distance of some 3,000 miles. The author's foreword makes it clear that the book is based on a six-month trip Flynn took on the first *Sirocco* in 1930 with some friends. The story is illustrated with photographs taken on the earlier trip. The novel ends with the complete wreck of the ship and the death of one of the crew. This did not occur in real life – Flynn mentions in his autobiography that he sold the *Sirocco* to raise funds for a tobacco plantation. The ship was a fifty-year-old vessel not really suited for a trip of this kind and all the crew, including Flynn at the time, were inexperienced sailors, but they made it. There was a lot of drinking, womanising and misadventure on the way and its makes an interesting story.

Beam Ends, which was followed by a number of magazine articles on his experiences in Hollywood, is written in a lucid, lively way. It is very much in Flynn's own voice at the time – that of a worldly English public schoolboy. Curious this, because Flynn had been at school in England for at most three years (1921–4) and one of the schools he says he attended – and from which he said he was expelled, aged fifteen, has never actually been identified. [120] About 75,000 words in length, the book carries the reader along rapidly and seems too short. Here is part of a description of a brawl in a café:

[EXT]
Undoubtedly, the idea is to win at all costs in a street brawl. Any ethical considerations of fair play are only a handicap. But that last blow was sheer brutality. Johnson was already falling, finished and blind with blood when it was struck. Forgetting all about my cherished role of

---
film The Lady from Shanghai (1948).
120 Probably the schools he attended in Australia were also very British in character.

spectator, or of peaceful prudence, I was into the fray with one burning desire – to avenge Johnson. Every rule went by the board. I hit with everything I had and was on top of him the moment he reached the ground. We rolled over together and I felt the wonderful exuberance of clutching his windpipe in both hands – a marvellous feeling of satisfaction that quickly changed to dim detachment as something hard hit me on the back of the head.
[EXT ends]

There are some vivid turns of phrase:

[EXT]
The Captain's wife was the first white woman I had seen for two years. She was fair, fat and fifty, with no teeth of her own to speak of, but to me she seemed the most beautiful thing I had ever seen. My eyes stuck out so far that the captain could have knocked them off with a stick.
[EXT ends]

Beam Ends, no doubt helped by the author's screen reputation, was fairly well received and went into a paperback edition (it is still in print). There was also an abridged version which appeared in *Cosmopolitan* magazine. Flynn's second book and final novel did not appear until nine years later in 1946, heavily cut down from the length of the original manuscript. It is another semi-autobiographical book, this time about film-making and the sea in New Guinea – written in the same lively style but much less well sustained as a narrative. It was less successful, too, than his first novel. Flynn saw it as a failure and was never to complete another book on his own. Tony Thomas (1980) points out that writing is hard work and that despite his talent Flynn did not put enough effort into the book. Acting, by contrast, Flynn found very easy and the money was obviously vastly better.

Flynn would only achieve bestseller status with his posthumously published autobiography. For some time he had had a contract for the book and wrote about 50,000 words, but could not complete it. The publishers lost patience and insisted on calling in outside help. Eventually *My Wicked, Wicked Ways* (1959) was put together by Earl Conrad,[121] an experienced author with several novels and non-fiction works to his credit, including an autobiography with Dorothy Dandridge. Flynn and Conrad worked together for ten weeks at Flynn's property in Jamaica with Flynn dictating to a stenographer. The two men liked one another.[122] Conrad did a very good job in only one year (1958–9) and was able to retain Flynn's style and voice. The deal was that Flynn would be the sole credited author. According to McNulty, threatened lawsuits from Michael Curtiz, Lili Damita and Maureen O'Hara led the publishers to reissue the book with deletions soon after publication. *My Wicked, Wicked Ways* contains some amusing tales: most of these stories are probably true, for example, how Flynn shot and killed a native in New Guinea in self-defence and was charged with murder but got off; that he left a toy snake in Olivia de Havilland's bloomers in her dressing room and hired two models to stroll naked through a press conference at his house.

There is some false information about Flynn as well as by him. Charles Higham (1980), who wrote many good books on Hollywood, wrote a bad one claiming that Flynn was a Nazi spy. The book contains no convincing evidence for this except

---

121 Dorothy Dandridge (1922–65) had a short and tragic life, see Chapter 9.
122

for Dr Erben's friendship and the fact that the FBI had files on both of them. Erben did admit in a court in Shanghai that he was a German spy but denied that Flynn was connected with any pro-German activities (Valenti, 1984). Tony Curtis, in his second autobiography, had a photograph of himself and Flynn, who has a cup of tea in his hand. Curtis commented that he would want to see a picture of Flynn having tea with Hitler before he could believe he was a Nazi (2008).

Another false story about Flynn was that he avoided military service out of cowardice. In truth, he was rejected for military service in February 1942 as he was suffering from tuberculosis. He also had malaria, contracted in New Guinea. Neither the studio nor Flynn himself wanted to publish anything that would detract from his swashbuckling image. Flynn felt very badly about his rejection by the army and tried, unsuccessfully, to get a role in the diplomatic service, according to McNulty. Matters were made worse by his appearance in a number of contemporary war films, including Desperate Journey (1942) and Objective, Burma! (1945). The latter caused trouble because it did not mention Britain's role in that conflict. Flynn was so ashamed of his absence from the war that it required considerable courage on his part to go on USO tours to entertain the troops, however much the soldiers loved him.

Flynn was largely self-educated and read widely, especially when on his own in New Guinea. In *My Wicked, Wicked Ways*, there are speculations about the differences between the sexes, the nature of the universe, the meaning of life, the nature of acting, film-making and other things. These passages have been taken as evidence of Flynn's intellectual capacity, and indeed they are, but it is all very self-centred stuff: everything is considered only from his own point of view. There is no general search for objectivity and yet despite that, Flynn seems to see *himself* objectively. He recognises that he is a mass of contradictions:

> I want to be taken seriously, I feel that I am inwardly serious, thoughtful, even tormented, but in practice I yield to the fatuous, the nonsensical . . . I have a zest for living, yet twice an urge to die . . . I am alternately, very kind, very cruel . . . I want to be loved but I may myself be incapable of really loving. I hate the legend of myself as phallic representation, yet I work at it to keep it alive . . . (Flynn, 1959)

Flynn was never able to have a satisfactory relationship with his mother and blamed her for that. At times he hated her, yet he loved and respected his father. Both parents were baffled by what his father called the 'enigma' of their son. But trying to understand Flynn was futile for them, and for us. As he recognised himself, there were two sides to him and 'Contradiction is neither true nor false. It *is*.' Some observers have considered his life a waste and a tragedy. His daughter Deirdre, however, took a different view. Barry Norman (1979) quotes Deirdre as saying in an interview: 'I think, in fact, that he probably led two lives in one. It was very free, his life. And he actually did what he bloody well wanted to do. I don't see that as a waste at all.'

Although his life cannot be properly described as 'tragic', there is nonetheless a sad side to Flynn's story. He enjoyed enormously sailing the seas, his estate in Jamaica, his children, his gallons of vodka, girls, parties and practical jokes, and even, at the outset, his writing and acting, but he was never socially acceptable.[123] Rory Flynn's official website for her father, *In Like Flynn*, rightly laments that 'In his lifetime Flynn received no recognition from his peers at the Academy of Motion Picture Arts and Sciences. He never attended a ceremony in his honour and was not nominated (for an Oscar).' Flynn, in short, was politically incorrect.

---

123 Raymond Massey, in his autobiography (1979) says that Flynn was not really acceptable as a member of the British colony (see Chapter 4 above), not only as an Australian but because of his 'erotic antics'. Massey points out that: 'similar activities, conducted with greater discretion on the part of a young actor named David Niven, were viewed with tolerance if not envy by the elder brethren of the colony'.

CHAPTER 7

The Dark Side

HOLLYWOOD'S MOST BEAUTIFUL women in the Golden Age became world famous, were treated lavishly by the studios and were courted by male stars and millionaires. Yet their lives were often marked by tragedy, stress, broken marriages, and often they failed to find any lasting personal happiness.[124] Some people have spoken of the curse of beauty; the idea being that the beautiful become spoiled and have things too easy or are exposed to more temptation than plainer mortals. Whilst it is not at all clear that the problems of Hollywood beauties were necessarily connected with their looks, it is nonetheless true that the most beautiful were often very unhappy and unlucky, Marilyn Monroe being the classic case. In this chapter we discuss some of the sadder glamorous actress/writers and one cheerful survivor. Marlene Dietrich, who was beautiful but in no way a sad case, was covered in Chapter 3.

---

124 Of course, misfortune and tragedy were not confined to women or to the beautiful. Bette Davis and Joan Crawford both big stars suffered, unjustly, from criticism in public from their children about their upbringing (see Chapter 4). Several children of big stars, such as the sons of Kirk Douglas, Gregory Peck, Bing Crosby, Tony Curtis, Charles Boyer and Paul Newman, committed suicide or died of an overdose of drugs in later life, perhaps because they could not live up to the image of their father (Douglas, 2007).

◄ HOLLYWOOD LIVES

Ava Gardner: Dr Macro.

Gene Tierney with Dana Andrews in *Laura* (1944): Dr Macro/20th Century Fox.

Gene Tierney (1920–91), among Hollywood's great beauties, was certainly the most unfortunate. She was described as 'the most beautiful woman in movie history', though similar accolades were awarded to Hedy Lamarr, Yvonne de Carlo and Ava Gardner.[125] There are no absolute standards of such a subjective thing as appearance. Tierney's beauty (which apparently was, unusually, even greater off-screen than on) is exceptionally difficult to convey in words. Indeed, any detailed description undermines it. She had wonderful green eyes and soft features, with full cheeks that become more pronounced as she aged. She had a lovely figure, though she had broad shoulders and was a little thick at the ankles. Also she had an overbite (buck teeth), but somehow these minor imperfections only served to increase her fascination. The figure did not come easily; the studio told her that to photograph well she needed to lose weight and she had to diet. Tierney wrote in her autobiography: 'For all of Hollywood's considerable rewards, I was hungry for most of those twenty years.' Her unpretentious autobiography (Tierney, 1978), which was written with Mickey Herskowitz, is notable for its simplicity and straightforwardness, it is a sad tale but with a happy ending.

Gene Tierney is perhaps best remembered for two films: *Laura* (1944) and *Leave Her to Heaven* (1945). These two films demonstrate that she could act as well as having a great screen presence. In *Laura*, she played the title role of a woman who goes away on her own to her cottage for a few days without mentioning it to anyone. In her absence, a corpse

---

[125] The quote is by Darryl Zanuck cited by Vogel (2005). Others, probably also studio heads, have described Ava Gardner, Lamarr and de Carlo at different times as the most beautiful women in the world. In her autobiography Tierney wrote that 'show business is partly a flesh market, and the subject of beauty, male or female, preoccupies us'.

of a woman is found in her apartment, the face obliterated by a shotgun blast, and it is first assumed that the body is Tierney's. Meanwhile a tough and cynical police detective (Dana Andrews), in the course of the investigation, gradually falls in love with her portrait which hangs over the mantelpiece in the apartment.[126] The detective falls off to sleep in an armchair to be woken with a start by Tierney returning. He then has to determine not only who killed the victim but also who that victim was. The scene of this awakening to reality is enhanced by the haunting melody composed by David Raksin and with lyrics by Johnny Mercer –elements which the director introduced. The magic which Preminger was to create was not apparent in the script and the producer, Darryl Zanuck, had to persuade a very reluctant Tierney to take the role. She refused it at first, presumably as Jennifer Jones had done before her, when she was offered the same part, because Laura is not on screen for half of the film. Despite excellent performances from two murder suspects (Clifton Webb and Vincent Price), in the final outcome Tierney, even when absent from the screen, dominates the picture.[127] She was perfect for the role of Laura because her dreamy beauty conveys the essence of the 'ethereal existence of a woman who seems unreal, mysterious, alluring', an essence which the music evokes and which the detective comes to love (Vogel, 2005).

In *Leave Her to Heaven*, Tierney plays the very different role of a psychotic, jealous and vindictive woman. Her father has just died and there is a scene in the high desert near Taos, New Mexico, where she rides around distributing her father's

---

126 In fact, during filming it was discovered that the portrait of Tierney did not come out well and a touched-up photograph that looks like an oil painting was substituted.
127 Vincent Price (1911–93) was to appear later with Tierney in Dragonwyck (1946). Price wrote I Like What I Know: A Visual Autobiography (1959), which is not about his stage and screen career but about his hobby – art.

ashes from an urn. She looks very good in jodhpurs. Tierney seduces her future husband (Cornel Wilde), deliberately allows her husband's crippled brother to drown and then coolly falls down stairs to abort his unborn child. Finally she poisons herself, leaving evidence that points to the responsibility for her death with her adopted sister Jeanne Crain and her husband for her murder. In this way her evil influence is felt even after her death.[128] This terrible story is made credible by Tierney's performance. She was nominated for an Academy Award for Best Actress, but lost it to Joan Crawford for *Mildred Pierce* (1945). This had been Tierney's only chance for an Oscar, but she did not expect it and in her modest way claimed that winning the nomination was excitement enough. It is interesting, given her later mental problems, that she also achieved an exceptional performance in another film, *Whirlpool* (1949), in which she played an unbalanced woman. This film, like *Laura* and *Where the Sidewalk Ends* (1950) was directed by Preminger and turned out to be among her last significant roles.[129]

Gene Tierney was born in Brooklyn, New York, and brought up there and in rural Connecticut. Her father at the time was a very well-off insurance broker and she was educated at the best schools, including Miss Porter's, Farmington, which numbered such wealthy debutantes as Jackie Kennedy and Barbara Hutton among its alumni. Gene was also at a finishing school in Switzerland for two years from 1936. Tierney, with her whispery diction, was as literate and as polished as

---

[128] Cornel Wilde (1912–89) was a former Olympic fencer who performed a variety of roles in romantic and action films of the 1940s and 1950s. He was nominated for an Oscar for his performance as Chopin in A Song to Remember (1944).
[129] Otto Preminger (1905–86) was a very versatile director, Austrian in origin. The film noir mentioned here were among his best, but he made some clunkers, for example Exodus (1960), which could have been so good but which was overambitious, overlong and miscast.

the socialites she often later played. While still under eighteen, and on a tour of Warner Brothers studios arranged by her father, she was identified as having potential for the screen. She was offered a contract but her father insisted that she go on the stage first. Against the odds (she had absolutely no experience of acting), she got a role as an Irish girl in a play on Broadway. She was then offered a contract by Columbia and accepted, but after a brief period there, frustrated by the lack of any role, she returned to the stage. There, she was seen by Darryl Zanuck of Fox, who promised her good parts. Her first film for Zanuck was a Western, *The Return of Frank James* (1940) with Henry Fonda. She went on to demonstrate versatility with *Hudson's Bay* (1940), and in *Tobacco Road* (1941), a steamy Southern drama in which her beauty is ill-concealed by a coating of olive oil and dirt. These three films were all good and successful but then she was grossly miscast in *Belle Starr* (1941) as a 'bandit queen' and in *Sundown* (1941) as an African princess – both awful films, despite good supporting actors.

Tierney had plenty of screen work, but the hard knocks in her private life took their toll. Her father, who had first run into trouble with his business whilst Tierney was at school in Switzerland, had been siphoning off assets from the company he set up to manage her career. Gene had idolised her father and the betrayal was a bitter blow. When she signed her next contract it excluded her father as agent and he unsuccessfully sued her for damages. Her parents had separated when Gene moved with her mother, Belle, a former gymnastics teacher, to Hollywood and they divorced later. Belle, who never remarried, refused alimony and supported herself for the rest of her life. Gene's father remarried to a wealthy lady who paid off his debts. (The father's Christian name was Howard and his son

'Butch' was also christened Howard. Perhaps significantly, Gene's second and enduring husband, Howard Lee, had the same Christian name.)

Gene was also courted for a while by Howard Hughes (who appears frequently in actresses' autobiographies) and who later in life was to perform a great kindness for her. Gene described Howard Hughes as 'gentle and well-bred' but realised that he was elusive and offered no prospect of a permanent relationship, which was all she was interested in. Future President John F. Kennedy, with whom she had a relationship after the break-up of her first marriage, was also given the boot when he told her that he could never marry her (she was divorced and he was a Catholic). She did fall in love with Oleg Cassini, an honourable but tempestuous titled dress designer working for Paramount.[130] Cassini was then twenty-eight, a divorcée and generally regarded as something of a playboy. This relationship did not meet with her parents' or the studio's approval and all three joined forces against them when they eloped and married in 1941. Cassini was fired by the studio and for a while was ostracised by Hollywood society. He was too temperamental, active and outgoing to be a suitable partner for Gene, who suffered physical and mental stress disorders all her life and yearned for peace, quiet and security. In a fit of jealousy, Cassini once destroyed Tyrone

---

[130] Oleg Cassini (1913–2006) was born in Paris of a Russian diplomat and an Italian countess. He was quite a character, proud and ambitious but prone to jealousy and fistfights. During the Second World War, he first enlisted in the US Coastguard, where he cruised with Victor Mature in the latter's yacht, looking for enemy submarines in the Pacific. (Like Ernest Hemingway's similar expeditions in his motor cruiser Pilar, the searches proved a failure but lots of fun.) Cassini's adventures, recounted in his enthralling autobiography, included later service in the US Cavalry, a family tradition, and an engagement to Grace Kelly who gave him up for Prince Rainier. Cassini, through talent and determination, built a successful fashion business, was personal couturier to Jacqueline Kennedy and a confidant of JFK himself. Cassini can be seen briefly as the dress designer in Where the Sidewalk Ends (1950).

Power's dressing room suspecting (wrongly) that Power and Gene were having an affair. Cassini was never after Gene's money and at the outset, when he was poor, signed a document renouncing any future claim on her. He was, moreover, loyal in his own way, suave and polished (they could speak French together) and they remained married for ten years. Their ultimate divorce was at Gene's wish, not his, though the last five years were marked by infidelities and attempted reconciliations on his side. Cassini never remarried.

The next and cruellest shock of all was the premature birth of Gene's daughter, Daria, in 1943. The child appeared normal at first but eventually was revealed as partially deaf, dumb and blind and mentally retarded. Many doctors were consulted; Howard Hughes heard about the problem and flew in a specialist in infant disease. The anguished parents did everything they could but after four years Daria was placed in an institution.[131] After the birth, Gene returned to the studio and produced some of her best work. Her problems, however, were only being suppressed and her mental illness first emerged during the making of *Way of a Gaucho* (1953) at a time when she had filed for divorce from Oleg. She continued to work, however. At the age of thirty-two she was in the physically demanding role of a Russian ballerina, opposite Clark Gable, in *Never Let Me Go* (1953), a film made in Britain.[132]

---

[131] About a year after Daria's birth, Gene was approached at a tennis party by a woman whom she had met briefly when she had been in the very early stages of pregnancy at the Hollywood Canteen. The woman, a Marine, confessed that she had broken camp quarantine because of German measles because she so much wanted to meet her. This irresponsible act was the cause of Gene's infection and Daria's problems. Curiously, Oleg met the same woman by chance some ten years later and she, unaware of the tragedy she had caused, told him the same story which Gene, to spare him, had not revealed.

[132] Tierney was contemplating marriage to Aly Khan (later killed in a car accident), but decided against it. In her book she says that her relationship with Khan was not the cause of her breakdown.

THE DARK SIDE

She made several more films, but working on *The Left Hand of God* (1954) her symptoms were continuing to worsen – with abrupt personality changes, bad-tempered outbursts, feelings of persecution and difficulty with remembering lines. Humphrey Bogart, her co-star, recognised the symptoms and warned the studio that she needed rest and treatment, but they wanted her to continue. She says in her book that it was Bogart's patience and understanding that carried her through the film – her last until 1962, many years later. At the time Bogart himself was suffering from terminal cancer.

Tierney returned to Connecticut and New York where she was admitted to one sanatorium, then another and another. She was released and worked in a dress shop as a form of therapy, but then readmitted, finally finding a degree of mental stability. From one of these sanatoria she escaped and was chased and recaptured. It is painful to read her account of this and of the treatments she received. She was given electro-convulsive shock therapy (ECT) in which an electric shock is administered to the brain. She also received 'the cold pack' in which 'I was wrapped from the neck down in icy wet bedsheets, my arms strapped to my sides. It was like being buried in a snowbank. Tears poured down my cheeks as the minutes ticked away. I couldn't move. I lost the feeling in my hands and feet. My mind was in a panic' (Tierney, 1978). It seems that the short-term result of these apparently humiliating and barbarous treatments was effective and ECT remains in use today, although it is highly controversial.

Tierney had earlier met and become engaged to Howard Lee, an oil tycoon, and he remained supportive during her hospitalisation. Lee was in the process of an acrimonious divorce from none other than Hedy Lamarr, on whom more later, and had been reluctant to meet another actress – but he did and their relationship took off quickly. They married as soon as he was free in 1960. With him, Gene's life entered calmer waters, though she did have short periods of relapse into illness. She had not worked since 1955 but was signed up for *Advise & Consent* (1962) by Otto Preminger. Tierney made two more films, in one of which she played Dean Martin's mother-in-law, as they were about the same age. Her film career was over and her last twenty years were spent quietly in Huston with her husband. He died in 1981 and she survived him by almost ten years. Tierney's second daughter, Christina Cassini, in her Foreword to Michelle Vogel's 2005 biography of Tierney, wrote that her mother 'was a woman full of genuine kindness' but 'unfortunately, did not have the necessary aggressiveness to resist all that she was confronted with in life'.

❦

Hedy Lamarr (1913–2000) was perhaps the most beautiful of them all.[133] She had a lovely, shield-shaped face and her dark hair was usually parted above the centre of her forehead, emphasising the pleasing symmetry of her features. She was quite tall (5'7") without apparent imperfections. *Celebrity Sleuth* magazine noted her measurements as 33-22-34 inches in 1933 and 33-23-35 inches in the 1940s. Very early on she wanted to become an actress and showed great determination in becoming one. She smuggled herself into a film studio in Vienna and was noticed and hired by a director. She went to Max Reinhardt's drama school in Berlin and made one silent and one sound film before the notorious *Ecstasy* (1933), in which she appeared completely naked, reputedly the first screen actress ever to do so. In the film, she appears in the nude, running in the trees by a lake.

---
133 Hedy Lamarr (Hedy is pronounced to rhyme with 'lady') was born Hedwig Eva Maria Kiesler and her screen name was given to her by Louis B. Mayer. Her father was a director of the Bank of Vienna.

She dives in but her clothes are taken away by a young man. (The idea for this scene was subsequently photographed, with more decorum, many times in Hollywood, often in Westerns.) She pursues the man to a cabin where there is a love scene in which she simulates an orgasm. This was given some realism, according to her book, by being pricked by the director in the buttock with a pin. Her autobiography (Lamarr, 1966) includes shots from the film and the book is entitled *Ecstasy and Me*. The picture was filmed in Czechoslovakia: even the producer found it over-erotic and cut many thousands of feet from the film before it was released.

Hedy Lamarr, a portrait taken soon after her arrival in Hollywood, late 1930s: Finler/MGM.

The next major event in Hedy's life was marriage to Fritz Mandl, a wealthy Austrian munitions manufacturer. This was the first of many unsuitable marriages. Mandl turned out to be madly jealous of his wife and tried to buy up all the copies of *Ekstase*, as the film was known in Austria. This attempt was frustrated since the word got round and more copies of the film were made. Mussolini was supposed to have one of them and refused to part with it. Mandl kept Hedy under close supervision and gave her no freedom. She was obliged to be the hostess at long, boring dinners, late into the night, with arms buyers and diplomats. Finally she escaped with all the jewels she had been given. Subterfuge was necessary, so she deliberately hired a maid who resembled her and one afternoon drugged the girl and left her in the house while she left to catch a train to Paris. After arranging a divorce in Paris, she moved to London. There, through an agent, she met Louis B. Mayer, who was in Europe talent-spotting. He offered her a contract, which she declined. Then she arranged to take the same boat back to New York as he did. Inevitably they met again on board and the offer was renewed and finally accepted at a much higher salary.

If we are to believe Hedy's autobiography in which she described herself as 'over-sexed', her life in Hollywood was indeed dominated by sexual relationships, including a few lesbian encounters, and six marriages.[134] The book, in its loose construction, is not unlike Marlene Dietrich's, though possibly more open and truthful in some respects.

---

134 Only one of these marriages was to a film star and that was John Loder; he did not want the divorce but she found him 'boring'. Howard Lee was her fifth husband and the only one apart from Mandl who was really rich. We have seen that Gene Tierney was happily married to Lee for twenty years, but Lamarr's divorce from Lee was accompanied by accusations of physical violence on both sides. Hedy's last husband, conveniently, was a lawyer, but he did not last either.

THE DARK SIDE

It is anecdotal, includes excerpts from press reports about her activities, and has a last chapter of encapsulated wisdom in the form of aphorisms, for example: 'It's funny about men and women. Men pay in cash to get them and pay in cash to get rid of them. Women on the other hand, pay emotionally coming and going. Neither has it easy' (Lamarr,1966).

Strangely, the autobiography, subtitled *My Life as a Woman*, has a preface and an introduction by two psychologists, one of whom says that Hedy's exploits were the fruit of 'a great beauty on the make' – which is hardly a supportive statement. The other, more sympathetically, dwells on the stresses of the life of a film star. The book sold very well but according to Walters (2005), Hedy's son John said the book was 'a real shock to Hedy, it's what blew her into seclusion'. Stranger still, Walters records that Hedy sued the publishers several years after publication, saying that *she did not write it* and that it was obscene and shocking and damaged her reputation. Her lawyer claimed that it was the work of a ghost writer, Samuel Post (though he received no credit in the printed book). The case was settled out of court.

The films of which, eventually, she made about twenty-five, are none of them very distinguished, although quite a few made money for the studio. *Boom Town* (1940) with Clark Gable was one of the most popular she appeared in, though she did not add a great deal to it and critics murdered it. Lamarr's best remembered Hollywood role was in Cecil B. DeMille's *Samson and Delilah* (1949) with Victor Mature. In his own autobiography (1959), DeMille pays the two stars a somewhat back-handed compliment when he wrote of his reactions on seeing the rushes:

'I knew, if I had not known it before, that the talents of Victor Mature and Hedy Lamarr are more than skin deep.[135]

Hedy obviously had strong passions and a wilful personality but somehow it does not come across in her pictures and her beautiful face registers little. Eyeman (2010) describes it as a 'perfect, if frozen, face'. In *Samson and Delilah* she was at the peak of her career and of her beauty, and both declined thereafter. She retired to Florida in the late 1950s. She was highly litigious and involved in a number of court cases in addition to the one against her publishers and those following her marriages. There were eight of these law suits, some of them relating to the unauthorised use of her image in advertising. Two of her court cases followed her arrest for shoplifting, one in 1966 and another in 1991, but in one she was cleared by a jury; in the other she was bound over. Her book rather gives the impression that she was relatively poor towards the end of her life. She died, of natural causes, alone, watching television in bed in her Florida home. There was, however, a further surprise when it was revealed that her estate was valued at over $3 million. Where this money came from is not clear: she claimed in her book to have made and spent $30 million over her lifetime, but possibly the money came from some oil assets which she was granted following her divorce from Howard Lee.

The really extraordinary thing about Hedy Lamarr, which is not mentioned at all in her book, was that she was one of the early pioneers of spread spectrum radio, the basic tech-

---

135 Victor Mature (1913–99) was of Italian origin, a big fellow with heavy-lidded eyes, who made a lot of films in addition to biblical epics. Mature was ill served by critics and the roles he was given. He has been quoted may times as having said, on being denied membership of a golf club which banned actors, 'I'm no actor and I've sixty-four pictures to prove it.' However, Mature made several films of note including: I Wake Up Screaming (1941); My Darling Clementine (1946 as Doc Holiday); Kiss of Death (1947); Violent Saturday (1955) and After the Fox (1966) a comeback in which he showed a good sense of humour by satirising himself.

nology behind mobile phones and the wireless connections between computers. This story is recounted in detail by Rob Walters (2005), who had to do a lot of research to get it. Hedy filed a patent in the name of Hedy Kiesler Markey (her married name at the time) in 1942. It was primarily the result of her work and that of George Antheil, a musical composer. Hedy and George hoped that the invention would allow the US Navy to radio-control electrically driven torpedoes by means of a secret communications system. This system was invulnerable to jamming and could not be broken into by the enemy because it incorporated a means for hopping, seemingly at random, between radio frequencies. The pair had to engage the services of a university professor to translate the idea into patentable language. It is not clear how Hedy made her contribution, though George always maintained that the basic concept was hers. Unfortunately, the patent did not contribute to the war effort at the time as Hedy hoped, partly because of the lack of credibility of the patent holders and bureaucratic inertia and also because electrically driven torpedoes only came into service in the US Navy later on. The Germans did use them, however, and it is possible that Lamarr got her idea from overheard conversations between arms specialists at her first husband's interminable dinners. In any event, fifty-five years after the patent was granted, Hedy's achievement was finally recognised. In 1997, she was granted a Pioneer Award from the Electronic Frontier Foundation and others followed in Austria and the US. The awards were accepted in her absence by Hedy's son, Anthony Loder. Her reaction apparently was, 'about time'.[136]

---

[136] Lamarr was not the only inventor among the ranks of film stars, however. According to a recent press report (Sunday Times, 10 July 2011), Marlon Brando had a patent lawyer, who has said that, among many other things, Brando had invented a tuning device for conga drums which was registered by the US Patent Office.

In retrospect, Hedy Lamarr could not be described as a tragic figure. She remains a major figure in post-war cinema – Walters mentions that in 1999 she was named as one of the top 100 sexiest stars of the century in the January issue of *Playboy*. Certainly there were no other Hollywood stars who made a major, or indeed any, contribution to science! If she could not act, that did not matter. Alistair Cooke wrote:

[EXT]
The most profitable screen heroine that a studio can create ... is that of a heroine whose beauty is so overwhelming that it allows her own character never to come into play and therefore never to be called into question. (Cooke, 1940)
[EXT ends]

While Tierney was ethereal and Lamarr exotic, Lana Turner (1921–95) represented – in her youth at least – simply luscious American femininity. She was one of the wartime studio-polished glamour girls of the 1940s and 1950s, along with Betty Grable, Linda Darnell and Rita Hayworth. Born in Wallace, Idaho, tragedy struck early when her father was murdered for his winnings in a crap game (he had planned to spend them on a bicycle for Lana). Her parents had drifted around in the Depression era and ended up in San Francisco. Lana's mother, who had her daughter partly brought up in foster homes, eventually found work in a Los Angeles beauty parlour and settled there.

In Lana's first film, *They Won't Forget* (1937), made when she was just sixteen, she is seen dressed in a clinging sweater and pencil skirt walking down the street from a café. As

THE DARK SIDE

Basinger (2007) described it, 'her hips swayed, her buttocks jiggled and her breasts bounced'.[137] Lana had earlier lived a similar situation in real life. Slipping away from Hollywood High School one day, she crossed the road to the Top Hat café for a Coke and was seen by W. R. Wilkerson, publisher of the *Hollywood Reporter*. After his approach had been checked out by her mother and friend, Wilkerson recommended Lana to Zeppo Marx (one of the Marx brothers, no longer a performer but then a successful talent agent). She was rapidly signed up by Mervyn LeRoy, a producer/director at Warner's, and straight away cast in the film he was directing. This was how it often happened in those days, when someone appeared just right for a role and passed a screen test, they were put straight into it and learned on the job. *They Won't Forget* was one of Warner's gritty social dramas, in this case a story of the rape and murder of a school girl and a lynching. After this, LeRoy took Lana with him when he moved to MGM and acted as her mentor. She had a small part in *The Adventures of Marco Polo* (1938), on loan-out to Samuel Goldwyn. The film starred Gary Cooper but she never met him on the set at the time. Being underage, Lana had lessons at MGM's famous Little Red School House with Judy Garland and Mickey Rooney and appeared with them in *Love Finds Andy Hardy* (1939). In this film, Lana is a girl who likes to kiss boys (innocently of course, this was MGM).

Already receiving fan mail and being promoted as 'the sweater girl', Lana was beginning to enjoy an active social life of dining and dancing, which included going out on 'official dates' organised by the studios. Later it ceased to be necessary for the studios to generate publicity for Lana – as

---

137 David Niven (1975) happened to be present during Lana's unsuccessful screen test for Scarlett O'Hara. He wrote, 'She had a perfectly packed little body and a behind that signalled a most beguiling message of welcome when she walked.'

we shall see, she made a good job of it herself. Her first big chance came in *Ziegfeld Girl* (1941), with Judy Garland and Hedy Lamarr as hopefuls in show business. Lana plays Sheila Regan, a budding actress whose nights out with stage-door Johnnies turn her into an alcoholic, and in making a dramatic entrance scene falls down a grand staircase. It was a role of a kind she would repeat several times in the future, notably in *The Bad and the Beautiful* (1952) with Kirk Douglas. In that film and the earlier *The Postman Always Rings Twice* (1946), she makes an impact as a mature woman. In *Postman*, Lana plots with John Garfield to murder her husband, an unlikely subject for MGM. Her sex appeal blazes off the screen in this film. She appears platinum-blonde in brief and brilliant white shorts and top with a bare midriff and a white turban.[138] Turner often looked tall and statuesque in her films but in fact was only 5' 2½", which is why she usually wore four-inch heels. Her measurements in 1940 were 34-26-34".

Turner made many films and was always in demand. By the 1950s her beauty and career were beginning to fade somewhat and she continued, often in fallen-woman roles, most notably in *Peyton Place* (1957), which revealed the steamy secrets of small-town America. This picture earned her an Oscar nomination (though not an award). *Imitation of Life* (1959), a tear-jerker about racial prejudice, was her comeback movie. *Madame X* (1966) was another tear-jerker in which a mother is on trial for murder, and her defending lawyer, unknown to either of them, is her own son. This was the last memorable film Turner was to make. She had a very long career, some forty-three years from her beginnings as a schoolgirl in 1937 to her last feature film in 1980. She had appeared with most

---

[138] Turner's natural hair colour was dark auburn but was frequently dyed and often elaborately styled. The basic story of Postman was made several times, even more successfully in Double Indemnity (1944).

of the big stars of the day, including Brian Aherne, Mickey Rooney, George Murphy, Hedy Lamarr, Ginger Rogers, Ray Milland, Kirk Douglas, Ricardo Montalbán and Anthony Quinn, to mention only some of her fellow autobiographers. She also starred with some of the all-time greats who did not write books, including Clark Gable, Spencer Tracy and John Wayne.[139]

Throughout, her life had been a rollercoaster of scandal and emotion – with seven marriages, all short-lived.[140] Only two of her husbands were in show business: Artie Shaw and Lex Barker. Artie Shaw (1910–2004) only appeared in two films, one of which was *Dancing Co-ed* (1939) with Lana. Artie was a clarinettist and band leader and something of a prodigy who wrote several books and was a crack-shot. Shaw, already twice married when he met Lana was to have eight marriages, even more than Lana. Shaw's wives included Ava Gardner and Evelyn Keyes. The marriage between Shaw and Turner in 1940 was the shortest of all, only eight months. Lana had a long affair with Tyrone Power, but this did not end in marriage: to her grief, he wed Linda Christian, whom we encountered in Chapter 6. In her autobiography (1982), Lana wrote that Power was her 'one true love' and devotes considerable space to their relationship; alas he was to die at the young age of forty-five. Lex Barker (1919–73), whose nickname was 'Sexy-Lexy', played the lead in five Tarzan films. He came from a wealthy family and had earlier been married

---

139 It is surprisingly difficult to measure star popularity. According to one study, Turner appeared in five of the Top Ten films by rental income in the period 1946–65. This compares with ten for Elizabeth Taylor, nine for Gregory Peck, seven for John Wayne and five each for Ingrid Bergman and Doris Day, so she was certainly among the higher echelon of stars in this period (Sedgwick and Pokorny, 2005).

140 She married Stephen Crane – the father of her only child – twice, the second time made necessary by her pregnancy and doubts about the legality of their first union.

to Arlene Dahl. Lana's fourth marriage ended abruptly when it was discovered that Barker had been sexually molesting her daughter, although this was subsequently hushed up (Crane, 2008).

Immediately following her divorce from Barker, Lana fell for Johnny Stompanato, who was later discovered to be the bodyguard of mobster Mickey Cohen and known to the police for exploiting wealthy, lonely women. One night in April 1958, her fifteen-year-old daughter Cheryl heard angry voices; her mother was being threatened with disfigurement by Stompanato, who had previously beaten her up many times. Cheryl went into the kitchen to get a knife and then rushed upstairs to the bedroom. Her mother opened the door and Stompanato came up behind her and, according to Cheryl, 'ran onto the knife in my hands'. It was a fatal wound and he died within minutes (Crane, 2008).[141] The juvenile court took the view that it was 'justifiable homicide'. Lana explains in her book that she had not tried to get away from Stompanato earlier because he had threatened to harm her, her daughter and her mother, if she left him. She feared that with his underworld connections he could easily arrange a killing and be miles away with an alibi at the time. She was also terrified of publicity, though after the court case there was a tremendous furore in the media, reinforced by the recent release of *Peyton Place* (1957). Lana was fearful that the studios would drop her, but in fact that did not happen. On the contrary, film land was increasingly putting her in movies which, in various ways, paralleled her own tempestuous life.

Turner's marriages and divorces continued until the last.

---

[141] Lana's account (Turner,1982) differs: she says 'I saw Cheryl make a sudden movement. Her right arm had shot out and caught John in the stomach.' It was clear, nonetheless, that Cheryl was defending her mother and possibly saved her life.

THE DARK SIDE

In 1969 she wed Ronald Dante, a night-club hypnotist who was to defraud and rob her. Lana was, in fact a lonely woman who never found the lasting companionship she wanted, but she had great courage, professional pride in her work and a great deal of zest for life. She writes ruefully in her book that she had hoped for seven children and one husband but it turned out to be the other way around.[142] Despite her fears, her public remained loyal to her throughout all her ups and downs. In 1981 Turner was honoured with a retrospective of her films in Paris and was selected as one of the recipients of the Artistry in Cinema Award by the American National Film Society.

☽☽☽

Carroll Baker (1931–) had the qualifications for glamorous roles (blonde hair and a 35-24-35" figure, with a girlish face) as well as training at the Actors Studio, but she became typecast as a petulant sexpot for a while. Her first film was a small part in an Esther Williams' vehicle, *Easy to Love* (1953), but then she plunged into three major productions with well-known actors: *Giant* (1956), *Baby Doll* (1956) and *The Big Country* (1958). All were good roles but she got fed up with her stereotyped image: the daughter of Rock Hudson and Elizabeth Taylor who falls for James Dean; the virginal child-bride of Karl Malden, seduced by his enemy Eli Wallach; and the spoiled rich girl who loses out to Gene Simmons for Gregory Peck's affections, respectively. *The Big Country* was, like *Giant*, a colour wide-screen epic. She was lucky to get the part because she had been suspended from Warner's for refusing the role of a nymphomaniac in *Too Much, Too Soon*

---
[142] I have omitted details of some of the other tragic events in Lana's life, including a suicide attempt, several miscarriages and her abortion of Tyrone Power's child.

(1958). Dorothy Malone instead took that role, supported by a fading Errol Flynn. Carroll was to make a lot more films but none of them were as good as her first three. She did well as her stereotype in *The Carpetbaggers* (1964), a story suggested by the life of Howard Hughes and which was Alan Ladd's sad final appearance. She was also good as Debbie Reynolds' sister and James Stewart's mountain-man wife in the Cinerama epic *How the West was Won* (1962). In John Ford's tedious *Cheyenne Autumn* (1964), she played a schoolteacher sympathetic to the Indians.

Carroll had built up a significant leading star position, but at her second husband's insistence, she sent a telegram with demands to Paramount Pictures – who promptly fired her. Having bought herself out of her contract with Warner's in 1959, she was dogged by debt and after the firing she was blackballed by the other studios as 'too difficult'. She had two nervous breakdowns, one in 1959 and a second in 1966. She started making films in Europe though they seem to have been mainly potboilers.

Baker's autobiography is well written, if harrowing, and has some good word-portraits of James Dean, Elizabeth Taylor and Robert Mitchum (one can never read enough about Mitchum, who did not write a book of his own). Baker's book opens with a graphic description of her second breakdown which lasted almost three years: 'I have always lived too much inside my head . . . but somehow I managed to function fairly well for some thirty years until one day my inherent repression suddenly took over and imprisoned me within the confines of my mind . . . I locked myself in a pitch black room in a strange hotel in an unknown or since-forgotten city and called out for my mother' (Baker, 1983).

The book goes on to sketch her early life. Born in

THE DARK SIDE

Johnstown, Pennsylvania, and after early experience in vaudeville she was introduced to Louis Ritter, a wealthy man (a furrier), 'a lot older than my father', who promised to get her into movies. A virgin, she was raped by him on the train to the West Coast. Brought up as a Catholic, Carroll believed she had to marry him which, after her bullying, he reluctantly did. In Hollywood she was introduced to the producer-director Gabriel Pascal, apparently a friend of Ritter's[143]. After an audition Pascal said: 'You are very unlucky, poor child, because you have a great talent. So great a talent that it will forever make you unhappy' (Baker, 1983).

Ritter turned out to be quite mad and, like Hedy Lamarr's first husband, kept her a prisoner. Again like Hedy Lamarr, Carroll sold the jewels and things she had been given and escaped to get a room on her own. She soon got a role in a Broadway play which starred Brian Aherne and got into the Actors Studio, paying the fees for her tuition by doing a TV commercial.[144] At the Studio she met her second husband, Jack Garfein, a child-survivor from Auschwitz, and another mistake that would prove unfortunate, to say the least. She appeared in another Broadway play and on television. Carroll was noticed by George Stevens, then casting for *Giant,* and hired after a screen test which he said was a mere formality to gauge the clothes and lighting she needed. She was not im-

---

[143] Gabriel Pascal (1894–1954) was a Hungarian film producer who won the confidence of George Bernard Shaw. The great writer was very difficult about giving permission to screen his plays. Pascal made Pygmalion (1938) with Leslie Howard and the costly disaster Caesar and Cleopatra (1945), both based on Shaw's plays. Pascal wanted to remake Pygmalion as a musical but Shaw refused – though it was done long after Shaw's death in the enormously successful My Fair Lady (1964), directed by George Cukor for Jack Warner.

[144] Brian Aherne (1902–86) started on the English stage as a child and had a long stage and film career. His autobiography (1969) seems to have something telling to say about so many things. After several trips for stage appearances, he became a US resident in 1933 and stayed there.

pressed with Hollywood, however, which she found looked 'so ordinary' (which it did, and still does), but enjoyed the life at the studio and meeting some of the screen people she had dreamed about.

After completing her three big films, Carroll had her first breakdown in 1959, following her ruinous break with Warner's. Her second mental breakdown was in 1966 when, after being fired by Paramount, she was again under enormous personal and professional pressure. She wrote towards the end of her book: 'My entire existence, for as long as I could remember, had been controlled by chauvinistic men: from a strict father to mad Louis Ritter, to power-orientated studio executives and producers, to my cripplingly submissive relationship with Jack Garfein. Only never had I been able fully to express my own personality' (Baker 1983).

After Paramount fired her, she found that she was blackballed by the studios as 'difficult' and forced to seek movie work in Europe. At last this was to free her from Jack who was pursuing his own career in New York. When she came to write her autobiography in 1983, she had made more films in Europe than in the USA. Though the films were not distinguished, life took a turn for the better. The outcome of her long standing contractual dispute with Paramount was that the courts awarded her a large capital sum. Although she did make some more films in America, she settled in London and married a British actor, Donald Burton, a relationship which lasted until his death in 2007.[145]

---

[145] Our account here of autobiographies of tragic beautiful actresses is not exhaustive. Mention should be made of Frances Farmer (1972), who spent time in jail and eight years in a state mental institution, where her sufferings – including rats and rape – were even worse than those endured by Gene Tierney. See also Chapter 9 for Dorothy Dandridge's tragic life.

THE DARK SIDE

Yvonne de Carlo: Dr Macro

After the vicissitudes of Tierney, Lamarr, Baker and Turner, it is something of a relief to turn to Yvonne De Carlo (1922–2007). She was promoted as 'the Most Beautiful Girl in the World' at the time of her title role in *Salome Where She Danced* (1945), her first major picture. Often in exotic dramas (Westerns and Easterns) she appeared in minor parts in twenty films before *Salome*. In *This Gun for Hire* (1942), her second film, she is a showgirl in a nightclub scene. Like most people, De Carlo's life had its bad moments but was not darkened by tragedy like those of Tierney and Turner, and she overcame

169

the many obstacles she encountered.[146] Born in Vancouver in a thunderstorm (appropriately enough given her success towards the end of her career as a housewife-vampire in the television series *The Munsters*, 1964–6), her father deserted the family when she was three years old. At the age of fifteen she was performing in nightclubs and at eighteen won a prize in the Venice (US) beauty contest. In her very readable, cheerful and witty autobiography (1971), De Carlo wrote that her father's desertion did not make her turn away from men; on the contrary she 'developed a strong attraction for just about anything masculine'. She was married only once, to stuntman Bob Morgan in 1955, but had many affairs. Morgan was very seriously injured in a train crash only three years later. Already contemplating divorce at the time of the accident, she stayed loyally with him, paying his medical bills and they did not divorce until 1968. There were two children.

Her screen name, De Carlo, was her mother's maiden name; her grandfather was of Sicilian origin. During her screen career she was pursued by the usual crowd (Aly Kahn, Artie Shaw and Howard Hughes) and had a crush on Sterling Hayden, though he was not responsive, so nothing came of it. She appeared in a long run of mostly 'B' pictures. *Salome* was not a biblical epic but a spy story set in Arizona and nothing to shout about. A decade later, she did appear as Charlton Heston's wife in DeMille's *The Ten Commandments* (1956). She produced a very good performance as Burt Lancaster's double-crossing ex-wife in *Criss Cross* (1949) and showed her talent for comedy in *Hotel Sahara* (1951), a British film with Peter Ustinov in which the hotel changes its loyalties (and pictures on the wall) as opposing armies pass through.

---

146 For those who must know, Yvonne was 5'4" tall and her measurements in the 1940s were 34-23-35".

THE DARK SIDE

The Captain's Paradise (1953), another British comedy and a better one, has Alec Guinness as the Captain running a ship between Gibraltar and Ceuta, who has a wife in each port. There is a homely one in Gibraltar, Celia Johnson, who provides regular meals, early nights and carpet slippers, and a glamorous Moroccan one (De Carlo) with whom he dances in nightclubs until late. She reprised another comic role as the lusty housekeeper for John Wayne in *McClintock!* (1963) at Wayne's personal invitation. The housekeeper innocently arouses jealousy in Maureen O'Hara, Wayne's estranged wife. (Perhaps this jealousy was felt in real life since neither De Carlo nor O'Hara mentions the other in their respective autobiographies.)

Unlike Tierney and Baker, De Carlo did not have breakdowns at moments of stress such as her divorce, her mother's illness and her son's motorcycle accident, though she did suffer partial amnesia briefly, three times. She wrote: 'I couldn't take time out for a nervous breakdown of my own – I had to work', which she had consistently done throughout her life, not only films and television but also in the theatre and in nightclubs. Yvonne says in her book that having had to cope with being alone for most of her life, 'If I can't have the best, I'll be content to do a single.'

CHAPTER 8

Sensitive Tough Guys and the Genres

LIKE THE STAR system, the genres of film (for example, horror, war, musicals) were an aid to audiences in identifying what pictures they wanted to see. Most actors were not very much interested in the films in which they appeared – what they wanted were 'meaty roles' in any genre that maximised scope for their talents; the best and most popular actors appeared in all kinds of pictures. Chapter 9 looks at musicals, while this chapter deals with some generalist actors and two kinds of film, *noir* and Westerns, both of which required the appearance of a certain toughness in their actors.

Chapter 7 examined the difficult lives led by many beautiful actresses, but many men in Hollywood also suffered severe stresses. Acting necessitates intelligence and sensitivity and the men who played it tough on the screen also experienced difficulty in their personal lives –sometimes to an extent that their real lives were as tough as those on the screen.[147]

---

147 For example, Robert Wagner (2008) endured divorce, remarriage and then a further loss with the drowning of Natalie Wood. David Niven lost his first wife in a fatal accident (see Chapter 3). Yet neither Niven nor Wagner could be described as having had tragic lives and it is difficult to think of male actors who suffered on the scale of the women discussed in Chapter 7. William Gargan (1969), in his autobiography, tells how his screen career was brutally terminated by the loss of his voice through cancer at the age of fifty-five.

It is interesting that there are far fewer actors in Westerns and film *noir* who wrote autobiographies than the generalists or those who specialised in musicals. In the case of *noir*, the scarcity of autobiographers may be partly explained by the fact that this genre flourished for only a limited period of time, while Westerns, one of the oldest genres, relied on a breed of men who were noted for a laconic style that did not lend itself to literacy.

Anthony Quinn: Finler.

We begin with two male actors who in their long careers played virtually every kind of role: Anthony Quinn (1915–2001) and Kirk Douglas (1916–), both of whom wrote exceptionally good books. Their autobiographies are frank and revealing and after putting them down the reader feels that he has lived a life alongside the authors. Quinn and Douglas were born within a year of one another in very different circumstances but had several things in common. Quinn was in a crash-landing during the making of *Lawrence of Arabia* (1962); in 1991 Douglas survived a mid-air collision between a light plane and the helicopter he was in. Each appeared in a wide range of films: Douglas, for example, made films *noir* and a musical (*Young Man With a Horn*, 1950) as well as Westerns; Quinn's roles were equally varied, though he never made a musical, unless you count *Zorba the Greek* (1964).

Both actors had problems with their fathers and had pangs of guilt about the upbringing of their own children. Tragically, one of Douglas's sons committed suicide and one of Quinn's drowned, aged three, in a swimming pool.[148] Quinn agonised over his compulsive infidelities and Douglas over his Jewishness and the upbringing of his children. Douglas was the steadier of the two; Quinn had ten children by three marriages and two more out of wedlock. Douglas wrote, 'We made *Lust for Life* together (1956), the story of the painter Van Gogh and the title of that movie would be a good summary of Tony's own story.' Both were born into very poor families: Douglas's father was a ragman with a horse and cart in the streets of New York; while Quinn's father left home when his mother was pregnant to fight with Pancho Villa's revolutionaries and their home in Chihuahua, Mexico, was little more than a hut without a toilet. Physically they were not alike at all, however. At 6'1" and much heavier, Quinn was four inches

---

[148] Suicide among the children of Hollywood actors was not unusual. In Douglas's last book (2007) he gives a list of twenty-one stars whose sons or daughters died by suicide or drug overdose, including Marlon Brando, Gregory Peck, Paul Newman and Jill Ireland.

taller than slim, athletic Douglas. While Douglas looked like the Easterner he was, Quinn had sallow good looks which, in his youth, were compared with those of Ramón Navarro.[149] Quinn was to become a multi-purpose foreigner in the movies. He was the lead in *Zorba the Greek* (1964), a Mexican in *Viva Zapata!* (1952), an Arab in *Lawrence of Arabia* (1962), a Frenchman (Gauguin) in *Lust for Life* (1956), and in other roles he played Hawaiian, Irish and Spanish.

Douglas started on the stage and was not in a movie until after he completed his service in the Navy. He made his mark in *The Strange Love of Martha Ivers* (1946). In his manner, Douglas always seemed stressed like a bow-string and he had the sad but resilient quality that was essentially Russian, where his origins in fact lay. He wrote, 'I have made a career playing sons of bitches.' Judging by his book, he is not an unsympathetic person at all, though he has been criticised for his egotism. Always fit, Douglas became a star as a boxer in *Champion* (1949), for which he was nominated for an Oscar, one of three nominations, although he never won the award, even for his role as Van Gogh (for which Quinn, in a minor role lasting only eight minutes of screen time, won an Oscar). Douglas played the lead in *Spartacus* (1960) and a wide range of other roles, including at least five films *noir* and many Westerns. In one of the best of these, *Last Train from Gun Hill* (1959), he appeared with Quinn. One of his last roles, at the age of seventy, was in *Tough Guys* (1986), as one of two elderly train robbers released from prison; the other one was

---

149 Ramó Novarro (1899–1968) was a romantic lead in the 1920s and a rival of Rudolph Valentino (1895–1926), an Italian-American whose premature death and funeral led to extraordinary scenes in Hollywood. Novarro was Mexican by birth. His most famous film was the earlier version of Ben-Hur (1925). His films were made mostly in the 1920s and 1930s, but he made a comeback in the 1940s. A homosexual, he died a violent death, murdered by two teenagers he had invited into his home.

played by Burt Lancaster, who was eighty-one. Douglas was proud of doing his own stunts and in this film he ran along the top of a moving train.

Douglas married twice and one of his four children is Michael Douglas, the actor. Kirk Douglas had a facility for writing and obviously enjoyed it, writing eight books in all, in addition to *The Ragman's Son* (1988). His other autobiographical books included *Climbing the Mountain* (1997), which was about his religious explorations, and *Let's Face It* (2007), about his old age. He has also written children's stories and novels. In the Foreword to *Ragman's Son*, Douglas says that in writing the book he found 'that the story is the search for myself, the telling is the discovery'. It was a search that he continued in his other books. He commented that he had not written the book his fans wanted, but one with much in it about his unhappy childhood. In fact, *Ragman's Son* is full of fascinating insights into the making of his films and his recollection of other actors and proved to be a bestseller.

Quinn's two autobiographies are also clearly an exercise in exploring his true self. Like Douglas, at intervals he uses the device of himself as a childhood figure who criticises and scorns him. His first book, *One Man Tango* (1995) and his earlier version, *The Original Sin* (1972), both dwell on inner conflicts and guilt[150] (the sin in his title is an inability to accept love). Quinn was born in Mexico but brought up in Los Angeles. After earning a living as a porter, labourer, boxer and other things, he got a part as an American Indian in a Cecil B. DeMille film, *The Plainsman* (1937). (This was not his first film; previously he had had a bit-part in *Parole*, 1936.) For

---

[150] Only the second autobiography acknowledges a co-author. The two books are quite similar, although the second is obviously more up to date and is structured around flashbacks on a cycle ride near his home in Italy, the first around sessions with a psychiatrist.

The Plainsman he had won the role of an American Indian by pretending to be one and speaking Indian-gibberish. He nearly got fired on the first day when he criticised the way DeMille was directing a scene, but was saved by the intervention of Gary Cooper. The great director accepted Quinn's correction, which was about the difference between a white man's fire and an Indian's fire. This was clearly a critical moment in his life because on the set that day was DeMille's adopted daughter, Katherine, whom he was later to marry.[151]

The Westerns in which Quinn, and especially Douglas, appeared are an important part of American culture because they connect with the last frontier of expansion as settlers and economic activity spread west from the East Coast, a process which ended just over 100 years ago. Westerns have been made since the early days of the movies and some of the best were made towards the end of the Golden Age in the 1950s.[152] These films were popular among audiences who loved to see their heroes triumphing over evil in the final reel. Westerns could be cheap to make since, after the industry moved west, the necessary terrain was readily accessible. The Western myths were capable of almost infinite variation. There were various sub-categories: serials, comedies, singing cowboys, historical, psychological, and even *noir* and Italian.

151 On his admission, it was a difficult marriage but it lasted twenty-eight years and five children before it ended in divorce. Quinn always felt that DeMille had never accepted him as a suitable son-in-law and although everyone expected him to do so, DeMille did not use his influence to get Quinn work. There was little empathy between CB and his son-in-law. Evelyn Keyes (see below) began an affair with Quinn but was told by DeMille 'stay away from that half breed'. Quinn's next role was the result of a favourable mention by Carole Lombard, who also introduced him to a new agent, Charles Feldman.

152 Most people will have their own list but many classic Westerns date from that time: High Noon (1952); Shane (1953); The Searchers (1956) and The Magnificent Seven (1960). All but the first of these was made in colour, which is particularly attractive in Westerns. However, there are some pre-war black and white Westerns which are memorable, for example Stagecoach and Union Pacific, both released in 1939.

None of the major stars who wrote autobiographies restricted themselves to Westerns, though virtually all of them played in at least one. Two of them, James Cagney and Ronald Reagan, spent much of their leisure time on horseback, but rarely did so on the screen. Reagan always regretted this. Charlton Heston very much liked Westerns and would probably have done more given the chance of good roles. He was excellent in *The Big Country* (1958), one of the last of the big budget Westerns of the period by a major director. He also made *Will Penny* (1968), a film he very much wanted to do and which he described as 'one of the great parts of my life', but it was not a commercial success. In his autobiography Heston wrote:

[EXT]
Along with jazz, the Western is the only totally indigenous American art form. Nobody else can do it, and now some of us have lost the touch. That's too bad. More than any other kind of film, the Western cries out for a camera and uses it most gloriously . . . The Western is utterly unavailable to the stage, not because it can't contain the wide Missouri in flood, or a war party of mounted Sioux braves, but because the stage is, finally, the domain of the spoken word. . . . I never knew an actor who didn't like making Westerns. (Heston, 1995)[153]
[EXT ends]

There were some actors in Westerns of the second rank who wrote books, for example Woody Strode (1990)[154] and several of

---
153 Heston does not include musicals as an indigenous art form, nor does he mention The Squaw Man (1913), DeMille's first film which started as a successful play (see Chapter 1).
154 Stuntmen and women (stunt doubles) were essential in Westerns if only because many generalist actors were not skilled horsemen; Spencer Tracy, Gregory Peck and Robert Stack were among the exceptions. I have already mentioned Buster

the stuntmen who leapt across galloping stagecoach teams, vaulted onto horses and rode down cliffs and fought on top of moving trains, also wrote autobiographies. Yakima Canutt (1895–1986) was generally regarded as the greatest of these men (although a few women did the job too). Canutt was not Indian, as his name suggests, but of mixed European origins. He started in movies in 1919 as an actor and before that he was a rodeo champion. Over time he graduated to the roles of action- and second-unit director, winning an Oscar along the way. Canutt's autobiography (1979) shows that, for him, it was a matter of engineering to make stunts safe for actors and animals. He writes of belts attached to wires to pull riders backwards off their horses when they were 'shot', medieval weapons such as maces in rubber, telescopic lances which collapsed on impact, tubes of 'blood' and balsawood rifles. Canutt did the stunts or directed them in many of John Wayne's early pictures, as in *Stagecoach* (1939), doubled for Robert Taylor in the jousts in *Ivanhoe* (1953) and supervised the chariot race in *Ben-Hur* (1959). Canutt also doubled for Clark Gable as he rode through the flaming Atlanta streets in *Gone with the Wind* (1939). None of the big Western stars, including John Wayne and James Stewart, wrote books, although a great deal has been written about them, nor did some leading men who did only relatively few Westerns but nevertheless made a memorable mark in the genre, such as Spencer Tracy, Richard Widmark, Glenn Ford and

---

Wiles' autobiography (1958) in Chapter 3. Martha Cantarini (1928–) is the latest stunt double to have written an autobiography (2010). She is beautiful and was not limited to stunt work or to the horses in which she specialised. Cantarini doubled for Jean Simmons and Carroll Baker in The Big Country (1958), among many other films. On the rare occasions when unintended violence broke out on film sets it was stunt men who were called in to break it up. Obviously highly dangerous work, there were accidents, but surprisingly few. One horrific case was that of a stuntman who jumped from a helicopter. His chute got tangled up and he landed on his feet with such force that his leg bones were driven through the soles of his boots and several inches into the ground. He later died from his injuries (Canutt, 1979).

SENSITIVE TOUGH GUYS AND THE GENRES

Alan Ladd.[155] The one notable autobiography, which is all about Westerns, is that of Harry Carey Jr, *Company of Heroes* (1994).[156] Carey Jr (1921–) was the son of Harry (really Henry) Carey with whom he appeared in Howard Hawks ' *Red River* (1948), Jr's first major film.[157]

John (often Jack) Ford (1895–1973) was an Irish American who appears in several of the star autobiographies. In his later career he made a number of films with John Wayne, including a trilogy on the US Cavalry in the Old Wild West. Carey Jr appeared in these Westerns and in other films, including *Mister Roberts* (1955). As a director, Ford specialised in Westerns, though he made many other notable films such as *The Informer* (1935), *The Grapes of Wrath* (1940), *How Green Was My Valley* (1941) and *The Quiet Man* (1952), all of which won him Oscars. None of

---

155 We should mention two other actors, Karl Malden (1912–2009) and Robert Stack (1919–2003), who wrote autobiographies (1997 and 1980 respectively). Both were good actors, Malden especially, but producers did not seem to know what to do with them, and they played a wide range of roles without achieving significant stardom. Both had conspicuous success on television, however, especially Stack who starred in no less than 118 episodes of The Untouchables about gangster hunting. Malden was awarded an Oscar for A Streetcar Named Desire (1952) and was nominated for his role as a priest in On the Waterfront (1954). Both did not get going in films until the Second World War, although Stack gave Deanna Durbin her first screen kiss in First Love (1939). He went on to play very different roles in such films as The Bullfighter and the Lady (1952) and Written on the Wind (1956), for which he was nominated, and The High and the Mighty (1954), an aviation drama with John Wayne, and a lot of mediocre stuff, including Westerns. Stack was a champion skeet-shooter (hitting clay pigeons ejected by machine). Paul Picerni, Stack's co-star in The Untouchables, wrote a charming memoir (2007) which has insights into several of the films and actors mentioned in this book.

156 Woody Strode's autobiography includes much on his John Ford Westerns (see Chapter 9).

157 Harry Carey Sr (1878–1947) was a big star in the silent Westerns of the 1920s (though not as big as William S. Hart, 1870–1946). Carey Sr started with D.W. Griffith at the Biograph Company in 1908 after being expelled from law school. Much later, his long career continued as a character actor. Carey Sr worked with John Ford at Universal in some of Ford's early films. Carey Sr combined stern looks with great personal warmth.

his Westerns won an Oscar, though he was nominated for *Stagecoach* (1939).

Carey Jr made over a hundred films but his book is mainly about the seven that he made with Ford, from *3 Godfathers* (1948) to *Cheyenne Autumn* (1964). Ford liked to work with actors that he was familiar with and he had what Carey calls a 'stock company', which included Wayne, Ward Bond, Ben Johnson and others, and of which Carey was the junior member. Ford was, to say the least, eccentric. He could be quite vicious to his actors even though he expressed love for them. Maureen O'Hara (2004), who was in many of Ford's films, described him as an 'incredibly complex man' and devotes a lot of space to him in her book.[158] Carey quoted Ford, who insisted that he be called 'Uncle Jack', as saying more than once: 'You're going to hate me when this movie is over, but you're going to give a great performance.' Carey summed up his character: 'He was bearable or unbearable, never nice.' Egged on by Ford, Carey had to learn how to 'Roman Ride' for *Rio Grande* (1950). This involved standing with one foot on each of two horses running together at up to 35 miles an hour and was obviously very dangerous.

Carey's book is very readable and really gives the reader a feeling for what it was like playing in Ford's Westerns. He had not wanted to follow in his father's footsteps; his ambition was to be a classical singer but fate and his talents dictated otherwise. He wrote that it seldom works when an 'actor who

---

158 O'Hara mentions in her book, apparently on the basis of one incident, that Ford was a suppressed homosexual, which may explain some of the torture he clearly went through. Her book is very frank and well written. It is amusing to see how – although she talks about herself as being tough and outspoken – she was pushed around and exploited quite a bit by several people, including her husbands, as well as by Ford himself. Wilcoxon (1991) says that Ford was the opposite of Cecil B. DeMille, who drove his actors hard but was nice to them, while Ford drove them hard and was not nice.

SENSITIVE TOUGH GUYS AND THE GENRES

is established as playing one type of role puts on a whole new face, so to speak, and tries something different. The public wants him to stay what they made him.' He was not writing of himself here but about Tyrone Power who played an athletics trainer at West Point in Ford's *The Long Gray Line* (1955). Power hoped to establish himself as a character actor in contrast to his usual romantic roles. Producers knew that the public liked actors in familiar roles, but typecasting often resulted in considerable frustration on the part of the players themselves.

As with Westerns, no front-rank actors who wrote books specialised in film *noir*, and among those actors that did appear in many *noir* films, remarkably few produced autobiographies. This was clearly mainly because front-rank actors, unless they died prematurely (like Tyrone Power), had long careers and the *noir* period was in full flood only from the immediate post-Second World War period to the mid-1950s.

We gave a general definition of film *noir* in Chapter 1. A rough definition is all you can make because the whole subject is full of controversy and film academics and sociologists have had field-days with it. The French critics who first named the phenomenon, Raymond Borde and Etienne Chaumeton, took eight pages in their book on the subject to outline the characteristics of film *noir* (literally 'black film') many years, some would say a quarter of a century, after American filmmakers initiated it (Silver and Ursini, 1966).[159]. Film *noir* reached its highest stage of development immediately dur-

---
[159] French critics discovered film noir belatedly because they could not see them during the Occupation. Their contribution to noir criticism has proved to be more enduring, however, than the auteur theory from France which holds that the director is primarily the author of a film (this only applies to a few directors, as pointed out in Chapter 1). Once invented, no genre ever seems to die and contemporaneously we now have neo-noir, such as L.A. Confidential (1997).

ing and following the Second World War. There were many influences on the genre, for example, German Expressionism imported by exiled directors, and the work of the great detective story writers such as Dashiell Hammett and Raymond Chandler. One theory is that the series of *noir* films also reflected the straitened conditions of the period when film stock and electricity were rationed (most *noir* films were shot in black and white and often at night) and disillusioned returning war veterans were creating new social problems (Kerr, 1986). Technical developments also had an impact, for example the use of hand-held movie cameras which allowed film-makers to get out onto the streets (*noir* films were essentially urban in character). Not to be confused with the gangster pictures which were popular in the inter-war period, *noir* films generally had morally ambiguous heroes and often crisp dialogue. They also provided good opportunities for female stars either in the role of femmes fatales or redeeming innocents. Nonetheless, *noir* films were an important and welcome development and were to have a lasting influence, even though they were rarely made after the mid 1960s.

As mentioned, good actors did not remain long in *noir* films, which were mostly 'B' pictures, though many had experience of them as a training ground. Alain Silver and Elizabeth Ward's *Film Noir Encyclopedia* (1980) has an appendix listing actors with the titles of the *noir* films they made. It is striking that, although many actors – men and women – made quite a lot of *noir* films, none of them wrote books: Humphrey Bogart, Charles McGraw, Robert Mitchum, Dan Duryea, Elisha Cook Jr, Robert Ryan and Raymond Burr all made ten or more *noir* movies. Women prominent in the genre made fewer *noir* titles: Gloria Grahame, Shelley Winters and Lizabeth Scott each made seven; Evelyn Keyes and Joan Bennett four and

Veronica Lake three, for example. Four of these women did write books but said little about their *noir* experience as such.

Veronica Lake with Alan Ladd in *This Gun For Hire* (1942): Dr Macro/Universal.

At the time, the actors did not realise they were making film history. Veronica Lake (1971) wrote *'This Gun for Hire* [1942] didn't seem to be much of a film.' *The Blue Dahlia* (1946) she dismissed as 'an interesting whodunit'. Of these now minor classics, she wrote 'Today's film buffs look for things in films that we didn't when I was making films.' Lake felt she was really mostly decoration in these pictures and lamented her role in *Sullivan's Travels* (1941), which was an opportunity to act, as she saw it. But she underestimated herself because in these films and others she communicated sympathetic warmth as well as beauty and a true comedic sense. The public loved her, but at the peak of her fame she quit film-making at the end of the 1940s, out of frustration. Lake wrote that the price of stardom was too high for her, but nevertheless she showed no bitterness. She did not want to go the way of Alan Ladd and Gail Russell (1924–61), who she felt had been destroyed by Hollywood.[160]

Evelyn Keyes (1916–2008), though a very different character from Lake, had a similar attitude. For example, all she had to say about her role in the classic *noir*, *Johnny O'Clock* (1947), was that her colleagues on the set seemed to have had an unfavourable reaction to her marriage to John Huston that took place during filming. 'There were congratulations, but with a distinct lack of enthusiasm. Dick Powell and Bob Rossen, were particularly lukewarm, almost resentful, as if I had somehow double-crossed them.' Keyes was married four times, including to Charles Vidor (1900–59), the director, John Huston and Artie Shaw (1910–2004), the musician, all three brilliant and successful men, but in no case did the marriages last. Unusually, Keyes wrote a successful novel, *I Am a Billboard* (1971), before her two autobiographies (1957, 1991). She had a journalistic background and after she retired from filming, wrote scripts and articles for the press. Her books are well written, compulsive and funny, though she is a bit too snooty about the films she made. Like those of Shelley Winters, Keyes' books are of the 'tell-all' kind but shorter (both Keyes and Winters' first autobiographies were bestsellers.[161] Keyes had had affairs

---

160 Russell – beautiful, sensitive and with a sad, haunted look – died of alcoholism, as did Alan Ladd. Russell made several films with Ladd and they were both close colleagues of Lake.

161 Shelley Winters (1920–2006), originally Shirley Schrift, was a stage and screen actress remembered for A Place in the Sun (1951). She was a character actress but a good one, who won Oscars for The Diary of Anne Frank (1959), and A Patch of Blue (1965). She was nominated twice for A Place in the Sun and also

with both Quinn and Kirk Douglas, among very many others. As a sample of her style, this is what she had to say about Douglas, who was between marriages:

> And there was Kirk Douglas, in and out–in more ways than one. Our – uh – whatever it was – lasted no more than four months, but in that short time Kirk was responsible, directly, or indirectly, for two very important decisions in my life: I went to a psychoanalyst, and I broke my contract with Columbia. (Keyes, 1977)

Keyes made her debut in the forgettable *Buccaneer* (1938) and became well known when she was selected to play Scarlett O'Hara's younger sister in *Gone With the Wind* (1939), actually only a bit part. Her best films were *Here Comes Mr Jordan* (1941), *The Jolson Story* (1946) and *The Prowler* (1951), a *noir* film. She wrote that she had never realised her potential as an actress.

Clifton Webb (1893–1966) did two film *noir*: *Laura* (1944), which made him a star and for which he was nominated for an Oscar, and *The Dark Corner* (1946). Webb had three successive careers, on stage as a dancer (of the Astaire not Kelly type) in the 1920s and as a stage and screen actor. He made many other kinds of film, including *The Razor's Edge* (1946) and *Sitting Pretty* (1948), for both of which he was nominated but never awarded an Oscar. Although versatile as an actor, off-screen Webb was

---

for a brilliant performance as an overweight lady who has to negotiate a tricky manoeuvre in the bowels of a luxury liner in the disaster movie, The Poseidon Adventure (1972). Winters' two books are very long – too long – and packed with the kinds of anecdotes about the stars she met in the course of her long career which ran from 1943 to 1999. She was successful on television as a raconteur and wrote a play, among her other activities.

apparently just like his character in *Laura,* an urbane, cynical *mondain* with a waspish tongue, but unlike that character he was kind and loyal to his friends. Webb lived with his mother, Mabelle, all his life and outlived her by only six years. He left six chapters of an autobiography and many notes, which were very effectively put together with researched interpellations by David L. Smith (Webb, 2011). The book reveals that Webb put so much into his role in *Laura* in its ten weeks of filming that he ended up in hospital when it was finished.

Joan Bennett in *Scarlet Street* (1945): Dr Macro/Universal.

Joan Bennett (1910–90) is credited with four *noir* films by Silver and Ward, but made more; in fact she has been called the Queen of *noir* probably largely on the basis of two films with Edward G. Robinson, which were her best.[162] Joan actu-

---
162 The two films with Robinson were The Woman in the Window (1944) and

ally thought she was best in comedy and did make some light comedies. She hailed from a long line of actors and her two sisters, Constance and Barbara, as well as her father, were on the stage. Joan started off as a blonde in silent films but ended as a brunette, in which guise she bore a remarkable resemblance to Hedy Lamarr. Her autobiography (1970) is not just about her own story but that of her family. In her own life, in 1951, Joan had a *noir* episode when her husband Walter Wanger, the well-known producer, thought – wrongly – that she was having an affair with her agent and shot and injured him in a car park. The famous lawyer Jerry Geisler (who defended Errol Flynn; see Chapter 6) managed to get his client off with a prison sentence of only four months, of which he served only three. Joan says in her book that the accompanying scandal destroyed her career in motion pictures, concentrating after the events of 1951 mainly on the theatre and television, though she did make a few more films.

Scarlet Street (1945). Bennett's other noir include The Scar (1947; Hollow Triumph in the US) with Paul Henreid.

CHAPTER 9

Music and Prejudice

MUSICAL FILMS HAVE gone through phases. They were particularly popular following the birth of sound in the 1920s, in parts of the inter-war period and during the Second World War when audiences wanted to be cheered up. Of course, before sound came in there was live musical accompaniment in many theatres and dancing was not unknown in silent films.[163] The innovation of sound led to a flood of musicals from *The Jazz Singer* (1927) onwards.[164] Early musicals were mostly comedies adapted from stage shows but the genre was to develop in many different directions: backstage musicals; the geometric patterns of Busby Berkeley; the early Rooney/

---

163 Joan Crawford danced the Charleston in Our Dancing Daughters (1928). Cecil B. DeMille made three silent films with opera diva Geraldine Farrar in 1915. On the set, Farrar was accompanied by a live orchestra to put her in the mood for singing. The Farrar films were popular. Eyeman (2010), in his enormously detailed yet readable autobiography of DeMille, comments: 'An opera singer in silent movies would seem to be intrinsically absurd but Farrar would prove the exception to the rule.'
164 Since most sound films have music it is not obvious exactly what a musical is. For example, many noir films have one or more scenes in nightclubs with a torch singer, and even a dance number, but that does not make them musicals. Jewell (2007) quotes the definition from The Oxford Companion to Film: 'A musical is a film in which the elements of song and/or dance are so essential that to remove them would leave little or nothing.'

Garland movies which featured kids 'puttin' on a show'; the Shirley Temple and Deanna Durbin films; the Astaire–Rogers romantic series; and the very sophisticated musicals in the 1940s and later.

Roy Rogers: Finler.

Another variant was the singing Western, dominated by Gene Autry (1907–98) and Roy Rogers (1912–98). Edward Buscombe in (Griffin 2011) points out that the Autrey and Rogers movies were very different from the mainstream Westerns discussed in Chapter 8. Singing cowboys avoided shoot-outs of the one-on-one kind, were clean-living (no drinking, smoking or swearing), led restrained love lives and their films were set in the modern, not the frontier era. They wore elaborately decorated clothes with coloured shirts and piping, mother of pearl buttons, silver belt buckles and the like, and their boots were tooled and multicoloured. The singing Westerns flourished from the middle 1930s to the 1950s and were extremely popular, as were records and radio. Autry, who made some fifty films for Republic, made his debut in 1934; Rogers came later, and his first film was in 1938. Both wrote autobiographies (Autry in 1978; Rogers in 1994) and both shared their stardom with their horses – Champion and Trigger respectively.

In the last period of the Golden Age, musicals and movies generally moved out onto the street as in *On the Town* (1949). These were the heydays followed by the late flowering of *West Side Story* (1961). It seems very unlikely that the high standards of singing and dancing of the 1940s and 1950s will be reached again since they depended on a studio system which has now gone. But you never know: *Mamma Mia!* (2008), for example, was a great popular success.

The actor-autobiographies of the great days of the musicals are numerous (especially compared with those of the actors of film *noir* which flourished in the same period), but on the whole are not very interesting. Leslie Caron's recent book is a major exception. She was discovered by Gene Kelly in Paris, where she was a young ballet dancer and given a lead role in her first film, *An American in Paris* (1951). Her book is witty and literate and covers not only her romances with Peter Hall, Warren Beatty and others, but interesting accounts of her life during the German Occupation in France, the cultural shocks she experienced, her development as a serious actress, her work as an hotelier, and much else.

The only other really notable autobiography (2003) in this sphere is that of Betsy Blair (1923–2009). Blair did start as a chorus girl but never appeared in a musical film. She was a dramatic actress, well known for her role opposite Ernest Borgnine in *Marty* (1955). Her very readable book, however, provides a good portrait of Gene Kelly, her husband for sixteen years, who did not write a book of his own. Blair's book presents a sweetly nostalgic picture of the 1940/1950s Hollywood, a period overshadowed, however, by the Blacklist, which she says destroyed both her Hollywood career and her marriage. Nevertheless it is plain that there was more to it than that; politically active Blair was well to the left of Kelly and, perhaps more important, she outgrew him: 'He really wanted me to be the carefree sixteen year old he fell in love with.' Blair neatly surveys Kelly's career:

[EXT]
The revolutionary alter-ego number in *Cover Girl*, the artistry of the ballet in *An American in Paris*, the sexiness of the 'Apache' dance with Cyd Charisse (and her fabulous legs), the tenderness of his work with children, the Mexican girl in *Anchors Aweigh* and 'I got Rhythm' with a bunch of French kids, the humour and joie de vivre with Donald O'Connor and again with the Nicholas Brothers, all his numbers with Judy Garland, and of course, the sublime *Singin' in the Rain*, were accepted and embraced by the public . . . He was, for all his talent and intelligence, a man of the people . . . He democratised the dance in movies. (Blair, 2003).
[EXT ends]

The long list of mostly female actors who appeared in musicals produced few books of interest. Cyd Charisse

MUSIC AND PREJUDICE

(1922–2008) and her husband, singer Tony Martin, wrote their book (1976) (or told it to Dick Kleiner) in alternate chapters. This unique approach has not been emulated by anyone else and does not work well. Their sixty-year long marriage was only terminated by her death. Like other top dancers – for example, Leslie Caron, Shirley MacLaine and Ann Miller – Charisse had early training in the ballet. Female singers also wrote autobiographies, including Rosemary Clooney (a distant relation of George Clooney), Jane Powell (1988) and Ethel Merman (1955). Among the male singers, including Howard Keel(2005),[165] the only book that stands out is Mel Tormé's (1988), which has humour and good writing. All the singers' books discuss at length their personal traumas and Tormé explains that falling in and out of love is the main source of material for popular songs which, 'nine times out of ten usually has to deal with the subject of love' – though it has to be said that most non-singing actresses' books are also dominated by accounts of their love affairs.

Another singer who wrote autobiographies (1949, 1960 and 1970) was Maurice Chevalier (1888–1972). Just as David Niven was 'very British', Chevalier was very French and always had a heavy accent in English. Hollywood made Chevalier an international star but he never settled in the US. His stays in Hollywood began in the 1920s and continued almost until his death. He had made silent films in Paris, beginning as a boxer and circus acrobat. He was wounded in the First World War and spent two years in German prison

---

[165] Howard Keel (1919–2004) whose powerful voice and tall frame suited him ideally for such singing roles as in Annie Get Your Gun (1950) and Seven Brides for Seven Brothers (1954). His film career declined with the fashion of musicals but he appeared in the TV series Dallas (1981–91). His book was apparently completed by his wife who wrote an Epilogue after his sudden death from undiagnosed cancer.

camps, and at one point he was refused re-entry into the US because of supposed Communist affiliations but, like Chaplin, he was forgiven and awarded an Honorary Oscar for his career and his performance in *Gigi* (1958) with Leslie Caron. Chevalier was essentially a vaudeville artist and described himself as 'a simple sunshine salesman' (Chevalier, 1970).

Bing Crosby's autobiography (and also, in a different way, Chevalier's) is an exception to our generalisations about singers' books. Originally published in 1953 at the peak of his fame, Crosby's account has the distinction of being republished half a century later. This no doubt owes much to his enduring fame but also to the quality of the book which, although anecdotal and lacking a definite structure, compels attention. The book is human, amiable and relaxed, just like Crosby's performing manner.[166] These qualities come across in most of his performances but are perfectly, if briefly, encapsulated in his appearance in *Variety Girl* (1947), one of those shows put on by studios after the war to show off their premises and their talents (others included *Star Spangled Rhythm* (1942) and *Hollywood Canteen* (1944). *Variety Girl* also includes the shortest appearance by Sterling Hayden in a movie. Crosby (1903–77) was an enormously popular singer in the 1930s radio age, and in the 1950s on television. Many of his songs, such as 'White Christmas', have enduring

---

166 Crosby may not have been so amiable in his private life. One of his sons, Gary, a minor actor, wrote a book entitled Going My Own Way, published by Doubleday in 1983, which was critical of his father in a similar way to the books by the children of Joan Crawford and Bette Davis (see Chapter 2). However, his brother Phillip defended his father vigorously. Bing Crosby devoted an affectionate chapter to his children in his autobiography, written, of course, much earlier, in which he admits to being a strict disciplinarian. Two of Crosby's other children died by suicide. It seems that following in the big footsteps of famous Hollywood parents often created tremendous stresses for their children (see Chapter 8).

MUSIC AND PREJUDICE

appeal and command unprecedented sales. Crosby was, in fact, among the Top Ten box office stars from the 1930s to the 1950s and continued to be popular on television into the 1970s. Because Crosby still seems so contemporary, it is perhaps a surprise to read in his autobiography that he made short films for Mack Sennett, but this was in the late 1920s when the great silent comedy producer was in decline. Although most of his film appearances were in musicals and his film career began in the 1930s, Crosby later became a very successful straight actor and was awarded an Oscar for *Going My Way* (1944). For a singer to become a straight actor is not uncommon (think, for example, of Burl Ives, Dick Powell, Dean Martin and especially Frank Sinatra), but it does not seem to happen in reverse.[167] The autobiography of Dorothy Lamour (1914–96) discusses her *Road* films made with Crosby and Bob Hope and her book is very evocative of Hollywood in wartime. The book reflects her warm friendly personality, but conforms very much to the pattern of books by most musical singers and dancers mentioned above.[168]

Ginger Rogers' (1911–95) long and often tedious book does tell us about much other than her marriages and affairs. She started in Hollywood in 1931 and made nine films in partnership with Fred Astaire and many other films without him, and indeed without music.

---

167 Burl Ives' autobiography (1952) was published early in his career before most of his films, but he was a singer who became an actor. Tough guy Lee Marvin (1924–87) had a song in Paint Your Wagon (1969) which got into the charts, but this was a one-off event.
168 Lamour's book (1980) is unlike quite a few others in that it does have an index, with some 800 entries, most of them names of people. Noted for her sarong, Lamour appeared in films from 1936 to 1988. In Road to Morocco (1942), the stars sing 'Like Webster's dictionary we're Morocco bound!' Other destinations in the series included Singapore, Bali and Zanzibar; and the last was Road to Hong Kong (1962).

Ginger Rogers: Finler.

From the beginning Rogers had ambitions to be a dramatic actress and achieved this by winning an Oscar for *Kitty Foyle* (1940). There has been much speculation about Astaire and Roger's partnership in so many films. The fact is that neither of them wanted their series of musical films to last so long, but the public loved them. In their books, neither Astaire nor Rogers say much about the other, although there was clearly great mutual respect. It is difficult to resist the conclusion that each one resented the fact that their stardom was shared in that way. Eventually Rogers wanted to get back to drama, while Astaire longed for physically shorter partners who were not as well known as he was.

Fred Astaire (1899–1987) and Gene Kelly were the greatest male dancers of the silver screen. They were not competitors, however. Kelly said, 'Fred Astaire represents the aristocracy when he dances. I represent the proletariat.' Kelly was muscular and virile while Astaire was the epitome of elegance: with his loose-limbed, rhythmic movement he could charm an audience simply by walking onto a stage. Astaire's autobiography (1959), which he wrote himself in pencil at the age of fifty-eight, is a true reflection of himself – modest, debonair and reticent and, one might add, fairly short in length. Over half of the book is devoted to his early stage career (he started in partnership with his sister Adele, who married an English lord and thereafter gave up dancing). Astaire's life with his first wife, Phyllis, was obviously very happy and they did not entertain much with other show business people (Levinson, 2009).

Not only does Astaire say little about his deeper self, he does not have much to say about his dancing partners either. Ann Miller was 'a terrific performer'; Vera Ellen a 'brilliant dancing star'; Cyd Charisse was 'a terrific dancer'; while Rita Hayworth, who may in reality have been the best of all, 'danced with trained perfection'. Even Ginger Rogers was described merely as 'very attractive and talented'. In her book Rogers says that early on they went out together a few times. She also says that the statement attributed to her that she did everything Astaire did but backwards and in high heels was actually taken from a cartoon and was not her own remark. Astaire obviously thought Rogers was too tall for him (in high heels she was about the same height and Ann Miller was taller) and Rogers was certainly too heavy for him to lift. He does not make comparisons between his female partners; nor does he say much about his male co-stars. The best of all his male partners was certainly Donald O'Connor (1925–2003), and some people think that he was as good as Astaire in many ways. O'Connor was at his best in *Singin' in the Rain*, in which he showed his talent for comedy as well as doing astonishing back-flips off the wall. Astaire probably gives the impression of being lukewarm about partners because he really preferred to dance on his own.[169] For their part, his fellow dancers all respected and even revered him, though Rogers got impatient with Astaire's relentless attitudes to rehearsal and perfection. All found him difficult to get to know and remarked upon it. Jane Powell (1988) wrote that he was 'very sweet and very private'. She wrote that in a BBC interview about Astaire, she said, 'I'm afraid I have nothing to tell you because I never knew him,' adding that the interviewer replied that 'everyone felt that way'.

Astaire was an accomplished singer as well as dancer. He had practised singing from an early age and wrote lyrics and composed songs as a hobby. Towards the end of his career he turned to straight acting and wished he had done it sooner, but he missed singing and dancing and hardly knew what to do with himself when his wife died.

Ann Miller (1923–2004) replaced an injured Cyd Charisse in *Easter Parade* (1948), and acquitted herself well despite the fact that she herself was wearing a steel brace to support a seriously damaged back. To her regret, Miller never danced with Astaire again. As a dancer (and she was not much as an actress), Miller never got another chance as good as her role in

---

[169] In a press interview, Astaire reportedly said that Barrie Chase, a young dancer that appeared with him in his TV specials (1958–68), was his favourite partner. Chase (1933–) was a marvellous dancer, but she retired early after her marriage. She appeared in a number of movies, including Cape Fear (1961) and The George Raft Story (1961), but never as a lead dancer in a major film.

On the Town (1949), and was as a result perhaps underrated, though she had great success on Broadway. She says in her book that she could do 500 taps a minute, her only rival being Eleanor Powell (1910–82), who once described Fred Astaire as having a colourless personality. Miller was described by John Kobal (1971) as having a 'good-natured eroticism'. She was very proud of her long legs and goes into detail about them in her book, which also, inevitably, describes her three disastrous marriages, each one a terrible surprise to her.

Shirley MacLaine (1934–) wrote a much better autobiography than most of her women dancer peers. Her book (1968) reflects her funny, human and unconventional character, which also comes across well on the screen, for example in *Sweet Charity* (1968) and in her Oscar-winning performance in *Terms of Endearment* (1983). Drawing upon her apparently inexhaustible energy, she went on to write a total of thirteen books (only two mainly about her life in Hollywood), a record among the actors reviewed here. MacLaine, who, like Miller, believes in reincarnation, is the older sister of actor Warren Beatty and like all the other dancers explains how physically tiring and even dangerous dancing for the screen is. Most dancers (with the exception of Astaire) experienced injuries on the job, including bleeding feet and broken bones.

Shirley Temple (1928–), like Deanna Durbin, was a child star whose movies helped to keep their studios afloat in the bad times. One still hears her signature tune 'On the Good Ship Lollipop' from *Bright Eyes* (1934) on the radio from time to time. Like most child stars her career faded as she grew up, but she started very early – at the age of three. Her role in the films, as for other precocious stars, was to sort out the problems of the adults around her. She was pushed on, like quite a few other actresses, by her mother, who ended up earning

◄ **HOLLYWOOD LIVES**

$100,000 a year from the studio (Fox, later 20th Century-Fox) to manage her daughter.[170] The studio was outraged when Graham Greene wrote in a review of *Wee Willie Winkie* (1937) that '. . . middle-aged men and clergymen . . . respond to her dubious coquetry, to the sight of her well-shaped and desirable little body . . .' 20th Century-Fox successfully sued the publishers for implying, in effect, that the company had procured Temple for immoral purposes. Fifty years later, in her autobiography (1988), Temple adopted an amused tolerance to this nonsense.[171] She described it as 'immensely fruitful' since the publicity for the film quashed the rumour that she was a midget and that 'suddenly unemployed as a film critic, Greene was released permanently into the ranks of eminent novelists'. Her book is very long at some 175,000 words and a promised second volume has not been forthcoming. Her screen career ended in 1950 but Temple continued to help out with grown-up problems as US Ambassador to Ghana (1974–6) and to Czechoslovakia (1989–92) and was US Representative to the United Nations in 1969. She later retired to France where, like Olivia de Havilland, she has remained.

Mickey Rooney (1920–), unlike Shirley Temple, has never been an establishment figure. He started as a child actor appearing with his parents in vaudeville. He claims to have been in over 350 films and is probably the only living actor who

---

170 Others discussed in this book, whose mothers drove their early careers, include Ann Miller, Lena Horne and Gene Tierney. Except for those whose parents were in vaudeville, like Mickey Rooney, the boys mostly had to make it on their own. June Havoc (1912–2010) was pushed into vaudeville as a child by her domineering mother, who dominates her autobiographies too (1959, 1980). Havoc, whose sister Louise became Gypsy Rose Lee, was in many stage musicals, but in film she had mostly poor or minor roles, such as Gregory Peck's racist secretary in Gentleman's Agreement (1947) – though she was very good in that.
171 The absurdity of the Wee Willie Winkie case is not diminished by the knowledge that the film was directed by John Ford, who was most unlikely to wish to introduce eroticism of the sort alleged by Graham Greene (see Chapter 8).

◄ 202

has appeared in movies from the silent days up to the recent past. In his autobiographies he says that he earned $12 million before he was forty years old – but blew it all, finally filing for bankruptcy in 1962. He had eight wives (Ava Gardner was the first), but settled down in 1978 with his present wife, Jan Chamberlin, a country and western singer. Many of his films have been musicals; referring to the Andy Hardy series (fifteen of them) especially, Rooney says he was a fourteen-year-old child for thirty years thanks to his youthful appearance and short stature. Rooney has appeared in almost every kind of film. He played Puck in *Midsummer Night's Dream* (1935) and his later films included: *Boys Town* (1938) with Spencer Tracy; *National Velvet* (1944) with a juvenile Elizabeth Taylor; and *Words and Music* (1948), in which he played Lorenz Hart of songsters Rogers and Hart. Later, Rooney was in *The Bold and the Brave* (1956), a war picture, and *Breakfast at Tiffany's* (1961) as a Japanese man, Mr Yunioshi.

Rooney loves show business and even in 2007 did a tour of Britain (with his wife) with his own show of songs, reminiscences and film clips.[172] He has published two autobiographies (1965, 1991) and a forgettable novel (1994). The first of the autobiographies had a long and difficult history. The sports writer Roger Kahn, his collaborator, found it impossible to nail Rooney down to work on the book and finally had to sue him for breach of contract. This got Rooney moving, but when the book was completed he

---

172 London was not included in this tour but Lisa Minelli and Debbie Reynolds have appeared on the London stage quite recently. I saw Rooney's show in Weymouth, Dorset, on 27 August 2007: Rooney looked as if he had been pumped into his dress suit and his dancing amounted to little more than shifting his weight from one leg to another. He sang, played the piano, performed imitations (of Clark Gable and Jimmy Cagney among others) and made jokes about himself, but he still had that magical ability to hold an audience. Afterwards he told me that he and his wife were working on a new autobiography.

did not want it published. After another lawsuit, he went through the book and, according to Kahn, 'emasculated' it to the point at which Kahn took his name off it (Marx, 1986). His later, better, book acknowledges help from a lot of people, but Rooney is named as the sole author. Rooney's long life has been full of interest and covers his military service, his unsuccessful legal action against eight studios over residuals, the story of the Hollywood brothel with uncanny star lookalikes, and other things not well documented elsewhere.

Dorothy Dandridge in *The Decks Ran Red* (1958): Finler/MGM.

MUSIC AND PREJUDICE

Non Anglo-Saxon actors sometimes faced prejudice and discrimination – or, at best, very narrow typecasting. Attitudes in the autobiographies are entirely condemnatory to these forms of ethnicity, but various actors experienced the problem at first-hand and acutely in the years before the 1960s when racial attitudes began very slowly to change. Some actors had very little trouble; for example, Desi Arnaz (1917–86) as a Cuban immigrant who fled from the 1933 Batista revolution, did have to sleep in a rat-infested warehouse and clean out canary cages to survive in Miami at first, but his musical talents soon got him a job in a band, later with Xavier Cugat, and in a fairly short space of time a band of his own in New York. He went to Hollywood, having appeared on Broadway, and later Arnaz produced and starred in partnership with his first wife, Lucille Ball, in the *I Love Lucy* shows. They made enough money from this to buy up the real estate of the RKO studios and used them to produce more programmes for television. In the process, Arnaz invented the three-camera technique for filming the programmes, a big advance at the time. Desilu Productions, their television business, was later sold to Paramount. Unlike his wife, Arnaz appeared in only a few movies but became very well known, thanks to television. Arnaz wrote his autobiography (1976) himself, despite his admitted 'not too good knowledge of the English language' and very charming it is. Sadly Arnaz and Ball divorced in 1960: both remarried but kept in affectionate contact. Arnaz died three years before his first wife.

Lucille Ball herself (1911–89) had made arrangements to write her autobiography with Bob Thomas – but sadly died before it was started. After her death, to their surprise, her children found a manuscript that she had completed in 1964. This book was not published until 1996, thirty-two years later.

The family believe that Ball put the manuscript aside because it was so painful for her to write, or she may have not been satisfied with it. In any event, it is a fairly run-of-the-mill, show-business autobiography.

)))

Mexicans were treated badly in early Hollywood, even though it was Spain and Mexico that originally explored and developed the territory the film industry was based in. The prejudice against Mexicans was brought home to Ricardo Montalbán (1920–2009) on the very first day he entered the US by road with his brother. En route to California they stopped at a gas station, but at the adjoining restaurant they were confronted with the notice: NO DOGS OR MEXICANS ALLOWED. Later on, Montalbán was refused entry to a dance hall on the same grounds. Anthony Quinn, in his autobiography (1995), says that Mexicans were regarded as untrustworthy and that there were street fights between them and the Irish youths. Quinn, whose mixed parentage qualified him for either side, chose to fight with the Mexicans, the underdogs in the local community in Los Angeles. Montalbán got very angry about prejudice in his early days, but says that later on he tried to abide by the teachings of his Catholic priests to 'Hate the sin, but love the sinner'. He was to become the first President of a non-militant organisation, the Nosotros Foundation, dedicated to reducing tensions between Latin and other Americans and improving the opportunities for Mexican actors. The objective was to ensure that talent, not ethnicity, was the prime factor in choice by the studios.[173]

---

173 In a reference to The Magnificent Seven (1960), Montalbán accepts that Eli Wallach might be able to play a Mexican bandit better than he could, but wanted the opportunity to play a Mexican and other nationalities often portrayed by people of Greek and Italian origin. Wallach wrote his own autobiography

Montalbán got some criticism for speaking out in this way and cites the hate mail he received when he was seen kissing Lena Horne in the Broadway musical *Jamaica*. Before coming to Hollywood, he starred in Mexican films, which caught the attention of an agent who got him a contract with MGM. His first American film was *Fiesta* (1947), in which he danced with Cyd Charisse. In Montalbán's slim and lucid autobiography (1980) he reveals his frustration at being typecast as a Latin lover or American Indian and his lack of achievement on the screen. Actually he played a Japanese in *Sayonara* (1957) and an Italian major in *Hemingway's Adventures of a Young Man* (1962) and had a forty-year career in Hollywood and on television. His greatest personal successes included *Battleground* (1949) and *Sweet Charity* (1968).

Afro-Americans suffered the worst discrimination and the narrowest range of parts of all. In early Hollywood, black actors were restricted to menial roles as servants or as slaves – though sometimes these could be significant character parts, as in *Gone With the Wind* (1939). Remnants of this treatment left their mark on people in Hollywood well into the 1940s and 1950s. Betsy Blair recounts a story of a party in her and Gene Kelly's home. Blair went into the kitchen with Lena Horne to fix drinks and was followed by a showgirl acquaintance who, on being asked to get some glasses, pointed at Horne and said 'Why doesn't she get them?' Blair steered the girl out of the house immediately.

Woody Strode (1914–94), an Afro-American, saw himself primarily as an athlete before he hit success in films. He excelled at putting the shot, javelin and discus. As a football star, Strode, with others, was responsible for integrating the races

(2005). Anthony Quinn, an exceptional actor from Mexico, did of course get these opportunities to play various nationalities, though Montalbán does not mention this.

in major league football and he also did well in professional wrestling. In his acting career he was a member of John Ford's stock company and Ford was particularly fond of him, citing his friendship with Strode when he was accused, as he often was, of racial prejudice. Married for forty years to a Hawaiian princess, Strode made a number of outstanding movies, including his best roles in *Sergeant Rutledge* (1960) and in *Spartacus* (1960) in which last he is a slave forced to fight Kirk Douglas and in *The Professionals* (1966). He also appeared in the last film made by DeMille, *The Ten Commandments* (1956), as the King of Ethiopia. His autobiography (1990) is much less concerned with racial issues than those of the other black actors reviewed here, and less than a third of his book deals with his Hollywood career.

Sammy Davis Jr (1925–90), although he made quite a few films, was primarily a singer, dancer and comedian in cabaret – especially in Las Vegas.[174] Davis's father was in vaudeville and he first appeared on stage as a juvenile in the late 1920s. He had tremendous energy and produced no less than three autobiographies (1965, 1980, 1989). He lost his left eye in a car accident, but this did not slow him down for long; his nose had also been smashed by a white bigot in the Army. Once interrupted by someone complaining about discrimination, he responded 'You got it easy. I'm a short, ugly one eyed black Jew' (his adopted religion). He attracted criticism for having a relationship with Kim Novak, which was stamped on by Columbia Studios, and not in a nice way. He attempted to

---

174 Davis was the only member of the 'Rat Pack' group of entertainers to write books. Other principal members of the group were Dean Martin, Frank Sinatra and Joey Bishop, the comedian. All four appeared in Ocean's 11 (1960), a heist film in which Cesar Romero attempts to steal the loot and succeeds in stealing the film. This movie (recently remade with George Clooney) also starred Richard Conte and had a cameo appearance by George Raft in the original version.

rectify his 'error' by what he called a 'phony' marriage with a black actress, a marriage which lasted only just over a year. Later he married the Swedish actress, May Britt, which for a while seemed to be happy but ended in 1968 after eight years. His last marriage in 1970 to another black performer, Altovise Gore, only ended with his death. Davis helped to break down the colour bar in the entertainment world, especially in Las Vegas where initially he was not permitted to stay in the hotels in which he performed. In the end, however, Davis died penniless and in debt to the Internal Revenue Service (IRS).

Dorothy Dandridge (1922–65), like Davis, was a brilliant performer who also had a drive to cross the colour line. She attracted, among others, Otto Preminger and Curt Jürgens. She was the first Afro-American to be nominated for an Oscar as best actress. Dandridge made only a small number of films, including the all-black *Carmen Jones* (1954), which won her an Oscar nomination, *Island in the Sun* (1957) and *Porgy and Bess* (1959). She said in her autobiography (1970) that she had a mixture of English, Jamaican, American negro, Spanish and American Indian origins. This cocktail produced great beauty and a wonderful voice. All critics agree that she could have been an even greater star, but her promise went unrealised. Instead she died at age forty-two, brought down by failed romances, being made bankrupt by her crooked agent and above all by racial prejudice which, she said, 'denied her simple respectability'. According to her collaborator in the book, Earl Conrad, although she died from a drug overdose, it was an accident and not suicide. Nevertheless, this was 'murder that took a lifetime'. Her tragic life story is a painful read, ably told.

Lena Horne (1917–2010), another light-coloured and exceptionally beautiful and talented singer, suffered from some of the same problems as Dandridge but was tougher. Like Dandridge, Lena refused to conform to the negro stereotype. She appeared on Broadway and television but experienced reverse discrimination from other black people who resented her success. Like Dandridge, Horne crossed the colour line. Preceding and outlasting Dandridge, Horne was the first black sex-symbol and undoubtedly the best known of Afro-American actresses with her famous songs 'Stormy Weather' and 'The Lady is a Tramp'. When entertaining troops in the Second World War, she refused to perform for a segregated audience and the Army substituted German prisoners of war for white soldiers. In her films for MGM, Horne played peripheral roles and guest appearances so that her segments could be cut out for the sensitive US Southern States without ruining the film. This and other incidents, including her rejection for the role of Julie in *Showboat* in favour of Ava Gardner (whose singing voice was dubbed), are recorded in her excellent autobiography with Richard Schickel (1965). As the civil rights movement gained ground, Horne was able to score a notable success as a straight actress in *Death of a Gunfighter* (1969).

Sidney Poitier (1924–) has been the most successful black actor and has been honoured for it.[175] He has not hesitated to fight for the cause of racial equality but has approached it in a non-militant way and with a desire to be constructive. His performances have tried to show that black people can be exemplary human beings – an itinerant black carpenter helps a group of nuns to build a chapel (*Lilies of the Field* (1963); a black detective helps and gains the respect of a bigoted Southern sheriff in *In the Heat of the Night* (1967); and in *Guess Who's Coming to Dinner* (1967) the daughter of a well-

---

[175] He was awarded an Oscar for Lilies in the Field and was knighted by the UK in 1974, the Bahamas having become an independent nation within the Commonwealth at that time.

to-do white family says she wants to marry a black doctor.

Poitier, the son of a dirt farmer, came from Cat Island in the Bahamas but was born in Miami, Florida, during a parental visit to the mainland. In his teens he went to New York and, having been rejected by the American Negro Theater, returned later, having worked on his Bahamian accent, and was accepted. At first he was not committed to acting. He had responded to an advert by the theatre in the belief that it would be more congenial work than washing dishes, being a janitor and parking cars, which is what he had been doing. Once he had started he never wanted to do anything else. After a chance opportunity to appear on Broadway in *Lysistrata*, he was given opportunities in films and later directed many of them. Stanley Kramer deserves credit for making *Guess Who's Coming to Dinner,* it being very daring at the time for a white girl to be courted by a black person. Sidney Poitier's first autobiography appeared in 1980 when he was only fifty-six years old. It tells of his struggles to get established as an actor, his emotional life and the films he made. His second autobiography (2000) is an unconventional and beautifully written account of his moral development, which completely avoids pomposity and didacticism and inevitably reflects the fact that, at the time of its publication, when he was seventy-six, he had had the time to more fully digest his exciting and successful life than for the first book. Many actors wrote their books too early, in fact, and had to produce revised versions later.

CHAPTER 10

Hollywood Trials

MOST HOLLYWOOD ACTORS were not active in national politics, at least not before the 1960s. They did not have the time and the studios discouraged it for fear of alienating at least a part of their audiences. The Communist witch-hunts after the Second World War also gave an incentive for actors to keep their heads down in this respect. When all that was over, however, things changed and quite a few movie stars became active in Presidential campaigns. One actor – Ronald Reagan – became President himself. Another actor, Charlton Heston, also became very active politically, although he never sought office. Both Reagan and Heston, however, became prominent in the political field and wrote autobiographies. So did George Murphy, who preceded them by becoming a Senator for California in 1964, two years before Reagan was elected governor of that state.[176] Presidents love movie stars, like the rest of us, and several stars have dined at the White

[176] The trend towards political activism has continued. Arnold Schwarzenegger (1947–), a body-builder from Austria and star of the Terminator movies, was elected Governor of California in 2003 and served the maximum two terms. Jane Fonda (1937–), daughter of Henry Fonda and a strong civil rights and prominent anti-war campaigner, made exercise videos and some fine films, but like Schwarzenegger lies outside the period covered by this book.

House and supported Presidential election campaigns with personal appearances.

If we leave aside the anti-trust action which separated the studios from their theatre chains (Chapter 13), and racial politics (Chapter 9), the political developments which impinged most on the lives of Hollywood actors in the Golden Age were the struggles of unions, the related Communist scares of the 1940s and 50s and the associated blacklisting of writers, directors and actors. In this chapter we discuss the blacklisting and in the next we deal in more depth with Murphy, Reagan and Heston and their roles in politics.

The Communist scare reached its peak during the early part of the Cold War, but the roots of the post-Second World War troubles in Hollywood went back to the inter-war depression (Shindler, 1996). Hollywood as an industry suffered less than others in the early part of the Depression and at first the novelty of the talkies kept audiences up. By 1932 and 1933, however, audiences both at home and overseas had plummeted and the impact of the higher costs of making talkies brought the studios into heavy losses (except Columbia and MGM). Paramount and RKO went into receivership and in 1933 studio heads announced large pay cuts for their artistic personnel. Pressures from unions increased. In an attempt to head off union activity among artistic personnel, the industry had created the Academy of Motion Picture Arts and Sciences (AMPAS) in 1927, a studio- backed body for producers, directors, actors, writers and technicians. AMPAS, of course, still exists today and makes the annual Oscar Awards.[177] The

---

[177] AMPAS was initially promoted by Louis B. Mayer and has long-since ceased to be in any sense a labour union. Its first President was Douglas Fairbanks Sr and the first Oscars were awarded in 1929. The Screen Directors Guild, now the Writers Guild of America, was founded in 1938 and appears later on in this story.

threat of pay cuts, however, led to the formation of the Screen Writers Guild (SWG) in April 1933 and shortly afterwards of the Screen Actors Guild (SAG), though they were not to receive full recognition by the studios as negotiating bodies until 1937 for SAG and not until 1941 for SWG. By then all professional groups in Hollywood were unionised. SAG turned out to be a moderate organisation (though it achieved recognition only after threatening a massive strike), while SWG was much more militant. Other personnel, in addition to actors and writers, were involved in movie production and the craft unions, stage hands and technicians all had separate representative bodies. By 1946, workers in Hollywood were organised into forty-three separate craft and talent groups, the former being under the International Alliance of Theatrical Stage Employees (IATSE) (Balio, 1985). Extreme left-wing and organised crime groups gained control of IATSE and also promoted the Conference of Studio Unions (CSU) in competition with it. IATSE and CSU were eventually cleaned up, partly thanks to the efforts of SAG.

To understand how extreme left-wing groups emerged in Hollywood in the 1930s, and why there were fears of Communist infiltration, it is necessary to look at the background. When talking was introduced into the movies in the 1920s, the studios had to bring in not only stage actors from Broadway in New York who knew how to deliver lines, but also the writers who wrote their dialogue, tasks which were beyond some of the actors and most of the traditional (and less militant) talents involved in silent films. The writers, in particular, included many Jewish intellectuals many of whom were of leftish persuasion. These people were followed, both before and after Second World War by émigrés from Europe fleeing from fascist persecution (Franco in Spain, Hitler in

Germany and Mussolini in Italy). Many directors, actors and musicians as well as writers were among the émigrés (see Chapter 4).

Writers from Broadway were used to working on controversial subjects and to directors who kept close to the text of what they wrote. The status of writers in New York was high and writers like Lillian Hellman were just as valuable to theatre producers as the stage actors themselves.[178] In Hollywood, screenwriters came low down in the pecking order (after producers, directors and actors). Unlike actors, for example, who had their own dining room, the writers mostly had to use the Commissary (canteen). Writers had to work in offices and in writers' buildings and clock in and out, and could be laid off without pay just like factory workers. They also had to accept that what they wrote would be rewritten by others and it was common to use teams of writers on a screenplay, a practice introduced by Irving Thalberg of MGM. Shindler (1996) comments that 'Embarrassed by the ease and standard of living in Southern California and frustrated by successive professional humiliations, these men had only one weapon to fight the deadly onset of self-loathing. Politics, left-wing, radical politics within the bastion of entrenched privilege, was their escape

---

[178] Women writers seemed to adapt more easily to writing for the screen. Among the most successful was Lillian Hellman (1905–84), a playwright, the lover of Dashiell Hammett, who was also to become a suspected Communist later on. Hellman adapted some of her plays for Hollywood and wrote original screenplays. Her contemporaries included Anita Loos (1891–1981) of Gentlemen Prefer Blondes fame and Adela Rogers St Johns (1893–1988), a Hearst journalist who apart from screenplays also wrote an excellent autobiography, The Honeycomb which included her reminiscences of Hollywood. Hellman's adaptations included The Little Foxes (1941), Watch on the Rhine (1943) and The North Star (1943). The last mentioned, which depicted Russian villagers fighting the Nazis, later proved to be an embarrassment, though Russian and the US were allies at the time. The film was cited later as Communist propaganda by one HUAC witness because some of the villagers were seen to be smiling! Some of the best male novelists, however, such as William Faulkner and Scott Fitzgerald, were failures as screenwriters.

hatch. They fought the studio bosses and the Republicans with the same passion that they raised money to send ambulances to Spain and to bring Jews out of Germany.'[179]

With this background, quite a lot of writers and even actors were tempted to join the Communist Party during the Depression and after the Second World War. Betty Garrett, who played the stop-start cab driver in *On the Town* (1949), and who carried the shore- leave sailors around the city, wrote about her motives in joining the Communist Party (1998):[180] 'The more involved I became in the politics of the day, the more it seemed to me that the Communists, Socialists and other radical groups were the only ones who were really *doing* anything about discrimination, better housing, Spanish Civil War orphans, and so on.'

Garrett's motives, not as naive then as they would appear later, were typical of actor-moderates who joined Communist associated bodies. Sterling Hayden was another example, and remained in the party for less than a year because its meetings bored him terribly. There were also people, mostly writers, whose views were more extreme and who continued their association with Communism for longer: examples are writers

---

[179] The moguls, though of working-class origins and émigrés, were solidly Republican. Supported by the Hearst press, they worked hard to help defeat Upton Sinclair, a left-wing novelist who sought election as Governor of California in 1934. Sinclair wrote an exposé of the inhuman and unhygienic conditions in the meat-packing industry. The screen actors were more mixed in their political views and had a sizeable contingent of Democrats. SAG was far more moderate than the SWG and its board included some of the leading actors whose bargaining power was such that individually they did not need guild representation. In the early days Robert Montgomery, George Murphy and James Cagney all served as Presidents of the SAG Board, as did a little later Ronald Reagan and much later Charlton Heston. Not all actors commanded big salaries and the average income of all SAG Members was well below subsistence level. In effect, the big stars used their prestige to help the little guys.

[180] Garrett was to regret her brief membership of the Communist Party later when she and more particularly her husband, Larry Parks, received the attentions of the HUAC (see below).

HOLLYWOOD LIVES

Clifford Odets (1906–63) and John Howard Lawson (1894–1977). Odets was credited for the screenplay of *Humoresque* (1946) and *Sweet Smell of Success* (1957) and expressed very left-wing views in many plays in New York radical theatre. He was a member of the famous Group Theatre, which he helped to found in the 1930s, and its successor, the Actors Studio, founded in 1947 by Elia Kazan and others. The Actors Studio trained many famous theatrical/movie stars including John Garfield, Marlon Brando, Marilyn Monroe, Montgomery Clift and Lee J. Cobb.[181] Lawson was supposedly a committed Marxist whose credits included *Sahara* (1943), which starred Humphrey Bogart. Kazan, Lawson and Odets were to play prominent roles in the House Un-American Activities Committee (HUAC) hearings. After the Second World War, and as the Cold War went on, American opinion turned more and more against Russia and Communism and especially during the build-ups to the Berlin airlift (1948), the trials of alleged Soviet spies (such as the Rosenberg Case), and the Korean War (1950) when US (and British) troops were actually fighting Communists. It was a bad time for the studios because movie audiences were about to decline steeply. The anti-trust case that they had been fighting since 1938 culminated in a 1949 order to the big five studios to divest their theatres (see Conclusion).

There are some common misapprehensions about the HUAC hearings. There was not one but a whole series of post-war hearings which ran, with intervals from 1947 to 1958. After 1960, the Committee lost prestige and was eventually

---

181 As mentioned in Chapter 5, the Actors Studio under Lee Strasberg was to base its training on the ideas of Konstantin Stanislavski known collectively as the Method. Elia Kazan was also involved in the Group Theatre in the 1930s and later directed On the Waterfront (1954), which starred Brando, Cobb and Eva Marie Saint, all of whom trained at the Actors Studio.

abolished in 1975. It was actually first established in May 1938 when it investigated the Federal subsidies to theatre which were part of F. D. Roosevelt's New Deal, and the Special Investigation Committee was then chaired by Martin Dies. The whole Communist witch-hunt is associated with the name of Joe R. McCarthy, but in fact, although he later led that persecution to new heights, he was not involved in 1938 – or even in the 1947 HUAC hearings, which resulted in blacklisting and the imprisonment of the 'Hollywood Ten'. HUAC was set up by the House of Representatives, whereas McCarthy was in the Senate and his accusations of Communist infiltration were concerned with government, and especially the State Department, not Hollywood. McCarthy finally overreached himself when he focused on the Department of the Army. The turning point was Ed Murrow's television programme in 1954 in which he denounced the McCarthy investigations as a threat to civil liberties.[182]

The first HUAC sessions affecting Hollywood were the 'Hearings Regarding the Communist Infiltration of the Motion Picture Industry, 1947'. They were chaired by J. Parnell Thomas and Richard M. Nixon was a member, both of whom later got into trouble themselves. It will be noted that the title of the hearings assumed at the outset that Hollywood *had* been infiltrated and this set the tone of the proceedings which were, as Robert Vaughn described them, 'punitive' and not investigatory. The hearings produced no proposals for legislation.[183] They were supposedly focused on content, that is,

---

182 Ed Murrow's courageous role in defeating McCarthyism was dramatised in George Clooney's excellent film Goodnight, and Good Luck (2005).
183 Robert Vaughn, the actor (1932–) played the lead in the TV series The Man from U.N.C.L.E, but is equally well known for his roles in The Young Philadelphians (1959) The Magnificent Seven (1960), Bullitt (1968) and other films. Vaughn wrote a very good autobiography (2008), much of it devoted to his anti-war and other political activities. His first book, Only Victims: A Study of Show Business

an attempt to identify movies where Communist propaganda had been inserted – but none was found. The producers said they would never have allowed propaganda and some actors (for example, Robert Taylor and George Murphy) asserted that they would not speak propaganda lines. Those called before the hearings were classified into two groups: 'friendly' and 'unfriendly'. Friendly witnesses were those who were cooperative and willing, where appropriate, to name the names of Communists that they were aware of in the industry. The unfriendly were those who had made it clear that they were not prepared to cooperate and were prepared to cite their constitutional rights under the First Amendment in their defence. The Committee had compiled a list of people who were or were suspected of being Communists or had been investigated as such. Many of the people on this list were those who had joined the Communist Party during the Depression and later, like Sterling Hayden and Betty Garrett, had withdrawn or allowed their membership to lapse.[184]

In the first week of the 1947 hearings, which were held in Washington, friendly witnesses were called (there had also been some preliminary hearings in Los Angeles in the spring, but these, unlike most of the October hearings, were not held in public). In his testimony, Jack Warner asserted that there were some subversive elements in Hollywood and that he would be happy to help dig them out and get rid of them. Louis B. Mayer went further and called for national legislation

---

Blacklisting (1972), was based on his doctoral thesis and is one of the most useful things written about the HUAC Hearings.

184 According to one of the later witnesses in 1958, the list included the name of the child star, Shirley Temple, who was ten years old at the time she had been investigated in1938. The Committee afterwards protested that Shirley Temple had never been investigated but she had unwittingly allowed her name to be used in a French Communist newspaper, along with other stars, as sending anniversary greetings.

to regulate the employment of communists. Adolphe Menjou said that John Howard Lawson and Herbert Sorrell, head of the CSU, were Communists, or so he had heard, but named no actors. George Murphy and Robert Montgomery, former presidents of SAG, were more circumspect and asserted that communist influence was very minor. On the whole, the evidence presented by the friendly witnesses was vague and unconvincing, though they left no doubt about their sincerity and patriotism.

Most of the evidence was hearsay and some of it very trivial and silly. Lela Rogers, Ginger Rogers' mother, testified in the preliminary hearings that the phrase 'Share and share alike – that's democracy', spoken by her daughter in *Tender Comrade* (1943),was subversive – though neither Ginger nor her mother had complained at the time. In her autobiography Ginger does not mention that 'subversive' phrase but does note her approval for her mother's testimony and that of Adolphe Menjou, Gary Cooper and Robert Taylor, who were all 'in step' with her mother's views (Rogers, 1991). Ronald Reagan, then SAG President and wearing a white suit (traditional Hollywood code for being a good guy), introduced a sharper note, saying in response to the question 'What steps should be taken to rid the motion picture industry of any Communist influence?':

> [EXT]
> . . . we have done a pretty good job in our business of keeping those people's activities curtailed. After all, we must recognise them at present as a political party . . . In opposing those people the best thing is to make democracy work . . . Whether or not the Party should be outlawed, that is for the government to decide. As a citizen, I would

hesitate to see any political party outlawed on the basis of its political ideology. (Cited by Eliot (2008) with my excisions)

[EXT ends]

While all this was going on, a group of Hollywood artists – led by directors John Huston and William Wyler – worried about developments, formed the Committee for the First Amendment.[185] The First Amendment to the US Constitution, part of the Bill of Rights, protects freedom of speech and religion and the right to peaceful assembly. Support for the new committee grew to hundreds of artists who wished to defend the industry and protest against the HUAC, 'whose chosen weapon is the cowardly one of inference and whose apparent aim is to silence opposition to their extremist views, in the free medium of motion pictures' (Committee statement cited by Dmytryk,1996). A group of twenty-six stars from Hollywood, including Lauren Bacall, Paul Henreid, John Huston, Evelyn Keyes and Sterling Hayden, to mention only those whose autobiographies are discussed in this book, flew to Washington the day before the second week of the hearings of the 'unfriendlies' (ironically, the name of the chartered plane was *Red Star*). Their intention was to present a petition to the Speaker of the House and attend the hearings – which they did, a back row having been reserved for them.

The Committee for the First Amendment paid for this trip and also paid for two radio broadcasts in which stars, including Robert Ryan, Edward G. Robinson and Judy Garland,

---

185 There was some support for the hearings in Hollywood, though not necessarily for the way they were conducted. The Motion Picture Alliance for the Preservation of American Ideals was formed in 1944 by politically conservative people, including Walt Disney and the directors Sam Wood and King Vidor. Ward Bond, and Gary Cooper were members and John Wayne became its President in 1948.

spoke out. There were nineteen unfriendlies, but ten of them – suspected Communists who had made it known that they were not going to cooperate with the HUAC – were singled out and some of the remainder were not, in the event, called upon to testify.[186] En route, the planeload of supporters was greeted by cheerful crowds (in those days refuelling stops were still necessary). On arrival in Washington, however, they found a different atmosphere. The supporters made it clear that they were not there to defend the 'Ten' but simply to uphold constitutional rights. Humphrey Bogart issued a statement which said, in part:

[EXT]
This has nothing to do with Communism. It's none of my business who's a Communist and who isn't. We have a well-organised and excellent agency in Washington known as the FBI who does know these things. The reason I am flying to Washington is because I am an outraged and angry citizen who feels that my civil liberties are being taken away from me and that the Bill of Rights is being abused. (Quoted in Bacall, 1978)
[EXT ends]

All of a sudden, it became clear that public support for this position had ebbed away. An invitation for the group to lunch with President Truman was withdrawn at a day's notice

---

186 The Ten consisted of eight writers (Alvah Bessie, Lester Cole, Ring Lardner Jr, Albert Maltz, Samuel Ornitz, Adrian Scott and Dalton Trumbo) and two directors (Hans Biberman and Edward Dmytryk). There was an eleventh, Bertolt Brecht, the German writer, but he gave evidence that the Committee considered satisfactory and then prudently left the country. Charlie Chaplin, also not an American citizen, was subpoenaed but not called after he wrote to say that he had never been a Communist (Chaplin, 1964). Others not called included Samuel Goldwyn – to his annoyance because he did not approve of the proceedings at all.

and the press became hostile. It has never been entirely clear why this happened. It may be that the studios, fearful of the involvement of their stars in explosive and divisive politics were already beginning to switch sides, or that the proceedings of the HUAC were stoking up anti-Communist feeling – or it may have simply been that things were different in Washington where the impression had been gained that the group were there to defend the unfriendly 'Ten'. Evelyn Keyes (1978) wrote: 'We faced a hostile, sophisticated, worldly press who made us look like stupid children interfering with grown-up problems.' Paul Henreid (1984) wrote about the day after their arrival: 'We woke up next morning to find the press, which had praised us so fully, had done a complete about-face. We were no longer knights in shining armour. We were "dupes and fellow travellers", "pinkos" who were trying to undermine the country. Our brave crusade had become a disaster.'[187] The supporters returned to Hollywood separately. On the way back, via Chicago, Bogart gave a press conference in which he attempted to retract some of what he had previously said. He said that his participation was ill-advised and foolish and that he had been duped. This retraction is another mystery since Bogart had been the most vociferous of the group.[188] Henreid wrote, 'I felt Bogart's statement was a form of betrayal, and it was the end of our friendship – and the end of many of Bogart's other friendships. The rest of us stood firm.'

---

187 Henreid says that his wife Lisl had been keeping the books for the Committee for the First Amendment but that the book listing all the contributions, including studio heads, had mysteriously disappeared from their house in Hollywood with no sign of a break-in and nothing else missing. The Committee was soon listed as a 'Communist front'.

188 Lauren Bacall, Mrs Bogart, in her autobiography throws no light on the episode except to say that it was suggested that Bogart should issue a statement saying that he was not a Communist and denouncing the unfriendly witnesses and this he refused to do. It seems fairly clear, however, that Bogart succumbed to pressure from his studio, Warners.

HOLLYWOOD TRIALS

To the unfriendlies, the HUAC was quite brutal, refusing in most cases to hear prepared statements, preventing witnesses and their lawyers from criticising the hearings and from cross-examining the friendly witnesses, and repeatedly asking one question: 'Are you or have you ever been a member of the Communist Party?' The Ten were treated as if they were on trial without any opportunity to defend themselves. There was much pounding of Chairman Parnell's gavel and several witnesses who attempted to shout down the questioners, such as John Howard Lawson and Dalton Trumbo, were removed from the stand by guards before they had finished speaking. The audience of 400 cheered and booed and there was pandemonium. To cut a long story short, the Ten were, after a trial and an appeal to the Supreme Court (which refused to hear their case), sentenced to jail for contempt. Dmytryk and Biberman were sentenced to six months and a fine of $500; the others to one year and a $1,000 fine.[189]

Edward G. Robinson was not subpoenaed, but at his request and using influence through the Mayor of Los Angeles, appeared before the HUAC in the second week of the 1947 hearings on 27 October.[190] He asked for this appearance because he had been

---

189 Dmytryk's (1994) book is very interesting and contained, as we show later, some important revelations. He was placed in an open prison with the job of garage attendant. Amusingly he shows that many of the clichés of prison life used by him and others in films: prisoners were often innocent and not guilty (on 'bum raps'); unfriendly guards, and menacing 'jailbirds', turned out to be the opposite of the truth, however his prison may not have been typical. Edward Dymtryk (1908-1999) was the director of many fine films from 1935, both before and after his sentence, for example: Murder My Sweet (1944); Crossfire (1947) the first film about racial bigotry, with Robert Ryan and Robert Mitchum; Broken Lance (1954) with Spencer Tracy; The Caine Mutiny (1954) with Bogart, Jose Ferrer and Van Johnson and Mirage (1965).
190 Edward G. Robinson (1893–1973) had a long and distinguished career which started with stage appearances in 1913 and continued until the year of his death. He made his first movie in 1923 and appeared in a total of some eighty-five pictures, first becoming a big star in the 1930s with gangster films. His later films included Double Indemnity (1944) with Barbara Stanwyck and Fred MacMurray; The Woman in the Window (1944) with Joan Bennett; Key Largo

listed as a member of a number of what the Committee called Communist 'fronts', including the American Committee for the Protection of the Foreign Born, Progressive Citizens of America and the Committee for the First Amendment. He wanted to appear and clear his name because the allegations caused him anguish and, even at this stage, were leading to difficulties in getting work, even though there was then no blacklist as such. In his autobiography (1973), he wrote of the first two of the groups mentioned: 'Communist front organisations? Perhaps. I don't know. It never occurred to me. What occurred to me was that both groups were active in their passion for the deprived, the put-upon, the victims not only of Nazi terror but of our economic imbalance.'

Edward G. Robinson with Joan Collins in *Seven Thieves* (1960): GB/20th Century Fox.

(1948) with Humphrey Bogart; and House of Strangers (1949); his last was with Charlton Heston in Soylent Green (1973).

Robinson was very upset about the accusation of lack of patriotism, particularly because he had had a good record during the war. His sensitivity was heightened by the fact that he was a naturalised citizen, born in Romania. He was happy to testify that he had never been a member of the Communist Party, but what the Committee wanted was for him to say was that he had become a member of these 'fronts' because he had been duped – and he did not believe he had been. He actually appeared before the HUAC three times and did not get the clearance he wanted until 1952 when he finally agreed reluctantly to say that he had been duped. Matters had not been helped by the fact that, out of compassion, he had sent a cheque for $2,500 to Dalton Trumbo's wife. Trumbo was one of the Ten jailed for contempt and was still in prison; he had written to Robinson, asking for a loan because his family were short of money. Robinson never gave names of Communists Party members at the hearings and nor did he invoke his Constitutional rights. The Committee finally gave him the clearance he wanted, but not without a parting insult. The Chairman of the Committee at the time, Mr Francis Walter, said: 'Well, actually this committee has never had any evidence presented to indicate that you were anything more than a very choice sucker. I think you are a number one on the sucker list in the country' (quoted in Robinson, 1973).

The second series of HUAC hearings were held in 1951–2 ('Investigation of Communism in the Entertainment Field' under the chairmanship of John S. Wood). It is another twist to this extraordinary and unpleasant episode that Parnell Thomas was himself convicted for corruption (padding a government-funded payroll) after the first hearings and in 1948 ended up in the same prison as two of the Hollywood Ten. The second series of hearings began in March 1951 and continued for no less than ten sessions. A large number of people wanted to appear before the Committee to clear their names because of the threat or actuality of blacklisting and they appeared voluntarily, while others were subpoenaed. According to John Cogley, some ninety Hollywood figures appeared on the witness stand during the 1951 hearings.[191]

Early witness Howard da Silva took refuge in the Fifth Amendment and refused to answer questions relating to his political beliefs (the 1947 hearings having established that the First Amendment was an inadequate defence). The Fifth Amendment states that no one in a criminal case can be compelled to be a witness against himself. John Garfield and José Ferrer, who had also both been subpoenaed, said they were not Communists and were not sympathetic to their ideas, but avoided naming others or using the Fifth, as did, in a more forthright manner, Lillian Hellman. Larry Parks was the first entertainer in 1951 to raise the issue of whether it was morally right to name names. He admitted that he had long before been a member of the Communist Party but at first strongly resisted giving any other names, though under pressure he eventually did so in an executive session. Parks pleaded with the Committee: 'I chose to come and tell the truth about myself. So I beg you not to force me to do this. Don't present me with the choice of either being in contempt of this committee and going to jail or forcing me to really crawl through the mud, to be an informer.'

Sterling Hayden and Elia Kazan were friendly witnesses and gave names. Hayden greatly regretted it afterwards and Kazan worried about having done so for the rest of his life. Dmytryk, when he had finished serving his sentence, reappeared before

---

191 Report on Blacklisting, I, The Movies, Fund for the Republic, 1956, excerpted in Balio (1976).

the Committee and cooperated fully. As he explains in his book, he did this because he realised that he had been manipulated. He asserts in the book that the abortive defence of the Hollywood Ten had, in fact, been deliberately coordinated by the Communist Party in consultation with Moscow. His final view, as stated in his book (1996), was that 'The scoundrels were not members of the Committee or the Party, but fellows of liberal chic, the hypocrites who rated snitching a higher crime than treason and who, from no-risk positions, kept the conflict alive into the present decade, to the detriment of Hollywood and its chief industry.'

Whatever view one may hold about this, it is plain that the HUAC did terrible damage and achieved nothing. One of the motives of the Committee in choosing Hollywood for investigation was undoubtedly the opportunities it offered the members for publicity. Arthur Miller, the playwright and married to Marilyn Monroe at the time, was called in 1956. He refused to name names and was cited for contempt. Prior to this, Miller was told, through his lawyer, that he would not need to appear if he would arrange for a photograph to be taken of Chairman Walter and Marilyn. Miller had rejected this offer but the contempt charge against him was later revoked and he did not go to jail. From a later generation, Charlton Heston, who was not involved at the time, concluded in his autobiography (1995) that 'the hearings abused the democratic process and provided nothing useful in the country's confrontation with the Soviets'.

The damage to lives and careers has been much written about. Larry Parks, famous for his impersonations of Al Jolson and with a good career in front of him, was ruined as an actor and was forced to adopt a different career in property management – in spite of the fact that he had been a friendly witness. This 'reverse blacklisting', as his wife, Betty Garrett, called it, was to apply to others: the so-called 'unfriendlies' all lost out. One actor, Philip Loeb, committed suicide and J. Edward Bromberg, another actor, died of a heart attack following a summons before the HUAC while the stresses of the hearings at least in part may have also led to John Garfield's premature death from a heart attack.[192] Quite a few writers went abroad into exile, children of the Ten were taunted at school for having parents who were 'traitors', and wives and extended families were obviously adversely affected. Some writers were able to continue working on screenplays under pseudonyms at a fraction of their previous rates of pay. Some clearly quite innocent people, tainted with accusations, including Edward G. Robinson, were already finding it difficult to get work.[193]

The Waldorf Declaration was issued after a two-day meeting of the moguls and Hollywood financiers on 24–25 November 1947 at the famous hotel in New York. There were differences of opinion and Samuel Goldwyn and Dore Schary, the head of MGM, apparently were not in favour. Nevertheless the reaction of the terrified moguls as a group was clear: the declaration deplored the behaviour of the Ten

192 John Garfield (1913–52) was a much loved, and today underrated actor, originally with the Group Theatre, whose films included They Made Me a Criminal (1939); The Sea Wolf (1941); The Postman Always Rings Twice (1946) with Lana Turner; Humoresque (1946) with Joan Crawford; Body and Soul (1947), a boxing film; and Gentleman's Agreement (1947), an exposé of anti-Semitism, among others. Bogart and Bacall's version of To Have and Have Not (1945) was not as close to the heart of Hemingway's novel as Garfield's The Breaking Point (1950). Garfield turned down an offer by Elia Kazan to play the stage role of Kowalski in A Street Car Named Desire, which launched Marlon Brando as a star. His biographer, Larry Swindell (1975), says that Garfield was the forerunner of the 'anti hero rooted not in romance but in sociology', 'not one of the establishment but a rebel against it . . . and not a likely bet to win'. He was followed in this line by others such as Marlon Brando, Montgomery Clift, Steve McQueen and Paul Newman.
193 The atmosphere at the time and the view today of these events is well conveyed in Guilty by Suspicion (1990), with Robert De Niro as a hitherto successful film director, who is blacklisted and unable to work.

and stated forthrightly that 'we will not knowingly employ a Communist'. The resulting blacklist (which was actually an unwritten understanding) in practice was mainly used by the major talent agencies, who were soon invited into the studios for talks. The Screen Actors Guild helped to make the blacklist effective by adopting a by-law in 1953 that made members of the Communist Party, or other organisations 'seeking to overthrow the government by force', ineligible for membership.

However, from 1951 SAG did offer to help people clear their names, which meant getting clearance from the FBI or the HUAC. The anxieties of the studio heads were stoked by threatened boycotting of theatres showing movies starring or written by 'Communist sympathisers' by the American Legion and others. *Red Channels*, a privately published listing of suspected Communists, had appeared in 1950. It is very striking than none of the really big stars were affected by the blacklist – with the unjust exceptions of Robinson and Henry Fonda, who said that he was 'graylisted' for a time.[194] Perhaps the most disturbing feature of the period was the complicity of the big studios in the events that took place.

Robert Vaughn draws the title of his book, *Only Victims*, from a quotation from Dalton Trumbo made long after these events: 'When you who are in your forties or younger look back with curiosity on that dark time, as I think occasionally you should, it will do no good to search for villains or heroes or saints or devils because there were none; there were only victims.' The blacklist lingered into the late 1950s and was broken by Kirk Douglas, who courageously decided to give credit to Dalton Trumbo as screenwriter for *Spartacus* (1960), which he was producing. Although his friends thought he

---

194 Fonda did not discuss this in his autobiography (1981), but it has been reported in various other places, for example Collier (1991).

was crazy and that he was throwing his career away, Douglas went ahead and left a studio pass for Trumbo at the gate of Universal. In his autobiography (1988), Douglas says that 'It was a tremendous risk. At first nobody believed me. Dalton did. For the first time in ten years, he walked onto a studio lot. He said, "Thanks Kirk, for giving me back my name". The blacklist was broken.'

So there was, after all, a hero. But it took an even longer time before the industry, and the guilds in particular, acknowledged how badly so many actors and writers were treated during the blacklist era. In 1980 the SWG set up a committee to restore screen credits to blacklisted writers, but it took until 1997 to sort out the errors that had been made. In 1997, the fiftieth anniversary of the HUAC hearings, at a special event at the Academy, the presidents of SWG, SAG, the Directors Guild and the American Federation of Television and Radio Artists (AFTRA) spoke of their horror and shame at what had been done. Herbert Biberman, one of the Ten whose name had been removed from the official list of founders of the Directors Guild, and who had been expelled from the union he had helped to create, had his name restored, posthumously.

CHAPTER 11

Actors in Politics

GEORGE MURPHY (1902–92), Ronald Reagan (1911–2004) and Charlton Heston (1923–2008) were three actors who shared a passionate interest in national politics. The first two were of a different generation: Murphy's first film (1934) was only a little earlier than Reagan's, but Heston did not make his debut until 1950, towards the end of the Golden Age. Heston never sought political office and kept up his screen appearances until the end, while Murphy and Reagan both gave up the screen altogether, coincidentally, at the age of forty. The three had a few things in common, though: they came from lower middle-class families and had to work their way through college; they switched from the Democrat to the Republican Party and all three were physically active when younger. Murphy played football and baseball; Reagan was a swimmer and a football player though hampered by poor eyesight; Heston was a good tennis player and of the three did most to keep fit in his later years. All suffered health problems later on: Murphy's distinguished political career was terminated by cancer and he died of leukaemia; Reagan died after suffering from Alzheimer's for a long period; while Heston, who died of pneumonia, also had Alzheimer's.

George Murphy with Elizabeth Taylor and Mary Astor in *Cynthia* (1947): GB/MGM.

Murphy and Reagan had Irish charm and 1,000-watt smiles; Heston was quite humourless and more of a stoic, writing that he was 'too square for Hollywood'. None of the three would have described themselves as intellectuals and Reagan was sometimes crudely and (wrongly) described as a 'dim wit'. (Betsy Blair (2003) quotes herself as saying in an interview about Reagan's election, 'I didn't think he was smart enough to be President'.) Heston was the most literate and wrote a good autobiography without the assistance of a ghost-writer. But the other two books of his needed co-authors and the results were not distinguished. People often came up to Murphy – once he became a successful politician –with the question 'Didn't you used to be George Murphy?' and he used this as the title of his book. Reagan's first auto-

ACTORS IN POLITICS

biography was called *Where's the Rest of Me?* after a scene in one of his better movies in which he awakes in hospital after an amputation . Heston's title, *In the Arena*, is also very appropriate and echoes both his gladiatorial and his political exploits. Murphy and Reagan, on the whole, made competent but not very memorable movies. Actor, raconteur and wit Peter Ustinov said that the two were dispensable as actors but much more successful in politics. He went on to say that while actors had become politicians there was no reciprocal movement from politics into acting, a much more difficult career than politics.[195]

George Murphy grew up in Connecticut. His father was a well-known sports trainer who died when Murphy was only eleven; his mother died only four years later. Excelling in football and baseball, Murphy won an athletics scholarship to Trinity-Pawling, a famous private school in New York, and subsequently scraped through his examinations to enter Yale University, working on an assembly line in Detroit to help meet the costs. His subject was mining engineering, but he got disenchanted with this when he worked in a coal-mining firm during the vacation. When he found studying conflicted with his sporting activities, he dropped out during his junior year. Like Ronald Reagan, Murphy got his first taste of show

---

[195] Another polyglot, Theodore Bikel (1924–), a versatile stage and screen actor, guitarist and singer, wrote the most politically oriented of all the autobiographies reviewed in this book. Bikel devotes more space in his book to politics and world affairs than any of the others. He says he did not know what to make of inward-looking Hollywood. Bikel mentions that on the day the New York Times carried the headline 'H-BOMB TESTS TO BE RESUMED!', the just as large headline in the Los Angeles Times read 'ELVIS AILING!' Bikel was born in Austria, grew up in Israel and was educated in Britain. His first Hollywood film was The African Queen 1951. Others included The Defiant Ones (1958) and The Russians are Coming, The Russians are Coming (1966).

business at college and when he left Yale he went to New York to find work in the entertainment field. He started with a job as a 'floor manager' (effectively a bouncer) at a dance hall in Newark. Like others during Prohibition, he came into contact with rum-runners and bootleggers and was befriended by a gangster – but stayed straight.

Soon, Murphy formed a dance partnership with his girl-friend, Julie Henkel-Johnson, whom he was to marry in 1926. They played in nightclubs and eventually on Broadway – in quite a big way by 1929. Murphy's agent, to George's surprise, later came up with two Hollywood contracts. One was for a musical, *Kid Millions* (1934), with Samuel Goldwyn, who had seen Murphy on the New York stage. The other offer was for a year with Columbia. On their removal to Hollywood, Julie retired from her own career to devote her time to the family. After an uninspiring year with Columbia, Murphy met Louis B. Mayer, who signed him for MGM. George was now doing well and appeared with Eleanor Powell in a series of musicals: he was in *Broadway Melody of 1938* (1938), which made Judy Garland a star, and in *Broadway Melody of 1940* (1940), in which he danced with Fred Astaire. Musicals were still very popular but over time Murphy began to be offered serious roles as well, including *Bataan* (1943), and the big box-office success, *This is the Army* (1943). Murphy appeared as an FBI agent on the Mexican border in *Border Incident* (1949), in *Battleground* (1949) and in *Walk East on Beacon* (1952), another semi-documentary drama about the FBI exposing Communist spies. Murphy says in his autobiography (1970) that he made over forty-five films in his twenty-year career on the screen and lamented only that in these films he hardly ever 'got the girl'.

George Murphy's potential, and certainly his motivation

as an actor, seemed to be exhausted when he retired from screen roles in 1952. Well before this he had become more and more involved as a trouble-shooter and ambassador for the studio because, according to Mayer, he 'had a way with people'. He had also risen to the Board of the SAG and then to the Presidency (1944–6) and in 1951 received a special Academy Award for services 'in correctly interpreting the film industry to the country at large'. MGM kept him on salary until 1958 when he resigned to become Vice-President of Desilu Studios, the creation of Desi Arnaz and Lucille Ball. Two years after this he became a Senior Vice-President of the Technicolor Corporation. Though he seemed not to find the business side of show business too satisfying, politics was beckoning.

Murphy had probably never found acting very satisfying. Mary Astor (1971) wrote that he was not a song-and-dance man turned politician, but 'a politician who had earned his living at one time as a song-and-dance man'. When she worked with him on the set she relates that he bored his colleagues by always talking politics and that when he read the paper he never looked at the entertainment section. Echoing Ustinov, she went on to say that 'a good actor would never make a successful politician. Just in case you might be asked to consider George C. Scott for mayor of New York.'

Since 1939, Murphy had been increasingly involved in state and national politics and in that year had switched his allegiance from the Democrats to the Republican Party. He says this was because he became disenchanted with the role of bigger government under Franklin Delano Roosevelt's New Deal. In this he foreshadowed Ronald Reagan's belief when campaigning for his presidency that 'government was not the solution but the problem'. Murphy was also bothered by FDR's unsuccessful attempt to reform the Supreme Court, which had ruled some of his New Deal measures as unconstitutional. Partly through his observation of the struggles with the Hollywood unions, he became convinced that Communism was a real threat in the film industry. He claimed that he managed to convince Ronald Reagan of this (corroborated by Reagan in his first autobiography) and, as we have seen, both Murphy and Reagan were to give friendly (if muted) testimony at the HUAC hearings.

Murphy had helped to organise the Hollywood Republican Committee and in 1952 he assisted with the stage management of the Republican Convention and was to do this again in the 1956 and 1960 Presidential campaigns. He also helped with General Eisenhower's rallies and, when Ike was elected, the inaugural festivities. After this, he was appointed State Chairman for the Republican Party and was persuaded to run for the Senate. He was elected to the Senate in 1964, having conducted a successful campaign against Pierre Salinger, former Press Secretary in the Kennedy Administration. His term ended in 1971 and he stood for re-election, but this time was defeated, probably because the throat cancer which developed during his term of office, severely impairing his speaking voice. Murphy remained politically active, however, dying in Florida at the age of eighty-nine.

It has been said that Murphy helped to make Hollywood musicals into an art form and although he never became a megastar himself, he was a solid performer with a long and successful career. He was the first Hollywood performer to achieve national elected office and in this he paved the way for Ronald Reagan's attainment of the highest office in the land.

ACTORS IN POLITICS

Ronald Reagan in *The Bad Man* (1941): Finler/MGM.

Reagan was born in Tampico, Illinois, and grew up there and in other towns in the Chicago farmland belt. His parents were not well off – his father was a salesman in a shoe store – but he went to a local college, graduating in 1932 with a part scholarship, which meant that he had to pay his way by washing dishes and acting as a swimming coach and lifeguard. He became deeply involved in football and his ambitions to act emerged in the drama activities at the college. Through his own efforts, he got a short assignment as a sports commentator and then a staff job at WOC Davenport, a local radio station. This did not last but gave him the experience to get another role with WOC in Des Moines. In those days before television, radio was a big thing and was based in Chicago. Reagan called radio 'The Theatre of the Mind' – aptly because the listener has to use his imagination to fill out what he cannot see.

Keen on horses, Reagan enlisted in the Cavalry Reserve Corps and in 1937 qualified as a 2nd Lieutenant, something that required considerable equestrian skills. His eyesight was poor, which ruled out serious participation in baseball – which is why he had concentrated on football. He had to cheat in the eye test to pass the Army medical board, tests which, oddly, were administered only *after* training. In his first autobiography (1965), Reagan enthuses about riding and football and, of the latter's permanent fascination for him, wrote: 'the smell of sweat and taste of mud and blood do not change with the years'. Sports journalism followed naturally and he contributed a regular sports column to a local paper under the name of 'Dutch Reagan'. He was invited to attend summer camp on Catalina Island for the Chicago Cubs baseball team and on his second visit there he met an actress in Los Angeles who arranged for him to see George Ward of the Meiklejohn Agency. Ward got him a screen test at Warner Brothers. Jack Warner himself saw the results of the test and Reagan was signed for a seven-year contract with a six-month out-clause.[196] It all happened with amazing speed. He arrived in Hollywood on 1 June 1937 and started on his first film only three days later – *Love is on the Air* (1937), a 'B' movie in which he played a radio announcer. (In his second and third

---

[196] For the test Reagan was advised by his friend to remove his glasses. He claims that he was one of the first people in the US to wear contact lenses. These early lenses were uncomfortable and made him look pop-eyed, so he only wore them when absolutely necessary, such as for long-shots and stunts.

movies he also played sports or radio announcers.) He was kept busy, mostly in B pictures and by 1940 had made no less than eighteen films. One of these, *Dark Victory* (1939), in which he had only a minor role, was a triumph for Bette Davis.

In Hollywood, he was befriended by the exceedingly Irish Pat O'Brien, who helped to get Reagan the role of star football half-back, George Gipp, in *Knute Rockne, All American* (1940).[197] In this film, O'Brien played the Norwegian-born Notre Dame coach, Rockne, a much-revered character. Reagan only appeared for ten minutes in the film and dies prematurely, but his performance made audiences sniffle with emotion and he got good press notices. From *Rockne*, Reagan went straight into *Santa Fe Trail* (1940) as George Custer, but was overshadowed by co-star Errol Flynn. (Rather like George Murphy at this point, Reagan was often cast as the hero's best pal who does not get the girl.) *Santa Fe Trail* was a box office success but did little for Reagan's reputation as an actor. He had his agent, Lew Wasserman, to thank for his next part – in *Kings Row* (1942).[198] This is a gloomy story of incest disguised as madness and frustrated romance. In a tragic accident, Reagan has his legs amputated by a sadistic surgeon who resents his patient's rejection of his daughter. Reagan thought

197 Fast-talking O'Brien (1899–1983) had been a hit in Front Page (1931) and was very popular in the 1930s. In his autobiography, O'Brien says that after many mediocre roles, Knute Rockne made Reagan a star (O'Brien, 1964). O'Brien admitted Reagan to the hard-drinking 'Irish Mafia club' which included James Cagney, Spencer Tracy and Errol Flynn (who was not Irish but not really acceptable among the cliquey British ex-pats). Reagan was not a heavy drinker and had to conceal the fact in this company.

198 Lew Wasserman, then fairly recently arrived in Hollywood, was the local representative for the Music Corporation of America (MCA) and the best of a number of brilliant talent agents who helped to bring the studio system down by inflating star salaries and breaking up the contract system. He was to play a crucial role in Reagan's career and ended buying up Universal Studios when his company withdrew from the agency business. Wasserman headed up MCA when Jules Stein, the founder, retired.

it his best picture. In it, he is again the best pal of the leading character, Parris, who is rather weakly played by Robert Cummings. In *Desperate Journey* (1942), Reagan was reunited with Flynn, which he was not pleased about because Flynn tried, and often succeeded, in stealing his best scenes. This story of flyers shot down and captured in Germany, who escape to cause mayhem on the way, is surely a comedy, though the critics have not interpreted it as such. It has tremendous pace and humour and is very entertaining. It ends with Flynn, having foiled the Nazis, famously saying: 'Now for Australia and a crack at those Japs'. Reagan is little more than a stooge in this film but delivers some banal lines with dogged good humour.

During all this film-making, jilted by his first love, Mugs, from Illinois, Reagan enjoyed having dates – both for fun and for studio publicity purposes – with a large number of starlets, including Lana Turner. In his book he notes, not entirely with approval, that promiscuity among the hopeful starlets and actors and executives was condoned and indeed so widespread that his studio had an on-site abortion clinic to deal with the consequences. However, Reagan, who participated enthusiastically in all this, according to Marc Eliot (2008), was really after a serious, long-term relationship. In 1940 he married Jane Wyman, whom he had met two years previously when they appeared together in *Brother Rat* (1938) and later in *Tugboat Annie Sails Again* (1940). In the 1940s, Wyman (1917–2007), like Reagan, was not getting very far with her career, though he earned vastly more than she did. Button-nosed Wyman, who started as a chorus girl and in dumb-blonde roles, was to develop into a serious actress, far outpacing Reagan, who was her third husband. She received an Academy Award for *Johnny Belinda* (1948), a melodrama in which she played a deaf mute.

ACTORS IN POLITICS

The Second World War was to put a temporary stop to Reagan's career as a movie star. He was drafted into the Army Air Force and because of his poor eyesight not into a combat role but into the First Motion Picture Unit in Hollywood.[199] Although many stars did not, by accident or design, serve in the armed forces, or served in various film units, it seems possible that they were doing as much good for the war effort by overseas tours in combat zones and making films to boost morale, train and entertain. Although some of the biggest stars did serve at the sharp end (James Stewart, Robert Montgomery, Tyrone Power, Clark Gable and Robert Taylor, for example), it is interesting that none of them came to grief. Reagan, who could not normally serve in a commercial film while in uniform, was allowed to play in *This is the Army* (1943). In this film, he had a starring role as the son of a Broadway producer who puts on an Army musical stage show. (The father was played by George Murphy, made up to look older since he was in fact only nine years older than Reagan!). The film, intended to be a morale booster, was an enormous success. The Army personnel involved, including Reagan, received only their military pay and the proceeds –over $10 million – went to the Army Emergency Relief Fund.

Reagan was discharged from the army in September 1945. Resuming his contract with Warner, which had been suspended for the duration, he was given a number of mediocre films to do and one good one, *The Hasty Heart* (1949),[200] which

---

199 It is said that Reagan and Ann Sheridan were under consideration at this time for the roles that were ultimately played by Humphrey Bogart and Ingrid Bergman in Casablanca (1942). The reader may guess that the film would not have been the enormous success it was had the casting been different. The Army film unit was actually Jack Warner's idea and he was to work in it himself.

200 It was during the making of The Hasty Heart that Patricia Neal in her autobiography records that, when in her presence, Reagan 'was asked what he would most like to be in the whole world, and Ronnie laughed and said, "The President of the United States"'(Neal,1988). This was thirty-two years before his ambition was realised.

was made in England and made a star of Richard Todd. Less momentously, Reagan appeared in *Bedtime for Bonzo* (1951).[201] During the war, a number of younger actors had emerged, such as Peter Lawford, Van Johnson and Gregory Peck. Reagan was earning good money and was able to buy an eight-acre ranch in the San Fernando Valley where he could indulge his love of horses. Warner's were reluctant to put him into Westerns, which is what he would really have liked, and he did not make one until *Cattle Queen of Montana* (1954) with Barbara Stanwyck (and that was a flop). Wyman's career, in contrast, had taken off and although she wanted a second child (their first being a girl), did not want to become pregnant again, so they decided to adopt a little boy to complete their family. Wyman's absences on location and the opposing trajectories of their screen careers, and other incompatibilities (Wyman was bored with Reagan's developing interest in politics), however, led to divorce in 1948.

Reagan was invited to join the right-wing Motion Picture Alliance (MPA), dedicated to eliminating Communists from the industry – and then a secret organisation, though it went public later. The early supporters of the MPA included Sam Wood, a producer, Walt Disney, Adolphe Menjou, Ginger Rogers, Clark Gable, Ward Bond and Robert Taylor. However, Reagan declined to join them. He had been an inactive member of the Hollywood Democratic Committee and when this metamorphosed into the Hollywood Independent Citizens' Committee of the Arts, Sciences and Professions (HICCASP), he was invited to join the Board and accepted. With fellow

---

201 Bonzo was a chimpanzee being brought up as a human baby to test theories about the environmental influences on character. Reagan was to be ridiculed later for co-starring with an ape, but the film was successful enough to justify a later remake.

Board member, Olivia de Havilland, he found that control of the organisation had fallen into the hands of extremists and was effectively a front for the Communist Party. A motion that members of the organisation should be required to adopt a liberal statement of principles was rejected and Reagan and de Havilland resigned. HICCASP collapsed shortly afterwards.

Reagan had resumed his role as an alternate Board member of SAG which had begun in 1941 and had been suspended while he was in the army. Labour unrest had increased after the war and there was a particularly bitter strike of animators at Disney. In 1946 he was asked to investigate a strike by the CSU (mentioned in the previous chapter) which would have closed the studios had SAG supported it. Reagan reported that it was a jurisdictional dispute and that SAG should remain neutral and recommend its members to cross picket-lines which they did. He gave a powerful speech to the full membership on this – and while he was doing it the tyres of his car were slashed. Before the speech he had received threats of an acid attack: from then on he took to carrying a gun. In his autobiographies, he wrote that the gun was given to him by the police (Eliot could find no evidence for this and thinks it unlikely), but it is a fact that Reagan was asked to keep the FBI informed about the extremists. The SAG Board was so impressed by Reagan's efforts that he was elected its President in 1947, a position he retained until 1952. It was in that year that he negotiated a deal with the studios over residuals for films made after 1959 and a lump payment for SAG to establish a pension and welfare fund for its members. This arrangement did not please older members, who missed out on residuals for earlier films, but Reagan was convinced that it was the best deal that could be obtained and it was approved by the membership.

Reagan's films were to become fewer and in 1954 he found himself short of money. His agent and friend, Lew Wasserman, was able to get him a lucrative contract with General Electric to present the *GE Electric Theater* on television and to give speeches at GE plants all over the country.[202] His speeches generally had a serious political message and helped to make him newly familiar to the public. Meanwhile the TV show was very popular and lasted for ten years until the management changed. The new regime was less happy to see the corporation involved in the politics which Reagan refused to eliminate. In 1959–60 Reagan was recalled to become SAG President again because many of its senior Board members, such as Robert Montgomery and William Holden, were obliged to resign as a result of a by-law which prohibited them from participating in media production as well as acting. Independent production had become more common at the time, as bonds with the studios were broken, and for tax reasons it paid actors to form companies. In 1960 Reagan himself was given a 28 per cent financial interest in the GE Theatre in return for helping to produce as well as star and had to resign himself from the SAG Board. By this time he had remarried (in 1952), to Nancy Davis, who was expecting a baby.

But Reagan's film career was not yet over and he made four more films after 1954, including *Hellcats of the Navy* (1957), the only film in which he appeared with his second wife, Nancy, and his last film, a remake, *The Killers* (1964).[203]

---

202 In 1952, MCA which had earlier formed a production company (Revue) and was making TV films, received a blanket waiver by SAG to both produce and represent clients despite the obvious conflict of interest. Ten years later, the Justice Department filed an anti-trust suit against MCA, who were subsequently obliged to get out of the agency business altogether (see note on p. [9] above).
203 He was persuaded to do this late film because it was the only opportunity he ever had to play a villain, but the film – dwarfed, as many remakes are, by the 1946 Burt Lancaster/Ava Gardner version – flopped.

Meanwhile he was now on the track to election as Governor of California, a contest which took place in 1967. Then, after two unsuccessful attempts, he was elected as President of the United States in 1981 when he was seventy years old – and gained a second term in 1984. In his first autobiography, which appeared in 1965, before he ran for Governor, he gives full attention to his Hollywood career, interspersed with long accounts of his work at SAG and the union conflicts which already absorbed his interest.

Reagan actually spent more time as an actor, which he ceased to be in 1965 at the age of fifty-four, than as Governor and President. Yet in his 750-page second autobiography (1990), only about 20 per cent of it deals with his Hollywood years and gives only two sentences to his first wife, Jane Wyman, without even a photograph of her. Reagan's career as a politician was, of course, far more important than his career as an actor. His Hollywood years, though, were an excellent preparation for his Presidency; he also learned the art of negotiation from his work in SAG, and his scepticism about government and bureaucracy from his days in the Army. Like most Presidencies, his was controversial but nevertheless successful and productive – though there remain doubts about his frequent lapses of memory (as in the Iran–Contra affair), and indeed about his alleged pursuit of the interests of the producers over those of actors in the deals he made or influenced at SAG. Intellectuals have sneered at Reagan's supposed lack of elaborate reasoning for some of his actions and the weaknesses of what came to be called 'Reaganomics', but failed to realise that he was an intuitive politician and could not always explain fully why some courses of action were to him preferable to others (see Buckley, 2008). Reagan was his own man and not a weak President, though he believed in delegation; for example, when he began his negotiations with the Soviet leader Mikhail Gorbachev over disarmament, the Cold War adherents, which included the armed services and the State Department, were united in opposition.

Charlton Heston in *Ben Hur* (1959): Dr Macro/MGM.

Charlton Heston at his peak was 6 ft 3 inches tall and weighed 210 lbs, with a booming voice, blue eyes and well-defined muscles. He was an imposing, athletic figure, ideally suited for the epic historical movies and modern action-man films in which he mostly appeared. There was more to him than most actors: his well thought-out political views, his love of the classics, especially Shakespeare, his four books and his courageous political activism marked him out as somebody special in the Hollywood scene. Throughout his career as a superstar he took time out from film-making to perform plays of limited appeal to the mass audience. Always giving work his full commitment, Heston made a lot of films just to allow him the money to do what he called 'art'. He also found time to play a variety of roles in national politics, and in SAG, in which he followed Murphy and Reagan. He never accepted or sought political office (apart from being Honorary Mayor of Hollywood) and turned down invitations to run for the Senate – because he loved acting and realised that it was not compatible with high political office.

Heston's parents originally had a small house on the shores of Lake Michigan, where he had an idyllic childhood, wandering in the woods, shooting and fishing. His parents were divorced when he was about twelve years old, however, and he was brought up by his mother and a stepfather whose surname he took. His mother's second husband had a tough time earning money in the Depression but Heston admired him for keeping going and devoting himself to the family. They settled down in Wilmette, Illinois, where Heston attended New Trier High School. From there he got a part-scholarship to Northwestern University drama school, working at various jobs, including lift operator, to pay his way. Heston was a shy youth and something of a loner and acting helped him to come out of himself. He did military service with the 11th Air force, ultimately as a staff sergeant. Before going off to serve in the Alaskan Aleutian Islands, Heston married a budding actress, Lydia Clarke. At first, when Heston went to Hollywood, Lydia continued on Broadway and they led a 'bi-coastal life', but eventually she gave up her career to devote herself to the family of a boy and a girl. There were frustrations but they lived happily together until Heston's death in 2008.

At the outset, they lived in Manhattan and did the rounds of producers and agents seeking work. Both did odd jobs to survive, including modelling, but fairly quickly got stage roles. Heston did some live television and was noticed by the then independent producer Hal B. Wallis. Wallis gave him a flexible contract that allowed him to continue with theatre and television as well as to make films, an arrangement unheard of at the time.[204] Heston's first film, *Dark City* (1950), was an unusual film *noir* cum musical with Lizabeth Scott, by then a well-established actress. Heston hit Hollywood at the right time because the studios were beginning to abandon 'B' pictures and were introducing new technologies (Cinemascope and Vistavision) to make big films to compete with television. Cecil B. DeMille then cast him in the lead role of circus manager in *The Greatest Show on Earth* (1952). In this film Heston is injured in a spectacular train crash, as dangerous animals make their escape. While waiting for medical assistance, he bravely continues issuing instructions to his colleagues.[205] Heston made many more films and then DeMille cast him as Moses in *The Ten Commandments* (1956). This film, a Vistavision epic, which won an Oscar for Best Picture, was an

---

204 Hal Wallis (1898–1986) was a successful producer who made many box office winners, including Casablanca (1942), and discovered a surprisingly large number of stars, including Kirk Douglas, Burt Lancaster, Shirley MacLaine, Errol Flynn, Lizabeth Scott and even Elvis Presley (see his autobiography of 1980).

205 Among the many entertaining anecdotes in Heston's autobiography is the story of his driving into the studio in an open car and waving to DeMille, who liked the wave and called him in for an interview, and that was how he got the part that made him a star. Another is that a man wrote into the studio to say that the cast of The Greatest Show on Earth, which included Heston as the circus manager, Cornel Wilde as an acrobat and James Stewart as a clown, were wonderful, but expressed amazement 'at how well the circus manager did in there with the real actors'.

ideal showcase for Heston with his commanding presence, craggy face and stentorian voice, and made him an international superstar.

William Wyler's remake of *Ben-Hur* (1959), with its famous chariot race, consolidated Heston's stardom and gave him opportunities to throw a javelin, row in a slave galley, swim and ride. He subsequently appeared in several more historical epics, for example, *El Cid* (1961), *The War Lord* (1965), *The Greatest Story Ever Told* (1965), *The Agony and the Ecstasy* (1965; as Michelangelo) and *Khartoum* (1966; as General Gordon – in which he ends with his head on a stick). Heston's major pictures, however, were now tending towards modern settings and more variety. He made the excellent Western, *The Big Country* (1958), appeared as a Mexican police officer in Orson Welles' *Touch of Evil* (1958), and in a film set in the future, *Beneath the Planet of the Apes* (1969).

With all this activity he could afford to do a couple of films of Shakespeare's plays, which had long been his ambition (both, unfortunately, were commercial flops). Then came some disaster films, including *Airport 75* (1974), two naval pictures and much else right up to his retirement from public life in 2003. Some of these films made a lot of money and were enough to keep him in demand. Neither of the roles which Heston thought his best –*Khartoum* and *Will Penny* (1968) – were commercially successful, a fairly common situation in the struggles between actors and their bosses, the studio heads. Yet Heston's acting ability was limited, despite his portrayals of epic figures and his popularity owed more to his handsome face, body and voice than his ability to portray emotion in close-up.[206] This assessment would not have

---

206 Although he was, of course, playing a dedicated soldier, a good role for him, his early scenes with Ava Gardner in 55 Days at Peking (1963) are quite embarrassing and unconvincing. For an extended discussion of Heston's acting skills,

pleased him: he was very serious about acting and meticulous in researching for the roles he played; both his first and second autobiographies devote space to the craft of acting.

In politics, Heston's influence emerged over an extended period: at first he doubted that actors should become involved in politics at all. From 1961, when he became a superstar, he realised, we must suppose, that his fame gave him real potential influence over events and he was keen to exercise it. He was one of the first Hollywood actors to march in favour of civil rights for blacks and he supported the Democratic Presidential candidates (at first, not on the hustings, but later very actively). He was in favour of the Vietnam War and the Johnson and Nixon administrations and was appointed to the National Council on the Arts.[207] In 1965 he was elected President of SAG and remained in that post until 1971, helping SAG to return to the values earlier promoted by Ronald Reagan, whose campaigns for the national Presidency he also later supported. As the Democrats moved leftwards, he spoke out against affirmative action (quotas for racial minorities, for example) and against the 'political correctness' engendered by multiculturalism, though he did not formally become a Republican until 1987. In 1995 he formed a Political Action Committee (PAC) named ARENA to further his activism.[208]

Supporting the National Rifle Association, which was sloughing off its 'red-neck' reputation, Heston was elected President of the organisation in 1998 and used this national

---

and an interesting comparison with Gregory Peck, see R. Barton Palmer (2010).

207 Heston was anti-Communist, though he didn't make a big thing about it. It is interesting that, like Frank Sinatra and many others, he attended the famous lunch in Hollywood for Nikita Khrushchev in 1959, while Ronald Reagan pointedly declined the invitation.

208 PACs are private groups formed to raise money for election candidates. Corporations and unions are not permitted to contribute directly and the amounts which individuals may subscribe are limited. Governed by state and federal law, PACs are supervised by the Federal Election Commission.

platform to promote his cultural values, linking gun ownership to freedom and constitutional rights. His vigorous campaigning over freedom to possess arms attracted some ridicule in the press and certainly lost him some friends in Hollywood, but he persisted. In May 2000, he made a speech in which he held up a Revolutionary War musket and paraphrased the NRA slogan: 'I'll give up my gun when you take it from my cold dead hands', a phrase which gives the title to Raymond's (2006) thoughtful analysis of Heston's career and political evolution.

Heston was a hugely successful actor, partly because of the roles he played. There is a Hollywood joke that runs 'If God came to Earth he would not be believed unless he looked like Charlton Heston'. Both Heston and his wife Lydia had strong religious convictions but had to stop going to church when the living presence of Moses in the congregation caused a commotion. He said, 'I have played three presidents, three saints and two geniuses. If that doesn't create an ego problem, nothing does.' Raymond argues that Heston played a major part in the resurgence of conservatism (the neo-cons) in the 1970s that was to presage the Reagan revolution of the following decade. In this, paradoxically, he was not intellectualising things so much as promoting 'the cultural values that he personified in his movies: responsibility, individualism and conservative masculinity . . . The ultimate message in Heston's political activities was that Americans actually could live the ideals that he embodied in his films' (Raymond, 2006). The continuing success of actors in the political arena suggests that the American public relish Heston's view of their potential, however short of it reality may be.

CHAPTER **12**

Sterling Hayden: The Wandering Star

STERLING HAYDEN WAS a tall, gangling, powerful man with a resonant voice. Thomson (2002) describes him as 'a man with placid strength' and 'as calm as a Melville sailor who had seen great sights and was puzzled by the need to talk of them'. At the outset of his movie career he was promoted by Paramount as 'a blond young Viking god . . . the greatest find since Gable'. He was 6ft 5 inches in height and weighed 204 lbs at that time. He had a long, permanent scar on his left cheek, caused by a flying stranded wire on board ship; he also had a broken front tooth from a falling pulley block, but that was presumably soon rectified by the famous Hollywood dentists. The imperfection of the scar was still clearly visible in close-ups many years later, for example in *Dr Strangelove* (1963) and served to emphasise his appearance of toughness.

His taciturnity later found release in two long books of great quality: *Wanderer* (1963), his transparently honest autobiography, and *Voyage: A Novel of 1896* (1976), an historical novel. Hayden's restless three score and ten years included experiences as dramatic as any in his screen roles. He was to make some sixty-five films between 1941 and 1982 and was a big star in the 1940s and 1950s. And yet he had only distain for his movie career, and pursued it sporadically, mainly to raise money for his real love, which was sailing ships and the sea. Towards the end he descended into alcoholism and took on mostly cameo roles *(The Godfather, 1972)* for which his voice and imposing presence proved invaluable.

Sterling Hayden as the deranged general in *Dr Strangelove* (1963): Finler/Columbia.

Hayden is best remembered by critics for his roles in three films: *The Asphalt Jungle* (1950), *The Killing* (1956) and *Dr Strangelove, or, How I Learned to Stop Worrying and Love the*

STERLING HAYDEN: THE WANDERING STAR

Bomb (1963). *Asphalt Jungle,* directed by John Huston, was Hayden's first chance to work with a director who really appreciated his talent. In the film he plays Dix Handley, a hoodlum who joins a team engaged in a robbery cleverly planned by Sam Jaffe as an elderly criminal just out of jail. In the film, Jaffe says of Hayden's character: 'He impressed me as a very determined man and far from stupid.' A heist movie which provided inspiration for many others, the film also provided the first decent role for Marilyn Monroe and a superb part for her sugar-daddy, played by Louis Calhern, with whom Hayden got joint top-billing. In the film, Hayden is big, loose and confident, but things go wrong (as they always did in those days when the Code required it to be demonstrated that crime does not pay). He is the strong man that knocks out an armed night-watchman and carries a wounded safe-cracker to safety. Later, again saving the situation, Hayden has a shoot-out with double-crossing Calhern's wicked collaborator, but is wounded. The gunshot wound does not stop Hayden but he is losing blood and with his loyal girlfriend makes an overnight drive to his late father's farm in Virginia, only to die in a wrenching scene in the farm paddock, nuzzled by grazing colts. Hayden was ideal for this part, his personal favourite, which he played with strength and sensitivity, belying the judgement in the film of the police-chief in charge of the case that his character was an 'inhuman killer'. The film is gripping, not so much because of the action but because of the interplay between the vivid characters involved.

When Hayden was screen-tested for the part, Huston got him to play the scene in which he tells his girlfriend about his dreams of buying the farm back and how he once broke in a colt there and it was the only time his father was proud of him. Hayden (1963) quotes Huston's description of the character as follows:

[EXT]
Dix is a loner who hails from a Southern farm. Dix is you and me and every other man who can't fit into the groove. Some of us are lucky but Dix has never been. He is angry and doesn't know how to control it. So he does the only thing a man with his limitations can do – he becomes a hood . . .
[EXT ends]

After the test, Huston said 'The next time anyone says you can't act, tell them to call Huston'. In fact, Hayden could act, as he was to show again in *The Killing* six years later. Until then the parts he was getting gave him little opportunity. In *The Killing*, a racetrack robbery directed by Stanley Kubrick, another director who could not fit into the groove but who appreciated Hayden's talent. It was Kubrick who was to give him the role in *Dr Strangelove* another seven years on. Hayden got top-billing in *The Killing*. He played an ex-con who masterminds the robbery and recruits a team of wonderful characters to carry it out. The team includes an ex-wrestler whose job it is to create a diversion – that superb fall-guy of the 1940s and 1950s, Elisha Cook, Jr (the hood repeatedly disarmed by Humphrey Bogart in *The Maltese Falcon* (1941), who played 'Stonewall' Torrey who falls to gunfighter Jack Palance in *Shane* (1953). Despite meticulous planning and action (described in documentary fashion and voice-over by Hayden), the robbery itself goes well but things go wrong afterwards. At the end, Hayden gets to the airport and checks in only to see the bag containing his share of the loot fall off a trolley and get blown away in an aircraft jetstream.

There was universal praise for Hayden's portrayal of an over-zealous and paranoid air base commander, Brigadier General Jack D. Ripper, in the black comedy *Dr Strangelove*, in which Hayden is not at all outshone in his scenes by a very funny Peter Sellers. Hayden's role is essentially a cameo but is central to the film. The General rambles on confidentially in a cool low voice about a communist plot to sap 'our precious bodily fluids' and 'poison our water'. Their talk is interrupted by the sound of gunfire as the National Guard attempt to storm the base to stop him launching the bomb. With relish, the General says 'Looks like we're in a shooting war here'. Hayden plays his role with energy and skill and not without effort; apparently Kubrick made forty-eight takes of one scene because he wanted Hayden to exhibit a desperate look, which of course, he finally did. Monush (2003) says this was the greatest role of Hayden's career, but I disagree: his two earlier celebrated roles show more depth and subtlety than his portrayal of the General in *Dr Strangelove*, hilarious though that is. What *Dr Strangelove* did was to demonstrate Hayden's versatility – though sadly, as with his other peak performances, this did not lead to directors queuing up with good roles for him.

Very successful in France, though not in the USA, was Nicholas Ray's *Johnny Guitar* (1953), in which Hayden played the title role of a laconic gunfighter who loves the persecuted heroine (Joan Crawford). This has become a cult movie, though Hayden later said he had no idea what it was about, a sentiment I share. The film breaks some of the conventions of the Western and is notable for a gunfight between two female protagonists. It has an excellent supporting cast (Mercedes McCambridge, Ward Bond, Ernest Borgnine and Scott Brady) and Hayden copes well with all the ambiguity. In 1954 the film *Suddenly* was released, in which Hayden plays a contemporary sheriff who stands up to a psychopathic presidential assassin, brilliantly played by Frank Sinatra. *The Last Command* (1955) had Hayden as Jim Bowie at the Battle of the Alamo, an example of quite lavish production values (for this studio – Republic) but in which embarrassingly poor dialogue ties the actors down to mere cardboard cut-outs. Hayden himself picked out *Denver and Rio Grande* (1952) as the trough of his earlier movie roles. In this film, unusually, he plays an unsympathetic villain but he fares no worse than a spectacularly miscast one-time Shakespearean actor, Edmund O'Brien, as his adversary, a two-fisted railroad engineer – a truly awful movie.

Some of Hayden's less pretentious westerns, such as *Kansas Pacific* (1953) and *Terror in a Texas Town* (1958), were good entertainment. In the latter, Hayden plays a Scandinavian whaler (complete with accent) coming home to find that his father has been murdered. The unique show-down has the villain-gunman speared by the hero's harpoon. The overwhelming majority of Hayden's movies were land-based – he was never typecast as a sea captain or in pirate roles into which non-sailor actors like Paul Henreid (see Chapter 4) were shoe-horned.

Hayden was to further exhibit his versatility and what he termed his 'malleability', in his later cameo roles. He was the nasty police chief who is shot dead in The Godfather (1972). In The Long Goodbye (1973) he was an alcoholic suicidal writer-husband who gets bullied by a tiny doctor who is ineffectually treating his drink problem and writer's block. This overrated film marked the end of Hayden's career in major feature films – though his very last, Venom, a horror film which apparently was so bad that Hayden walked out before it was finished, did not appear until 1982. Hayden said of his movie career, 'I started at the top and worked my way down' (quoted by Halliwell, 2001).

Sterling Hayden was born as Montaigu Relyea Walter at Upper Montclair, New Jersey, in 1916. His father was also tall (6ft 3 ins) but thin and in poor health (and he died when Sterling was nine). In his autobiography, Hayden said that what he wanted was a father like his Uncle Mont Sterling, who boxed and taught revolver-shooting to the State police in New York. Sterling did badly at school and was finally expelled. Three years after his father's death, his future stepfather, James Watson Hayden, was to come into his life. Daddy Jim, who later adopted the boy, was an unsuccessful businessman, possibly a conman. He was always waiting for the next big deal to come off and the family moved from lodging to lodging, often leaving at dawn or at night to avoid paying. Daddy Jim even appropriated the boy's trust fund endowed by his Uncle Mont. For a while they lived on an island at Boothbay in Maine.

Sterling Hayden, an early picture, probably in the gym at Paramount: Finler/Paramount.

◄ HOLLYWOOD LIVES

It was there, at the age of twelve, that Hayden took to books and to the sea: 'both were distilled of silence and solitude', he wrote in *Wanderer*. Sterling spent most of his time alone, in a sail loft with a sail-maker friend and in the local library. At seventeen he ran away and got a job as ship's boy on a schooner, then another, trawling by dory on the Grand Banks off Newfoundland. After further experience, in 1936 he was given the job of first mate on a trip around the world with a paying crew under Captain Irving Johnson. The sailing ship was based in Gloucester where his parents then lived. The Captain and his wife were to write a book about this trip, which includes photographs of Hayden, then twenty, with a giant tortoise, curled up in a bunk too small for him and hauling on ropes (Johnson,1939). In his book, Johnson says that Hayden was a 'natural sailor'. In 1938, after a tall ship race, Hayden was photographed and an article appeared in the *Boston Post* under the headline 'SAILOR LIKE MOVIE IDOL', a prediction which was soon to come true.[209]

After more sea adventures, including his first command of a ship bound for Tahiti and an ill-fated expedition to Panama to buy the German Kaiser's yacht, Hayden, then twenty-four, was persuaded by a shipmate to see an agent in New York. After a few weeks he was given a screen test and soon offered a contract with Paramount, starting at $250 a week. He set up in Hollywood with his mother, who had now been abandoned by Daddy Jim. His first role was opposite Madeleine Carroll (who in 1935 had appeared in Hitchcock's *The Thirty-Nine Steps*, a very successful film that was to bring the director himself to Hollywood). The film, *Virginia* (1940), was a Technicolor post-Civil War melodrama with Fred MacMurray.

---

209 This account of Hayden's early days is based mainly on his autobiography, but that book is not easily mined for dates and dating events becomes even more difficult later. No biography of Hayden has ever been written.

◄ 262

It was not a resounding success, though Hayden was favourably noticed and he appeared in a second film with Carroll, *Bahama Passage* (1941). They had fallen in love but Carroll was involved with another man, a handsome bomber ferry pilot, and Hayden feared he would lose her. To impress her (so he said, but it might have been his old restlessness) he joined the forces himself.

Madeleine Carroll with Gary Cooper in *Northwest Mounted Police* (1940): Finler/Paramount.

The studio, in order to tie him in, had bought Hayden a boat he wanted, but nevertheless he walked away from filmmaking to go to war, first into the Office of the Coordinator of Information (COI), which involved commando training in England.[210] He did marry Carroll, who also went away on war

---
210 Despite its innocuous name, the COI and its successor, the OSS, were cloak-and-dagger organisations similar to the SOE in Britain. The head of both was

service, but they were to be divorced in 1946. Hayden went briefly back to sea after having been rejected for a commission in the Navy. He then joined the Marine Corps, which he did not like, so he wangled himself back into the COI, later the Office of Strategic Services (OSS), part of which in 1945 was to evolve into the CIA. With them he had an exciting time in behind-the-lines activities in the Mediterranean, including running guns for Yugoslav partisans under Marshal Tito. After this he was sent to Europe in a non-combatant role. He was awarded a Silver Star and received a personal citation from Tito. His military service was done under the name of 'John Hamilton' to distance himself from his film career.[211]

Back in Hollywood he was given roles in a number of forgettable movies until The Asphalt Jungle came along, and after that in more mediocre films. Meanwhile he had married again, in 1947, to Betty-Ann de Noon, who Robinson (2003) says he met on Laguna Beach. In the early 1950s Hayden fell foul of the House Un-American Activities Committee (HUAC, see below). He and his second wife were to have four children

---

Major General 'Wild Bill' Donovan (1883–1959). Donovan was a much-decorated combat hero in the First World War, a lawyer by trade who encouraged his loosely administered organisations to recruit unconventional persons of great ability, a profile which of course fitted Hayden well. Donovan had quite a good relationship with the President, FDR, but earned the enmity of General Douglas MacArthur, Edgar Hoover, the first head of the FBI, and Harry Truman. It was Truman who closed the OSS down immediately after the end of the Second World War. The CIA, its successor, was designed in line with Donovan's own proposals but he did not get the job of the first director (Waller, 2011).

211 It may be that Madeleine Carroll (1906–87) married Hayden, the second of her four husbands and ten years younger than herself, under the name Hamilton that he adopted in the armed forces. The OSS records have him down as Captain John F. Hamilton. According to Chamberlain (2010), Carroll's biographer, Hayden had admirable leadership qualities. In any case, Carroll joined the military Red Cross in 1939 when she left Hollywood and worked in field hospitals in Italy, France and Germany. Although her marriage to Hayden lasted for three and a half years, they lived together for only some four months. Born in England of an Irish father and a French mother, Carroll was decorated by General de Gaulle personally. Her last film was The Fan (1949), based on the Oscar Wilde play and starring George Sanders. Carroll died in Marbella, Spain.

and were divorced and married three times to each other, culminating in a bitter custody battle. It was during this dispute that Hayden defied a court order in 1959 and went off with the children on a voyage to Tahiti that was to provide the narrative frame for Wanderer. He did not remain unmarried for long and in 1960 he wed his third wife, Catherine McConnell (Kitty), a marriage which lasted until his death in 1986. It was in this period that he wrote his two books, experimented with drugs (marijuana) and slipped deeper into the alcoholism which may have fuelled his writing. Despite feeling it was unfair to Kitty, who liked a settled life, Hayden none the less spent part of the year in Europe on a barge, sometimes tied up on the Seine in Paris, where, he said, 'his romantic heart lay'. His wife had a house in Wilton, Connecticut, and he spent time there and also in a small apartment in Sausalito, California. In an interview with Gerald Perry (1984), he said 'The function of Gloucester in my youth has been supplanted by my place in Sausalito, which to me is the gem in the crown of the United States of America.' Poignantly, he was to die there of prostate cancer only two years later.

Wanderer is very different from most other movie biographies. Not only is it extremely well written but it devotes only a relatively small proportion of its 434 pages to Hayden's Hollywood career. It has no introduction, no index, no acknowledgements or photographs, except for an unflattering one on the dust-jacket (the later paperback edition of 1977 has a slightly better picture of the bearded author and does have an introduction. The book is divided into six sections and ninety-three short chapters and is interspersed with flashbacks and flash-forwards from the opening which has the author leaving on his 1959 voyage to the South Seas with his children. Hayden, always lucky, got away with breaching the court order, as he did much later when he was arrested for carrying drugs. In the latter case, the judge said, 'this is unusual but Hayden is an unusual man'. The non-linear structure and the colourful descriptions give the book a cinematic quality: it is varied and exciting enough to make a good movie. Here are some scenes from the book which the reader can easily imagine on the screen.

* * *

A flat broke Hayden is trapped with his ship in Tahiti and four armed gendarmes in white helmets and putties climb aboard, led by a plain-clothes security officer who shows him a note. Hayden fears this is the end and that he faces extradition for defying the court order, but it is only an instruction to the police to confiscate his credit card because he is delinquent' in the amount of $189.15. He happily complies.

* * *

In a flashback to his earlier, 1936, voyage with Captain Johnson among the islands north and west of Tahiti when he was twenty-three, Hayden sees moving toward him a schooner with about twenty beautiful girls arrayed around it on deck and in the rigging. Standing on the end of the bowsprit is a 'ravishing creature' in a bathing suit, her long hair moving in the wind. Truth being stranger than fiction, the girl turns out to be the daughter of the American Consul in Papeete, French Polynesia. They fall in love, both for the first time, and become engaged but Hayden's mother and uncle talked him out of it.

* * *

As a teenager at Boothbay in Maine, Hayden admires the local librarian, Esther. He describes her as beautiful with a lithe body but modest dress – low-heeled shoes and sweaters not too tight, delicate ears, thin ankles, soft and sweet, 'the kind of beauty a man would want in his wife'. He dreams of taking her off on a schooner but apparently says nothing because he is worried about the three-year difference in their ages. One night, wandering around the waterfront, Hayden sees through a lighted window a bald-headed man, whom he recognises as the cook at a local tavern, and the back of a woman.

[EXT]
I remembered having seen him before – he was cook at the Tinker Tavern. He got to his feet and dropped his pants as a girl stepped into his arms. She had nothing on and her hair flowed half round her face; I knew it was Esther even before he pushed her hair to one side. He stroked her back and she turned towards me , but only to get the drink. I shrank inside myself with one shoulder up as a shield, and the window was plunged into black. (Hayden, 1963)
[EXT ends]

This was a traumatic experience for Hayden, one he described in his autobiography, and used again about sixty years later in his novel, transmuting the experience that time to a voyeuristic ships' carpenter.

A hilarious scene in which Hayden's agent takes him to see a producer about a possible (but secret and unrevealed) role. The producer – who is not named – hedges around the subject for a while. The room is surrounded by pictures of Tarzan and his family and it dawns on Hayden that this is the role in question. He cannot conceal his revulsion and the producer, seeing this, attempts to argue that Tarzan is a free man who stands alone against the forces of evil, things which Hayden would like to stand for. Unconvinced, Hayden bolts for the fresh air and on the way out makes Tarzan noises to the studio cop at the gate. [212]

Hayden is remarkably frank in his autobiography and ruthlessly exposes his self-perceived weaknesses and dilemmas. He also reveals his philosophy of life (or is it a rationalisation of his fecklessness?) that a regular job and the illusion of security stifle a life. In a much-quoted passage, he writes that: 'To be truly challenging, a voyage, like life, must rest on a firm foundation of financial unrest.' In 1956 and 1957 he was earning an average of $160,000 a year, but he never invested his money 'because I don't believe in unearned income'. Despite his rejection of career and commitment, however, he still did not feel fully in control of himself and told his analyst: 'To survive, a man has to get his kicks some way, in his personal or his professional life. He can get along with one or the other, and damn few have both. Every last man

---

212 The producer was Sol Lesser (1890–1980), who took over the rights to Edgar Rice Burroughs' Tarzan stories from MGM. At the time of Hayden's story, Johnny Weissmuller (1904–84) had been playing the role since 1932 and was then about forty-three years old – twelve years older than Hayden. It is not well known that Weissmuller wrote a book about swimming, with some personal recollections (1930), though it was not an autobiography as such. Lesser had taken the series to RKO and from 1948 it was Lex Barker who took over the Tarzan role in place of Weissmuller. Weissmuller, who had been an Olympic Gold Medallist swimmer in the 1920s, went on to play a new role as Jungle Jim for Columbia, a role in which he could keep his shirt on (Weissmuller, 2002, a book by his son).

STERLING HAYDEN: THE WANDERING STAR

I know has one or the other. But not me. I'm all fouled up on both fronts' (Hayden, 1963). From childhood, Hayden felt there was something wrong inside him, despite his outward appearance of strength and resolution. He admits to feelings of fear during his war service (but don't all intelligent, courageous, men feel fear?). He seems to have been happy mostly when at sea, hating Hollywood and acting despite his admitted facility for 'saying other people's words'.

Hayden returned from the war with some admiration for Communism, as communicated to him by the Yugoslav partisans he fought alongside, men who, he said, when they saw social wrongs were willing to do something about it. He was recruited to join the Party by a girl from the studio and attended a meeting which seems to have bored him to tears. As an individualist he was not, of course, at all suitable material for the Party, though they did not initially detect this. Hayden soon drifted away, but later when the Communist witch-hunt was underway, he became fearful and approached the FBI for clearance in return for spilling the beans. This, having listened to him, they were not willing to do and he was subpoenaed to appear in 1951 before the HUAC (see Chapter 10). At the hearing, he named fellow members, all already known to the Committee, and thus qualified as 'a friendly witness'. His testimony allowed him to continue working and to avoid being blacklisted. The studio approved of his actions and he received a cable from Ronald Reagan praising him for his patriotism. However, his testimony, which was televised on CBS, was reviled by many and in his autobiography he expressed guilt and regret for what he had done. He explained that his cooperation was not out of patriotism but simply out of weakness. He was told, apparently by Hoover himself, that if he did not cooperate he would never get custody of his children. He also says that his analyst told him to testify – and of course he did not want to go to jail. Subsequently, he retracted his testimony publicly and became active in opposing the HUAC.

༄༄༄

Voyage, A Novel of 1896 (1976), Hayden's 250,000-word, 700-page, second book, took him many years to write, some of it in a rented tugboat and much of it in an 1896 Pullman railcar which he bought and located in Sausalito. Like *Wanderer*, the novel is set within the frame of a sea voyage, this time in a newly launched steel-hulled, four-masted square-rigger, *Neptune's Car*. The voyage is from Freeport, Maine, to San Francisco, around Cape Horn. The ship has a tough master, Captain Pendleton, an often desperate, partly shanghaied crew and a cargo of coal which begins to self-ignite in the hold. *Neptune* also has a brutal first mate, Otto Lassiter, and a murder to add to the tension. For contrast the reader sees things in the eyes of MacLeod, a Scottish intellectual who is travelling as the only passenger. The story is a paean to the age of the sailing ship and an indictment of the inhuman treatment of crews. Hayden's descriptions of the rough men who sailed in these ships hold nothing back: they expectorate, fart and vomit; lance boils with knives and treat wounds with tar; they fight and contemplate mutiny. The Captain is a match for them, however, and can outbox even the first mate. Here is one of Hayden's descriptions of Lassiter:

> [EXT]
> Otto Lassiter, huge in double banked oilskins, lurched into the messroom and scaled his Cape Horn derby at a peg on the forward bulkhead. Peeling off three layers of clothing, he kicked a stool to the bogey stove and spread

his hands to its belly. Sea cuts, deep and bloodless, scored either margin of the thick callous pads inside his fingers. His beard was an unkempt mat dusted with particles of salt that shone like coral sand. The balls of his eyes were smeared with red, and their pupils glowed like pine knots as he swung around, roaring "Steward! Where in hell's name's my cafay nore, ya hump?"
[EXT ends]

Parallel with the story of the *Neptune* is an account of the ship-owner's daughter and her effete husband. The couple make a voyage in a luxurious yacht to Japan, across to Hawaii and returning to San Francisco at the same time as *Neptune*. Also there is the story of the ship-owner himself, Blanchard, and his feelings about the election of the populist William Jennings Bryan as Democratic presidential nominee. In the presidential election, Bryan loses out to the Republican, William McKinley, an advocate for the Gold Standard.

This ambitious and powerful novel is therefore really the story of the haves and the have-nots, though both Captain Pendleton and Blanchard are portrayed sympathetically. Finally, in the story, there is a vampish rich girl, Lois, a friend and fellow passenger in the yacht of Cynthia, the ship-owner's daughter. Lois, who later exhibits sympathy for the *Neptune*'s crew, rebels against her family and stays on in Hawaii where she seduces Cynthia's husband. One of the characters, Harwar, an experienced and ageing mariner who signs on to dry out from his alcoholism, is clearly modelled in some respects on the author himself:

[EXT]
With the passage of the years, more and more and more,

he sensed he was losing his mind. Maybe it was lost already. Come to think of it, maybe he never had a mind – the kind, that is, that men were supposed to have. Hell, of course he had a mind. A good mind. Maybe too good. Maybe that was where the trouble lay: What was good enough for most men fell far short of satisfying Simon Basil Harwar. In any event he had never been able to harness himself or cause himself to function as most men did. The best he could do was to work in spurts. Short, sharp, bursting spurts sending him higher than anyone around him. What they used to call a ninety-day wonder. But now that he was no longer young he was beginning to come adrift inside. Enough to frighten any man. Let alone a coward. To say nothing of the King of All the Cowards, which he was – he thought.

[EXT ends]

The most important sources of Hayden's rich, exciting prose (the book is definitely a page-turner) cannot be known, but he was an avid reader from his childhood in Maine. In his autobiography, Hayden says that he carried 500 books with him on board his ships, lovingly collected over twenty-five years, including Melville. Conrad, London and Stevenson. Elsewhere he also mentions Richard Dana, author of *Two Years Before the Mast* (1840), and refers to other classics of poetry and politics (for example Emerson and Thomas Paine). The main source of his inspiration, however, is plainly his own varied life. (All extracts from *Voyage* (1976) reprinted by permission of SLL/Sterling Lord Literistic, Inc. Copyright by Sterling Hayden).

STERLING HAYDEN: THE WANDERING STAR

Sterling Hayden achieved distinction at sea, as a film actor and as a writer. Uniquely among movie stars, his greatest achievement was in writing and his autobiography is, from a literary point of view, the best of all those reviewed in this book. Both his books were bestsellers and still remain in print to this day.

Conclusion

MOVIE AUDIENCES TODAY – on reading about the past – might be forgiven for thinking that nothing much has changed since the 1940s. DVDs of the latest films often still begin with MGM's roaring lion, the Paramount mountain, Universal's revolving globe, Warner's shield and the other familiar logos. The sheer passage of time has naturally prevented the continued appearance of the movie stars of the classical age themselves but they have been replaced by younger generations, such as Robert De Niro and Nicole Kidman. Some of these contemporary stars are even related to those of the Golden Age – Jeff Bridges, George Clooney and Michael Douglas, for example.

In reality, there have been some fundamental changes. The big corporations that now own those famous logos make only a few pictures on their own account, instead they part-finance and distribute the productions of a shifting population of independents, often short-lived companies formed just to make one film. The classical studios, which owned chains of cinemas and were fully integrated with production companies, had arrays of stars on long-term contracts and made hundreds of films a year. In the New Hollywood, the big companies, now shorn of their theatres, rent out their sound stages or have sold them to others. The studio system was beginning to break down in the 1940s and had largely gone by the 1960s. The familiar brands, as mentioned, continue, but are now part of large media conglomerates created by diversification and acquisition. Some of these conglomerates are not even US-owned: Vivendi-Universal (France); Sony Corporation which owns Columbia-Tristar (Japan); and News Corporation (20th Century-Fox) (Australia). MGM now incorporates United Artists but it is weighed down with debt and has an uncertain future. The Walt Disney Company (the only one to have survived as a discrete entity under its original name) and Viacom, which owns Paramount, are the only two of the original studios which, with AOL Time-Warner, remain in American ownership (Scott, 2005).[213]

There were multiple causes of these changes: social and economic developments, including some overseas, changing tastes, the arrival of competition from television, the enforced divestiture of the theatre chains through anti-trust suits, the demise of the founder moguls and other factors. Which of these forces were decisive is far from clear but together they swept away the classical studio system for ever.

Certainly, one trigger for change was a sudden decline in cinema admissions in the US which fell continuously from 1946 to a low point of 0.8 billion in 1972 when a gentle recovery began. This decline cannot be blamed entirely on television – as few as 10 per cent of households owned TV sets in 1950 – and movie audiences had been declining for years. TV ownership did grow explosively to 34 per cent of

---

213 Disney has ploughed its own distinct furrow and now has, in addition to film studios, theme parks, media networks, including television, and makes toys and clothing. It is actually the largest of the media companies with a turnover of $40 billion.

US households by 1952, 65 per cent in 1955 and 90 per cent by 1962. Instead, commentators have pointed to the growth in real incomes and the post-war population boom which boosted urbanisation and suburbanisation, distancing audiences from first-run cinemas and creating and spurring the growth of new leisure activities. Many also believe that unfavourable publicity from the Communist witch- hunt turned people away from Hollywood. The McCarthy era did not really get underway until the late 1940s (see Chapter 10) but the unfavourable publicity which preceded it and controversy over censorship could have helped to reinforce the existing trend.

There were also striking demographic changes: between 1946 and 1950 numbers in the under-five age group grew by 57 per cent, the five to fourteen age group grew by 64 per cent while the next two age groups were static. As audiences declined, the proportion of younger people increased, with changes in film content to accommodate this (Sedgwick and Pokorny, 2005). These changes may have alienated older people, though Hollywood and the then ageing moguls were slow to react in terms of the types of films made. It took time for the effects of the demographic changes to work through and today it is very obvious that most films are aimed at younger people, with plenty of the violence and explicit sex which seem to appeal most to the young. The contrast between the types of films made before 1950 and now becomes obvious when the numerous remakes are considered and the latest versions are compared with the originals. Another factor in the demise of the studio system – and coming on top of the decline in domestic audiences – was that foreign countries, especially Britain, introduced measures to restrict the repatriation of film revenues and quotas to encourage local production. This process started immediately after the war end and encouraged location shooting abroad rather than in the home studio.

The ending of the studio system, therefore, was underway well before the anti-trust authorities enforced the separation of the studio theatre circuits. The threat of this anti-trust action had begun in earnest in 1938 when the five major studios 'were charged with combining and conspiring to restrain trade unreasonably and to monopolise the production, distribution and exhibition of motion pictures' (Michael Conant, 'The Paramount Case and its Legal Background' in Mast, 1982). The three minor studios, Columbia, Universal and United Artists, were joined in this action and charged with combining with the big five to restrain trade unreasonably and to monopolise commerce in motion pictures. Specific practices that were targeted included fixing minimum admission prices and block-booking and discrimination in favour of studio owned theatres. The independent exhibitors who brought the so-called Paramount case wanted the five majors to divest their theatres and to be given relief from the various restrictions on trade. (Conant in Mast, 1982). The outcome of the 1940 trials was a consent decree, affecting the major studios only and which prohibited blind selling, curtailed block-booking to five pictures and set up a system of arbitration tribunals to settle disputes. Under this decree, the court did not press for the divorcement of theatres but banned the majors from acquiring more of them. Neither side was content with this result and the case was reopened in 1944, resulting in 1946 in a further decree which prohibited fixing admission prices in the licenses to exhibit films and provided for a right to reject 20 per cent of the films subject to block-booking. Consideration of divestment was deferred but in 1948 the

CONCLUSION

Supreme Court on appeal finally did order the divorcement of theatres by the majors which then took place in the period up to the mid 1950s.

The studios had managed to hang on to their theatres for over twenty years after the threat of enforced divestiture was first raised. As mentioned in Chapter 1, in the mid 1940s the five majors had an interest in only 3,000 of the 18,000 cinemas in the country, but these – the best of the first-run theatres – accounted for about 70 per cent of domestic film rentals. The main result of the measures taken in the Paramount Case was a large increase in the number of independent producers as the big five laid off the enormously increased risk of producing movies without guaranteed outlets for them. Until then, more than half of pictures made failed to earn sufficient rentals to cover their production and marketing costs but the studios had been able to more than recoup this by revenue from the remaining films. It had been mainly the low-budget films which had failed and another important result of the case was continuing increases in film budgets as the studios concentrated on 'blockbusters' for which the inevitable failures were usually compensated for by a few runaway successes. The number of independent exhibitors declined as they were bought up by the big corporations that had acquired theatres from the studios.

In the 'New Hollywood' which emerged from the mid 1950s, the old studios became financiers of the independent producers and distributors for their products and the number of films they made themselves declined sharply. According to Sedgwick and Pokorny (2005), the ratio of the number of films for which the copyright was owned by the studios fell from 81 per cent in 1946–50 to 27 per cent in 1961–5. From 1953, encouraged by tax laws, the efforts of the talent agencies and the legal actions described in Chapter 5, the option contract system was dying and both stars like James Cagney and producer/directors like Hal Wallis increasingly went independent.[214] According to Bordwell et al. (1985), as early as 1946 every major studio except for MGM had some independent projects as part of their regular production schedule (MGM did not follow until 1956). The New Hollywood made films under the 'unit-package system' in which the stars, the distribution, the funding and other elements were assembled by independents and sometimes by the studios, talent agents or other players. The nature of movies also changed, accelerating the trend which started in the 1950s to bigger productions and a movement from 'films of sentiment to films of sensation' (Palmer, 2010), that is a movement from stories of everyday human life and relations to computer-enhanced spectaculars set in imagined worlds. The physical fabric of Hollywood has also changed. Although the region continues to prosper, inner Hollywood has become neglected and tatty, though there are efforts at restoration. The famous Hollywood sign high up on a hill is still there, an icon of the past and a symbol of an uncertain future.[215]

The actor-autobiographers, even when their period of stardom covered these events, do not say much about the process of destruction of the studio system – but they do bemoan the results. Ronald Reagan, in his second autobiography (1990), says 'I believe the government's decision to break up the studio system was wrong.' He explains that with seven studios

---
214 Scott (2005) cites sources showing that the number of professional actors under contract to Hollywood studios fell from 804 in 1945 to only 139 in 1960.
215 Leo Braudy's book (2011) about the Hollywood sign tells us that the uneven group of letters was put up in 1925 to promote a real estate development – Hollywoodland – and refurbished in 1947 and 'land' dropped a few years later. The sign was refurbished again in 1973, when it was declared an historic monument, and again in 1978.

CONCLUSION

it was not a monopoly. The public decided what films to see among competing products, but the ownership of theatres gave stability to the system and allowed studios to take risks, invest in stories and develop stars.[216] He expressed similar views in his first autobiography (1965), but the passage of time between then and his second book (1990) clearly led to a strengthening of his opinions: he widened the causes of the break-up to include the impact of censorship, the Communist witch-hunt and other official interventions which he thought combined to bring the system down, to the detriment of film-making. Reagan also emphasises the irreplaceable role of the individual moguls in building the system.

The Hollywood Sign: Finler.

As recounted in Chapter 1 above, Hollywood was the creation of two generations of moguls, and when they were all gone, a vital impetus left the system. Louis B. Mayer left in 1951, as his bluff offer to resign in a power struggle with

---

[216] Anti-trust interventions are sometimes counterproductive, usually because action is not based on a complete understanding of how industries function, as in the Paramount case. Interventions can be most damaging when made at times of economic change or incipient decline, when various forces are pushing for adjustment anyway, as in Hollywood in the late 1940s.

Nicholas Schenck was called. The youngest of the creator-moguls, Darryl Zanuck, left of his own accord for France to make movies there in 1956 (though he was to return six years later in an attempt to rescue 20th Century-Fox).[217] Custen (1997), in his excellent book about Zanuck, quotes him as saying, with foresight before he left: 'In a very short time, the business will be completely dominated by the stars and their agents' and 'they'll never run my business, because I won't be here'.

None of the autobiographers reviewed in this book seem to think that Hollywood has improved with the end of the studio system, despite that system's acknowledged faults. This could, of course, be partly a reflection of human nature's tendency to glorify 'the old days'. Still, the general tenor of these actors' books is that Hollywood and the movies made there are now very different from how they were in the Golden Age. Mickey Rooney, who, after all, lived and worked through the whole period before and after the break-up, wrote in his second autobiography (1991): 'Nothing makes me angrier these days than to think how far Hollywood has fallen.' The point made in many of the books – and others by directors and observers of the scene – is that the Golden Age was great because the people at the top loved movies and did not want to do anything else but make them. Today, the heads of 'studios are naturally more concerned with finance, marketing and distribution and less with the quality of the films themselves, or in developing new talent. Quality is now left largely to the independents, even though the studios are making their own blockbusters.

217 Zanuck was able to make The Longest Day (1962) his great film about the Normandy landings in 1944. He made the film as an independent producer and it was released through 20th Century-Fox. He was called back and elected President of the company with his son, Richard, in charge of production. He resigned from the company in 1971 but never had any significant ownership of it (Behlmer,1993).

CONCLUSION

Stars are no longer 'manufactured' by the studios but have to make their own way into the business from television, the theatre and other media, perhaps with the help of talent agents. I do not want to get into the question of whether films are worse now than they were in the past; obviously some good films are still being made. Audiences and standards are not the same as in the Golden Age and it is interesting that most of the autobiographers themselves, despite their nostalgia, are reluctant to make comparisons though most of them assert that stars of the quality and stature of the Golden Age no longer exist.

In this book I have been concerned, not only with what light the autobiographies throw upon the Golden Age, but also with the lives that the actors lived and the impact the studio system and the external world had upon them. I believe that the enjoyment of watching older films can only be enhanced by more knowledge of the background against which they were made. The qualitative judgements that I have made on the books themselves are determined as much by the contribution they make to this understanding, and the human condition, as to their literary quality. Some of the autobiographies, are well written and amusing to read but somehow tell us very little about the things we are mainly interested in (what was it really like to be a star in the period, how did the studio system work and what were the moguls and directors like?). The books of some fine actors, that of Joseph Cotton (1987), for example, for all its wonderful anecdotes and good writing, do not meet this standard as well of some of those by the less talented on the screen.[218]

---

[218] In a Foreword, Cotten says that 'Fact, per se, is valuable to the statistician, the research scholar, the detective; but let us be eternally thankful for the clouded memory that diffuses cold fact into colourful form, and the clouded memory that, abetted by time, transforms tears into laughter; and yes, even the clouded memory that often solidifies itself into a crystal ball of invention.'

Some of the books are simply a series of anecdotes – Bob Hope's autobiography (1990) is a case in point – and some, it has to be admitted, are the vacuous ego-trips that show-business autobiographies are often wrongly condemned as being. A few are intolerably long and hard-going (e.g. Gloria Swanson, 1980). The best – and I have identified, among others, those by Brian Aherne, Errol Flynn, Kirk Douglas, Anthony Quinn and Sterling Hayden, as well as those by younger stars such as Robert Vaughn, Robert Wagner and Leslie Caron and Betsy Blair – are of very high quality by our criteria. There is nothing wrong, of course, with books which are just about the actors, their marriages and their films and which are written in anecdotal fashion; fans of these stars will avidly read anything about them. This is an engaging and essential feature of the star system which *was* different in the Golden Age. Robert Wagner's excellent autobiography (2008) recounts in the Prologue how at the age of twelve he was playing by the golf course at the Bel-Air Country Club and saw in the distance a foursome heading towards him. He was to have an 'amazing experience', he wrote. As the group came into focus, he could see that it consisted of Cary Grant, Fred Astaire, Clark Gable and Randolph Scott, 'freshly minted'. People say, according to Wagner, that some movie stars are disappointing when seen in the flesh, but 'not these men. They inhabited life as securely as they inhabited the screen . . . I realised at that moment that I wanted to be in that club; looking back I see that this was when I made up my mind to be in the movies – to be an actor.'

Acknowledgements

OF THOSE WHO helped with this book, Kristen Harrison of www.artypeeps.co.uk is foremost providing both technical assistance and encouragement for some of what eventually proved to be a ten-year period between conception to birth of the book. Others who provided moral support included my fellow economists, Alan Peacock and the late Angus Maddison. My son, Laurent Bannock, provided technical back-up for the author who remains baffled by much of contemporary information technology.

Essentially an excavation of folk memories and fact, the book required extensive research and I gratefully acknowledge my use of the star autobiographies and the other books listed in the bibliographies, as well as the resources of the Internet and especially www.imdb.com .

Excerpts from Sterling Hayden's novel, *Voyage* 1976 are reprinted by permission of SLL/Sterling Lord Literistic, Inc. Copyright by Sterling Hayden.

Halliwell's Video and TV Guide and his *Who's Who in the Movies*, both now edited by John Walker, were invaluable and have been used as the sole authority for release dates for films and for birth and death dates, even though in many cases other authorities differ by a year or two.

The photographs were sourced partly from www.doctormacro.com and I wish to acknowledge the help of Jerry Murbach at Doctor Macro and for his permission to use their images. David Koppel took the photograph at the Night of 200 Stars, 1994, in the Prologue and kindly gave permission to reproduce it in this book. Many photographs come from the Joel Finler collection, London with permission and a few from my own collection. My friend Joel Finler, the film historian, also provided helpful advice. The studios that originated the stills and publicity material used have been credited throughout where known. They include: Columbia-Sony; Twentieth Century-Fox; MGM; Paramount Pictures; RKO Radio; United Artists; Universal Studios and Warner Brothers. Jane Robertson, the copy editor, eliminated many errors, but those remaining are the author's responsibility. Finally, the publication of this book was facilitated admirably by the services of www.outskirtspress.com.

References – General

Bach (1985) Steven Bach, *Final Cut: Dreams and Disaster in the Making of Heaven's Gate*, Jonathan Cape.

Balio (1985) Tino Balio, *The American Film Industry*, University of Wisconsin Press, 1976; revised edition 1985.

Balio (1993) Tino Balio, *Grand Design: Hollywood as a Modern Business Enterprise, 1930–1939*, Charles Scribner's.

Baxter (1976) John Baxter, *The Hollywood Exiles*, Macdonald and Jane's.

Beauchamp (2009) Cari Beauchamp, *Joseph P. Kennedy's Hollywood Years*, Alfred A. Knopf.

Behlmer (1982) Rudy Behlmer, *Behind the Scenes: The Making of . . .*, Frederick Ungar Publishing. New editions 1989 and 1990, the latter published by Samuel French.

Bordwell et al. (1985) David Bordwell, Janet Staiger and Kristin Thompson, *The Classical Hollywood Cinema: Film Style and Mode of Production to 1960*, Routledge.

Braudy (2011) Leo Braudy, *The Hollywood Sign: Fantasy and Reality of an American Icon*, Yale University Press.

Buckley (2008) William F. Buckley Jr, *The Reagan I Knew*, Basic Books.

Capra (1971) Frank Capra, *The Name Above the Title*, Macmillan.

Chamberlain (2010) Derek Chamberlain, *39 Steps to Stardom: The Life and Times of Madeleine Carroll*, Troubadour Publishing.

Collier (1991) Peter Collier, *The Fondas: A Hollywood Dynasty*, G. P. Putnam's Sons.

Connell (1955) Brian Connell, *Knight Errant: A Biography of Douglas Fairbanks, Jr.*, Hodder & Stoughton.

Conrad (1978) Earl Conrad, *Errol Flynn: A Memoir*, Dodd, Mead & Co, Robert Hales.

Considine (1989) Shaun Considine, *Bette and Joan: The Divine Feud*, Century Hutchinson and Time Warner Books.

Cooke (1940) Alistair Cooke, *Douglas Fairbanks: The Making of a Screen Character*, Museum of Modern Art.

Crane (2008) Cheryl Crane with Cindy de la Hoz, *Lana: The Myths, the Movies*, Running Press.

Custen (1997) George F. Custen, *Twentieth Century's Fox: Darryl F. Zanuck and the Culture of Hollywood*, Basic Books.

DeMille (1959) Cecil B. DeMille, Donald Hayne (ed.), *The Autobiography of Cecil B. DeMille*, W. H. Allen.

Dmytryk (1996) Edward Dmytryk, *Odd Man Out: A Memoir of the Hollywood Ten*, Southern Illinois University Press.

Eliot (2008) Marc Eliot, *Reagan: The Hollywood Years*, Harmony Books.

Eyeman (2010) Scott Eyeman, *Empire of Dreams: The Epic Life of Cecil B. DeMille*, Simon &Schuster.

Finler (1988) Joel W. Finler, *The Hollywood Story*, 3rd edition, 2003, Wallflower Press.

Flynn (2006) Rory Flynn, co-edited with William R. Bremer, *The Baron of Mulholland: A Daughter Remembers*, Xlibris Corporation.

Friedland (2009) Michael Freedland, *The Men who Made Hollywood: The Lives of the Great Movie Moguls*, JR Books.

Goldwyn (1923) Samuel Goldwyn, *Behind the Screen*, George H. Doran.

Gomery (2005) Douglas Gomery, *The Hollywood Studio System: A History*, BFI Publishing.

Griffin (2011) Sean Griffin (ed.), *What Dreams Were Made of: Movie Stars of the 1940s*, Rutgers University Press.

Halliwell (2001) Leslie Halliwell, *Halliwell's Who's Who in the Movies*, 14th edition, edited by John Walker, HarperCollins.

Halliwell (2006) Leslie Halliwell, *Film & DVD Guide*, 21st edition, edited by John Walker, HarperCollins.

Hancock and Fairbanks (1953) Ralph Hancock and Letitia Fairbanks Hancock, *Douglas Fairbanks: The Fourth Musketeer*, Henry Holt & Co.; UK edition, Peter Davies.

Hanut (1996) Eryk Hanut, *I Wish You Love: Conversations with Marlene Dietrich*, Frog/Vision.

Higham (1980) Charles Higham, *Errol Flynn: The Untold Story*, Doubleday.

Jewell (2007) Richard B. Jewell, *The Golden Age of Cinema: Hollywood, 1929–1945*, Blackwell.

Johnson (1939) Captain and Mrs Irving Johnson, *Sailing To See: Picture Cruise in the Schooner Yankee*, W.W. Norton.

Kemper (2010) Tom Kemper, *Hidden Talent: The Emergence of Hollywood Agents*, University of California Press.

Kerr (1986) Paul Kerr (ed.), *The Hollywood Film Industry*, Routledge.

Knight (1957) Arthur Knight, *The Liveliest Art: A Panoramic History of the Movies*, Macmillan.

Kobal (1971) John Kobal, *Gotta Sing Gotta Dance*, Hamlyn Publishing Group.

Korda (1985) Michael Korda, *Queenie*, Simon & Schuster.

Korda (1999) Michael Korda, *Another Life; A Memoir of Other People*, Random House.

Lanchester (1938) Elsa Lanchester, *Charles Laughton and I*, Faber and Faber.

Levinson (2009) Peter J. Levinson, *Puttin' On the Ritz: Fred Astaire and the Fine Art of Panache, A Biography*, St Martin's Press.

Lewis (1994) Judy Lewis, *Uncommon Knowledge*, Simon and Schuster.

Lord (2003) Graham Lord, *Niv: The Authorised Biography of David Niven*, Orion.

McNulty (2004) Thomas McNulty, *Errol Flynn: Life and Career*, McFarland and Co.

Mann (2006) William J. Mann, *Kate: The Woman Who Was Hepburn*, Henry Holt & Co.

Marx (1975) Samuel Marx, *Mayer and Thalberg: The Make Believe Saints*, W. H. Allen.

Marx (1986) Arthur Marx, *The Nine Lives of Mickey Rooney*, Robson Books (1987).

Mast (1982) Gerald Mast (ed.), *The Movies in Our Midst: Documents in the Cultural History of Films in America*, University of Chicago Press.

Monush (2003) Barry Monush, *The Encyclopedia of Hollywood Film Actors*, Applause Theatre and Cinema Books.

Munn (1993) Michael Munn, *The Hollywood Connection: The True Story of Organised Crime in Hollywood*, Robson Books.

Munn (2009) Michael Munn, *David Niven: The Man Behind the Balloon*, JR Books.

Norman (1979) Barry Norman, *The Hollywood Greats*, Hodder and Stoughton.

Palmer (2011) R. Barton Palmer (ed.), *Larger Than Life: Movie Stars of the 1950s*, Rutgers University Press.

Peary (1984) Gerald Peary, *Talking with Sterling Hayden*, Webcast.

Raymond (2006) Emilie Raymond, *From my Cold, Dead Hands: Charlton Heston and American Politics*, University Press of Kentucky.

Robinson (2003) Chris J. Robinson, *Don't be Bonin' Me: The Life of Sterling Hayden*, Webcast.

Schatz (1988) Thomas Schatz, *The Genius of the System: Hollywood Filmmaking in the Studio Era*, Henry Holt & Co.

Schickel (1977) Richard Schickel, *The Men Who Made the Movies*, Hamish Hamilton.

Scott Berg (1989) A. Scott Berg, *Goldwyn: A Biography*, Alfred A. Knopf.

Scott (2005) Allen J. Scott, *On Hollywood: The Place, The Industry*, Princeton University Press.

Sedgwick and Pokorny (2005) John Sedgwick and Michael Pokorny (eds), *An Economic History of Film*, Routledge.

Selznick (1972) Rudy Behlmer (ed.), *Memo From David O. Selznick*, Macmillan.

Selznick (1983) Irene Mayer Selznick, *A Private View*, Alfred A. Knopf.

Shindler (1996) Colin Shindler, *Hollywood in Crisis: Cinema and American Society 1929–1939*, Routledge.

Siegel and Siegel (2004) Scott Siegel and Barbara Siegel, *The Encyclopedia of Hollywood*, 2nd edition, Facts on File.

Silver and Ursini (1999) Alain Silver and James Ursini (eds), *Film Noir Reader*, 7th edition, 2003, Limelight Editions.

Silver and Ward (1980) Alain Silver and Elizabeth Ward (eds), *Film Noir: An Encyclopaedic Reference Guide*, Bloomsbury (2nd edition, 1989)

Sklar (1993) Robert Sklar, *Film: An International History of the Medium*, Thames and Hudson.

Slide (1998) Anthony Slide, *The New Historical Dictionary of the American Film Industry*, Fitzroy Dearborn Publishers.

Staiger (1994) Janet Staiger, *The Studio System*, Rutgers University Press.

Stephenson and Debrix (1965) Ralph Stephenson and Jean R. Debrix, *The Cinema as Art*, Penguin Books.

St Johns (1969) Adela Rogers St Johns, *The Honeycomb*, Doubleday & Co.

Swindell (1975) Larry Swindell, *Body and Soul: The Story of John Garfield*, William Morrow.

Taylor (1983) John Russell Taylor, *Strangers in Paradise: The Hollywood Émigrés 1933–1950*, Faber and Faber.

Thomas (1980) Tony Thomas, *From a Life of Adventure: The Writings of Errol Flynn*, Citadel Press.

Thomson (2002) David Thomson, *The New Biographical Dictionary of Film*, Little, Brown (1975)

Valenti (1984) Peter Valenti, *Errol Flynn: A Bio-Bibliography*, Greenwood Press.

Viertel (1969) Salka Viertel, *The Kindness of Strangers*, Holt, Rinehart and Winston.

Vogel (2005) Michelle Vogel, *Gene Tierney: A Biography*, McFarland.

Waller (2011) Walter Waller, *Wild Bill Donovan: The Spymaster Who Created the OSS and Modern American Espionage*, Free Press.

Wallis (1980) Hal B. Wallis and Charles Higham, *Starmaker: The Autobiography of Hal Wallis*, Macmillan.

Walsh (1974) Raoul Walsh, *Each Man in his Own Time: The Life Story of a Director*, Farrar, Straus and Giroux.

Walters (2005) Rob Walters, *Spread Spectrum: Hedy Lamarr and the Mobile Phone*, Booksurge Publishing.

Watson (2001) Coy Watson Jr, *The Keystone Kid: Tales of Early Hollywood*, Santa Monica Press

Weissmuller (2002) Johnny Weissmuller Jr, *Tarzan, My Father*, ECW Press.

West (1997) W. J. West, *The Quest for Graham Greene*, St Martin's Press.

Wood (2002) Ean Wood, *Dietrich: A Biography*, Sanctuary.

Yablonsky (1974) Lewis Yablonsky, *George Raft*, W. H. Allen, 1975.

Zanuck (1993) Rudy Behlmer (ed.), *Memo From Darryl F. Zanuck: The Golden Years at Twentieth Century-Fox*, Grove Press.

Zierold (1969) Norman Zierold, *The Hollywood Tycoons*, Hamish Hamilton.

Zukor (1954) Adolph Zukor with Dale Kramer, *The Public is Never Wrong*, Cassell & Co.

References — Books by Actors

Aherne (1969) Brian Aherne, *A Proper Job*, Houghton Mifflin.

Aherne (1979) Brian Aherne, *A Dreadful Man*, Simon & Schuster.

Allyson (1982) June Allyson with Frances Spatz Leighton, *June Allyson by June Allyson*, G. P. Putnam's Sons.

Arnaz (1976) Desi Arnaz, *A Book*, William Morrow.

Arnold (1940) Edward Arnold with Frances Fisher Dubuc, *Lorenzo Goes to Hollywood*, Liveright.

Astaire (1959) Fred Astaire, *Steps in Time*, Heinemann.

Astor (1971) Mary Astor, *A Life on Film*, Delacorte Press (UK edition, W.H. Allen, 1973).

Autry (1978) Gene Autry and Mickey Herskowitz, *Back in the Saddle Again*, Doubleday.

Bacall (1978) Lauren Bacall, *By Myself*, Knopf.

Bacall (2005) Lauren Bacall, *By Myself and Then Some*, Harper.

Baker (1983) Carroll Baker, *Baby Doll: An Autobiography*, Arbor House.

Ball (1996) Lucille Ball, *Love, Lucy*, G. P. Putnam's Sons.

Bankhead (1952) Tallulah Bankhead, *Tallulah: My Autobiography*, Victor Gollancz.

Barrymore (1926) John Barrymore, *Confessions of an Actor*, Bobbs-Merrill.

Bartok (1959) Eva Bartok, *Worth Living For*, G. P. Putnam's Sons.

Bennett (1970) Joan Bennett and Lois Kibbee, *The Bennett Playbill*, Holt, Rinehart and Winston.

Bergen (1984) Candice Bergen, *Knock Wood*, Hamish Hamilton.

Bergman (1980) Ingrid Bergman and Alan Burgess, *My Story*, Michael Joseph.

Bickford (1965) Charles Bickford, *Bulls, Balls, Bicycles and Actors*, Paul S. Eriksson Inc.

Bikel (1994) Theodore Bikel, *Theo: The Autobiography of Theodore Bikel*, Harper Collins.

Blair (2003) Betsy Blair, *The Memory of All That: Love and Politics in Hollywood and Paris*, Knopf, Revised UK Edition, Elliott & Thompson, 2004.

Blondell (1972) Joan Blondell, *Center Door Fancy: An Autobiography*, Delacorte Press.

Bloom (1982) Claire Bloom, *Limelight and After: The Education of an Actress*, Weidenfeld and Nicolson.

Bloom (1996) Claire Bloom, *Leaving A Dolls House: A Memoir*, Little, Brown & Co.

Borgnine (2008) Ernest Borgnine, *Ernie: the Autobiography*, Citadel Press.

Brando (1994) Marlon Brando with Robert Lindsey, *Songs My Mother Taught Me*, Random House.

Cagney (1976) James Cagney, *Cagney by Cagney*, Doubleday.

Cantarini (2010) Martha Crawford Cantarini and Chrystopher J. Spicer, *Fall Girl: My Life as a Western Stunt Double*, McFarland.

Canutt (1979) Yakima Canutt with Oliver Drake, *Stunt Man: The Autobiography*, Walker Publishing.

Carey (1991) Macdonald Carey, *The Days of My Life*, St Martin's Press.

Carey (1994) Harry Carey, Jr. *Company of Heroes: My Life as an Actor in the John Ford Stock Company*, Scarecrow Press Inc.

Carmichael (1965) Hoagy Carmichael, *Sometimes I Wonder . . .*, Alvin Redman.

Caron (2009) Leslie Caron, *Thank Heaven: Leslie Caron My Autobiography*, JR Books.

Chaplin (1964) *Charles Chaplin, My Autobiography*, Simon and Schuster.

Chevalier (1949) Maurice Chevalier, *The Man in the Straw Hat: My Story*, Crowell.

Chevalier (1960) Maurice Chevalier with Eileen and Robert Pollock, *With Love*, Little, Brown.

Chevalier (1970) Maurice Chevalier, *I Remember it Well*, Macmillan.

Christian (1962) Linda Christian, *Linda My Own Story*, Crown Publishers.

Clooney (1978) Rosemary Clooney, *This For Remembrance: The Autobiography of Rosemary Clooney, An Irish American Singer*, Robson Books.

Cotten (1987) Joseph Cotten, *Vanity Will Get You Somewhere*, Mercury House.

Crawford (1962) Joan Crawford with Jane Kesner Ardmore, *A Portrait of Joan: The Autobiography of Joan Crawford*, Frederick Muller, (1963).

Crawford (1971) Joan Crawford, *My Way of Life*, Simon &Schuster.

Crosby (1953) Bing Crosby as told to Pete Martin, *Call Me Lucky*, Simon & Schuster; new editions Da Capo Press 1993 and 2001.

Curtis (1993) Tony Curtis and Barry Paris, *Tony Curtis: The Autobiography*, William Morrow.

Curtis (2008) Tony Curtis, *American Prince: My Autobiography*, with Peter Golenbock, Virgin Books.

Curtis (2009) Tony Curtis with Mark A. Vieira, *Some Like It Hot: Me, Marilyn and the Movie*, Virgin Books.

Dandridge (1970) Dorothy Dandridge with Earl Conrad, *Everything and Nothing: The Dorothy Dandridge Story*, Abelard-Schuman.

Davis (1962) Bette Davis, *The Lonely Life: An Autobiography*, G. P. Putnam's Sons (UK edition, Macdonald, 1963).

Davis (1974) Bette Davis with Whitney Stine, *Mother Goddam: The Story of the Career of Bette Davis*, Berkley Books.

Davis (1987) Bette Davis with Michael Herskowitz, *This 'N That: A Memoir*, G. P. Putnam's Sons.

Davis (1965) Sammy Davis Jr and Jane and Burt Boyar, *Yes I Can*, Cassell & Co.

Davis (1980) Sammy Davis Jr, *Hollywood in a Suitcase*, William Morrow & Co.

Davis (1989) Sammy Davis Jr, *Why Me*, Warner Books.

Day (1952) Laraine Day, *Day with the Giants*, Doubleday.

Day (1975) Doris Day and A. E. Hotchner, *Doris Day, Her Own Story*, William Morrow & Co.

De Carlo (1971) Yvonne De Carlo with Doug Warren, *Yvonne: An Autobiography*, St Martin's Press.

De Havilland (1962) Olivia de Havilland, *Every Frenchman Has One*, Random House (UK edition, Elek Books, 1963).

Dietrich (1987) Marlene Dietrich, *My Life*, Ullstein Verlag, (English translation, Weidenfeld & Nicolson 1989).

Douglas (1986) Melvyn Douglas and Tom Arthur, *The Autobiography of Melvyn Douglas*, University Press of America.

Douglas (1988) Kirk Douglas, *The Ragman's Son: An Autobiography*, Simon & Schuster.

Douglas (1997) Kirk Douglas, *Climbing the Mountain: My Search for Meaning*, Simon& Schuster.

Douglas (2007) Kirk Douglas, *Let's Face It: 90 Years of Living, Loving and Learning*, John Wiley & Sons.

Fairbanks (1988) Douglas Fairbanks Jr, *The Salad Days*, Collins.

Fairbanks (1993) Douglas Fairbanks Jr, *A Hell of a War*, Robson Books.

Falk (2006) Peter Falk, *Just One More Thing: Stories from My Life*, Random House.

Farmer (1972) Frances Farmer, *Will There Really be a Morning?*, UK edition, Allison & Busby, 1974.

Flynn (1937) Errol Flynn, *Beam Ends*, Longmans, Buccaneer Books, 2002

Flynn (1946) Errol Flynn, *Showdown*, Sheridan House.

Flynn (1959) Errol Flynn, *My Wicked, Wicked Ways*, G. P. Putnam's Sons.

Fonda (1981) Henry Fonda, *My Life as Told to Howard Teichmann*, New American Library (UK edition, W. H. Allen, 1982).

Fontaine (1978) Joan Fontaine, *No Bed of Roses*, William Morrow.

Gabor (1960) Zsa Zsa Gabor, *My Story Written for me by Gerold Frank*, World Publishing Company.

Gabor (1991) Zsa Zsa Gabor, assisted by Wendy Leigh, *One Lifetime is Not Enough*, Headline Book Publishing.

Gardner (1990) Ava Gardner, *Ava: My Story*, Bantam Press.

Gargan (1969) William Gargan, *Why Me? An Autobiography*, Doubleday.

Garrett (1998) Betty Garrett with Ron Rapoport, *Betty Garrett and Other Songs: A Life on Stage and Screen*, Madison Books.

Gazzara (2004) Ben Gazzara, *In the Moment: My Life as an Actor*, Carroll & Graf.

Granger (2007) Farley Granger with Robert Calhoun, *Include Me Out: My Life from Goldwyn to Broadway*, St Martin's Press.

Havoc (1959) June Havoc, *Early Havoc*, Simon & Schuster.

Havoc (1980) June Havoc, *More Havoc*, Harper & Row.

Hayden (1963) Sterling Hayden, *Wanderer*, Alfred A. Knopf (paperback edition, Sheridan House, 1998, with Introduction by author).

Hayden (1976) Sterling Hayden, *Voyage: A Novel of 1896*, G. P. Putnam's Sons.

Henreid (1984) Paul Henreid with Julian Fast, *Ladies Man: An Autobiography*, St Martin's Press.

Hepburn (1987) Katharine Hepburn, *The Making of the African Queen or How I went to Africa with Bogart, Bacall and Huston and Almost Lost My Mind*, Knopf.

Hepburn (1991) Katharine Hepburn, *Me: Stories of My Life*, Knopf (UK edition, Viking).

Heston (1976) Charlton Heston, *The Actor's Life: Journals 1956–1976*, Dutton (UK edition, Allen Lane, Penguin Books 1980).

Heston (1995) Charlton Heston, *In the Arena: An Autobiography*, Simon and Schuster.

Heston (1997) Charlton Heston, *To Be a Man: Letters to my Grandson*, Simon & Schuster.

Heston (2000) Charlton Heston, *The Courage to Be Free*, Saudade.

Hope (1990) Bob Hope with Melville Shavelson, *Don't Shoot, It's Only Me*, G. P. Putnam's Sons (UK edition, Macmillan).

Horne (1965) Lena Horne and Richard Schickel, *Lena*, Doubleday & Company.

Hudson (1986) Rock Hudson and Sara Davidson, *Rock Hudson: His Story*, Weidenfeld & Nicolson.

Hunter (2005) Tab Hunter with Eddie Muller, *Confidential: The Making of a Movie Star*, Algonquin Books.

Huston (1980) John Huston, *An Open Book*, Macmillan.

Ives (1952) Burl Ives, *Wayfaring Stranger*, T.V. Boardman and Company.

Keel (2005) Howard Keel with Joyce Spizer, *Only Make Believe: My Life in Show Business*, Barricade Books.

Keyes (1971) Evelyn Keyes, *I Am A Billboard* (novel), Lyle Stuart.

Keyes (1977) Evelyn Keyes, *Scarlett O'Hara's Younger Sister: My Lively Life in and Out of Hollywood*, W. H. Allen, 1978.

Keyes (1991) Evelyn Keyes, *I'll Think About That Tomorrow*, Dutton.

Knef (1971) Hildegard Knef, *The Gift Horse*, Verlag Fritz Molden (UK edition, André Deutsch).

Knef (1975) Hildegard Knef, *The Verdict*, Farrar, Straus & Giroux.

Lake (1971) Veronica Lake, with Donald Bain, *Veronica*, Citadel Press.

Lamarr (1966) Hedy Lamarr, *Ecstasy and Me*, W. H. Allen, 1967.

Lamour (1980) Dorothy Lamour as told to Dick McInnes, *My Side of the Road*, Prentice-Hall (UK edition, Robson Books, 1981).

Lanchester (1938) Elsa Lanchester, *Charles Laughton and I*, Faber and Faber.

Lee (1989) Peggy Lee, *Miss Peggy Lee*, Bloomsbury Publishing (1990).

Leigh (1984) Janet Leigh, *There Really Was a Hollywood*, Doubleday.

Levant (1944) Oscar Levant, *A Smattering of Ignorance*, Doubleday.

Levant (1965) Oscar Levant, *The Memoirs of an Amnesiac*, G. P. Putnam's Sons.

Lindfors (1981) Viveca Lindfors, *Viveka...Viveca*, Everest House.

Loder (1977) John Loder, *Hollywood Hussar*, Howard Baker Press.

Loy (1987) Myrna Loy and James Kotsilibas-Davis, *Myrna Loy: Being and Becoming*, Bloomsbury Publishing.

McCambridge (1981) Mercedes McCambridge, *The Quality of Mercy: An Autobiography by Mercedes McCambridge*, Times Books.

McCambridge (1960) Mercedes McCambridge, *The Two of Us*, Peter Davies

MacLaine (1991) Shirley MacLaine, *Dance While You Can*, Bantam Books.

MacLaine (1995) Shirley MacLaine, *My Lucky Stars: A Hollywood Memoir*, Bantam Books.

Malden (1997) Karl Malden with Carla Malden, *When do I Start?: A Memoir*, Simon & Schuster.

Martin & Charisse (1976) Tony Martin and Cyd Charisse, as told to Dick Kleiner, *The Two of Us*, Mason/Charter.

Massey (1976) Raymond Massey, *When I was Young*, Little, Brown & Co.

Massey (1979) Raymond Massey, *A Hundred Different Lives: An Autobiography*, McClelland and Stewart.

Mayo (2001) Virginia Mayo as told to L. C. Van Savage, *The Best Years of My Life*, BeachHouse Books.

Menjou (1948) Adolphe Menjou and M. M. Musselman, *It Took Nine Tailors*, McGraw-Hill.

Merman (1955) Ethel Merman, *Don't Call Me Madam*, W. H. Allen.

Merrill (1988) Gary Merrill and John Cole, *Bette, Rita, and the Rest of My Life*, Lance Tapley.

Milland (1974) Ray Milland, *Wide-Eyed in Babylon: An Autobiography*, William Morrow.

Miller (1972) Ann Miller with Norma Lee Browning, *Miller's High Life*, Doubleday.

Montalban (1980) Ricardo Montalban with Bob Thomas, *Reflections: A Life in Two Worlds*, Doubleday.

Murphy (1970) George Murphy with Victor Lasky, *Say . . . Didn't You Used to be George Murphy?*, Bartholomew House.

Neal (1988) Patricia Neal with Richard Deneut, *As I Am, An Autobiography*, Century, Arrow edition, 1989.

Niven (1971) David Niven, *The Moon's a Balloon: Reminiscences*, Hamish Hamilton.

Niven (1975) David Niven, *Bring On the Empty Horses*, G. P. Putnam's Sons, Coronet 1976.

Niven (1981) David Niven, *Go Slowly, Come Back Quickly*, Hamish Hamiton.

O'Brien (1964) Pat O'Brien, *The Wind At My Back: The Life and Times of Pat O'Brien by Himself*, Doubleday.

O'Hara (2004) Maureen O'Hara with John Nicoletti, *'Tis Herself: A Memoir*, Simon & Schuster.

Palmer (1975) Lilli Palmer, *Change Lobsters –and Dance: An autobiography*, Macmillan.

Parrish (1976) Robert Parrish, *Growing Up in Hollywood*, The Bodley Head.

Picerni (2007) Paul Picerni with Tom Weaver, *Steps to Stardom: My Story*, Bear Manor Media.

Pickford (1956) Mary Pickford, *Sunshine and Shadow*, William Heinemann.

Poitier (1980) Sidney Poitier, *This Life*, Alfred A. Knopf, Inc.

Poitier (2000) Sidney Poitier, *The Measure of a Man: A Memoir*, Simon & Schuster.

Poitier (2008) Sidney Poitier, *Life Beyond Measure: Letters to My Great Granddaughter*, Simon & Schuster.

Powell (1988) Jane Powell, *The Girl Next Door and How She Grew*, William Morrow.

Price (1959) Vincent Price, *I Like What I know*, Doubleday.

Quinn (1972) Anthony Quinn, *The Original Sin: A Self-Portrait by Anthony Quinn*, Little, Brown

Quinn (1995) Anthony Quinn with Daniel Paisner, *One Man Tango: An Autobiography*, Hodder Headline.

Rathbone (1962) Basil Rathbone, *In and Out of Character*, Doubleday.

Reagan (1965) Ronald Reagan with Richard G. Hubler, *My Early Life or Where's the Rest of Me?*, Meredith Press (UK edition, Sidgwick and Jackson, 1981).

Reagan (1990) Ronald Reagan, *An American Life*, Simon and Schuster.

Reynolds (1988) Debbie Reynolds with David Patrick Columbia, *Debbie: My Life*, William Morrow.

Robinson (1973) Edward G. Robinson with Leonard Spigelgass, *All My Yesterdays: An Autobiography*, W. H. Allen, 1974.

Rogers (1991) Ginger Rogers, *Ginger: My Story*, Headline.

Rogers (1994) Roy Rogers and Dale Evans with Jane and

Michael Stern, *Happy Trails: Our Life Story*, Simon and Schuster.

Rooney (1965) Mickey Rooney, *I.E. An Autobiography*, G. P. Putnam's Sons.

Rooney (1991) Mickey Rooney, *Life is Too Short*, Random House.

Rooney (1994) Mickey Rooney, *The Search for Sonny Skies: A Novel*, Birch Lane Press.

Russell (1985) Jane Russell, *An Autobiography*, J & J Peoples, Inc. (UK edition, Sidgwick & Jackson, 1986).

Sakall (1954) S. Z. Sakall, *The Story of Cuddles: My Life Under The Emperor Francis Joseph, Adolf Hitler and the Warner Brothers*, translated by Paul Tabori, Cassell & Co. Ltd.

Sanders (1960) George Sanders, *Memoirs of a Professional Cad*, G. P. Putnam's Sons.

Stack (1980) Robert Stack with Mark Evans, *Straight Shooting*, Macmillan.

Strode (1990) Woody Strode and Sam Young, *Goal Dust: An Autobiography*, Madison Books.

Swanson (1980) Gloria Swanson, *Swanson on Swanson*, Michel Joseph, 1981.

Temple (1988) Shirley Temple Black, *Child Star: An Autobiography*, McGraw-Hill.

Tierney (1978) Gene Tierney with Mickey Herkowitz, *Self-Portrait*, Wyden Books.

Torme (1988) Mel Torme, *Mel Torme, An Autobiography: It Wasn't All Velvet*, Penguin Viking.

Turner (1982) Lana Turner, *Lana: The Lady, The Legend, The Truth*, E. P. Dutton (UK edition, New English Library, 1983).

Ustinov (1977) Peter Ustinov, *Dear Me*, William Heinemann.

Vaughn (1972) Robert Vaughn, *Only Victims: A Study of Show Business Blacklisting*, Limelight Editions.

Vaughn (2008) Robert Vaughn, *A Fortunate Life*, St Martin's Press.

Wagner (2008) Robert J. Wagner with Scott Eyman, *Pieces of My Heart*, William Morrow.

Wallach (2005) Eli Wallach, *The Good, the Bad and Me: In My Anecdotage*, Harcourt.

Watson (2001) Coy Watson Jr., *The Keystone Kid: Tales of Early Hollywood*, Santa Monica Press.

Weissmuller (1930) Johnny Weissmuller in collaboration with Clarence A. Bush, *Swimming the American Crawl*, Putnam & Co.

Wilcoxon (1991) Henry Wilcoxon with Katherine Orrison, *Lionheart in Hollywood: Life and Times with Cecil B. DeMille*, The Scarecrow Press Inc.

Wiles (1988) Buster Wiles with William Donati, *My Days With Errol Flynn: The Autobiography of a Stuntman*, Roundtable Publishing, Inc.

Williams (1999) Esther Williams, *Million Dollar Mermaid*, Simon & Schuster.

Winters (1980) Shelley Winters, *Shelley: Also known as Shirley*, William Morrow (UK edition, Granada Publishing, 1981).

Winters (1989) Shelley Winters, *Shelley II: The Middle of My Century*, Simon and Schuster.

Young (1961) Loretta Young and Helen Ferguson, *The Things I Had to Learn*, Bobbs-Merrill (UK edition, The World's Work 1913 Ltd, 1962).

Index

A

A&B pictures	14, 2,184
Academy of Motion Picture Arts and sciences	214
Acknowledgements	285
Acting	108-111
-Actors Studio	110n, 218n
-see also The Method	
Aadland, Beverly	138
Adventures of Robin Hood, The	125
Aherne, Brian	33, 68, 78, 80, 88-90, 99, 167
Allyson, June	104
An American in Paris	193, 194
Andrews, Dana	122, 144, 148
Anti-trust	278-9
Arnaz, Desi	205
-see also Ball, Lucille	
Arnold, Edward	35
Ashphalt Jungle, The	256-8, 264

Astaire, Fred	53-4, 195, 197-200
Astor, Mary	34-5, 232, 237
Autobiographies	xvi-xxii
-the best	284
Auteur theory	13
Autry, Gene	192-3

B

Baby Doll	165
Bacall, Lauren	224n
Baker, Carroll	165-8
Ball, Lucille	29, 107
-autobiography	205-6
Bankhead, Tallulah	34-5
Barker, Lex	163-4, 268n
Barrymore, John (Jack)	
-autobiography	34
-mythical joke about his corpse	68-9
Bartok, Eva	xii, 66n
Ben Hur	176n, 251
Bennett, Joan	22n, 184, 188-9
Bergman, Ingrid	77, 90-1
Big Country, The	165
Bikel, Theodore	235n
Birth of a Nation	17
black list, the	228-230
Blair, Betsy	104, 207
-Autobiography	194
Blue Angel, The	94-6
Bloom, Claire	38n
Bogart, Humphrey	xxi, 76n, 78, 82, 108, 113, 153, 223

Box Office Poison	96-7n
Brando, Marlon	108, 109-10
-inventions	159n
Brecht, Bertolt	223n
Brit, May	209
British actors in Hollywood	77-81, 84-86
Brook, Clive	79

C

Cagney, James	110, 115-6, 179
Cantarini, Martha	180
Canutt, Yakima	107, 134, 180
Capra, Frank	25
Carey, Harry Jr	181-2
Carey, Harry Sr	181n
Carey, Macdonald	66n
Caron, Leslie	
-autobiography	193
Carpetbaggers, The	166
Captain's Paradise, The	171
Carroll, Madeleine	79, 262-4
Casablanca	76-7, 243
Casini, Oleg	58, 151-2
Central Casting nationalities	84
Chaplin, Charles	24, 32, 77, 223n
-autobiography	36-8, 71, 78, 196
Charisse, Cyd	194, 199
Chase, Barrie	200n
Chevalier, Maurice	195-6
Children of the stars	45-6, 143, 175n, 178, 196, 268
Christian, Linda	128-9, 163

Citizen Kane	22n, 86
Clooney, George	195, 206n, 275
Cohn, Harry	24-7, 109n
Colman, Ronald	53, 77
Columbia	10, 24-7, 187, 214
Collins, Joan	226
Committee for the First Amendment	220-222
communist scare	
-see House Committee on UnAmerican Activities (HUAC)	
Conference of Studio Unions (CSU)	215, 245
Cooper, Gary	29, 161, 178, 263
Cotten, Joseph	283
Crain, Jeanne	149
Crawford-Davis rivalry	101
Crawford, Joan	44-7, 102, 149, 191n
Crosby, Bing	46, 196-7
Cummings, Robert	242
Curtis, Tony	107, 117-8, 142
Curtiz, Michael	76, 136-7

D

Dahl, Arlene	163-4
Dandridge, Dorothy	121, 204, 209
DaSilva, Howard	228
Davis, Bette	45, 105, 113-4, 135
see also Crawford-Davis rivalry	
Davies, Marion	17, 86
Davis, Sammy Jr	208-9
Day, Doris	109, 120-1
DeCarlo, Yvonne	169-171
DeHavilland, Olivia	112, 116n, 134, 245

Decks Ran Red, The	204
Cecil B DeMille.	3-8, 182n
DeMille, William	4
demographic change	277
Denver and Rio Grande	260
Denny, Reginald	84
Depression, inter-war	214
Destry Rides Again	97
Dietrich, Marlene	90-100
-autobiography	99-100,
Disney Company, Walt	276
Doctor Strangelov	255, 256, 258-9
Donat, Robert	133
Donovan, 'Wild Bill'	264n
Douglas, Kirk	118, 121, 174-8, 185, 231-2
Douglas, Melvin	45n
Downey, Robert	36
Dymtryk, Edward	223n, 225n

E

economics of film-making	xvii-xix, 9, 10, 14-15
Ecstasy	154-5
Edendale	7
Edison Trust, The	1-2, 3n

F

Fairbanks, Douglas Jr	ix, 41-44, 56
Fairbanks, Douglas Sr	39-40, 41, 214n
Farmer, Francis	168n
Feldman, Charlie	117, 118

Film Noir	22n, 183-9
Flying Down to Rio	21
Flynn, Errol	125-144, 241-2
-and David Niven	55
-and Olivia DeHavilland	116
-autobiography	141-2
-boxing	131-2
-directors of	135-6
-drinking and drugs	130-1
-novels	138-40
-rape case	127-8
-wives	127-30
Fonda, Henry	67, 213, 231
Fonda, Jane	213n
Ford, John (Jack)	181-2, 208
Four Star Television	59
Fox, William	2, 19
Freed, Arthur	104n

G

Gable, Clark	53, 121-2, 180, 284
Gabor, Zsa Zsa	88n
Gardner, Ava	122, 201, 208, 249n
Garfield, John	110n, 230n
Garbo, Greta	90, 92-3
Garden of Allah, The	96
Gargan, William	173n
Garland, Judy	161
Garrett, Betty	117, 217, 229
Gentleman Jim	135-6
Giant	165, 167

Gilbert, John	33
Goddard, Paulette	38
Goldwyn, Samuel (Goldfish)	4, 15, 28-30, 109n, 230
-and United Artists	24
-autobiography	30
-and Bernard Shaw	29
Gone With the Wind (GWTW)	14, 187
Grable, Betty	92, 93
Granger, Farley	109n
Greene, Graham	90, 202
Griffith, D.W.	4, 37
Gwenn, Edmund	74n

H

Harlow, Jean	122n
Hasty Heart, The	243
Hayden, Sterling	79n, 170, 196, 217, 228, 255-273
-and HUAC	220, 228, 269-70
Hellman, Lillian	216, 228
Hemingway, Ernest	136n
Henreid, Paul	68-78, 81-83, 224
-autobiography	83
Hepburn, Katharine	61-66
-autobiography	63
-and Spencer Tracy	64-5
Heston, Charlton	61, 67, 110, 233, 248-53
-on HUAC	229
-on Westerns	179
Hitchcock, Alfred	13n, 75n, 110

Hollywood, history of	1-47
-New Hollywood	279-80
-Hollywood Sign	280-1
Hollywood Independent Citizens' Committee of the Arts, Sciences and Professions (HICCASP)	244-5
Hollywood Ten, The	222, 223n, 225
Hope, Bob	284
Hopkins, Anthony	x-xi
Horne, Lena	209-10
House UnAmerican Activities Committee (HUAC)	64n, 217 et seq, 275, 277
Howard, Leslie	77, 80n
Hudson, Rock	64, 66, 105-7, 108-9
Hughes, Howard	22, 62, 65, 149, 151, 170
Hunter, Tab	109n
Huston, John	131-2, 186

I

International Alliance of Theatrical Stage Employees (IATSE)	215
In the Heat of the Night	210
Ives, Burl	197

J

Jannings, Emil	33, 95n
The Jazz Singer	191
Johnny Guitar	67n, 259
Johnny O'Clock	186
Johnson, Van	xi
Judgement at Nuremberg	97

◂ 320

K

Kazan, Elia	218, 228, 230n
Keel, Howard	195n
Kelly, Gene	112, 194, 199
Kennedy, J.P.	11
Keyes, Evelyn	58n, 186-7, 224
-autobiographies	186
-on Errol Flynn	127
The Killing	256, 258
Kings Row	241-2
Kitty Foyle	198
Kneff, Hildegard	92
Korda, Alexander	81
Korda, Michael	46, 55n
Kubrick, Stanley	258-9

L

Ladd, Alan	75n, 186
Lake, Veronica	103, 185-6
Laemmle, Carl	2, 8
Lamar, Hedy	154-9
-autobiography	155-7
-inventions	xix, 158-9
-on Errol Flynn	127
Lamour, Dorothy	197
Lanchester, Elsa	77n
Lasky, Jesse	4, 18, 19
Laughton, Charles	77
Laura	147-8, 187
Lawrence T.E.	100n

Lawson, John Howard	218, 225
Leave Her to Heaven	147, 148-9
Leigh, Janet	107-8
-on Errol Flynn	127
Lesser, Sol	268n
Levant, Oscar	88n, 121n
Lillies of the Field	210
Lindfors, Viveca	90n
Little Red School House	161
Loder, John	84-5, 154n
Loew, Marcus	15n
Lorre, Peter	77, 83
Los Angeles	2, 3
Love Finds Andy Hardy	161
Loy, Myrna	116
Lupino, Ida	79n

M

MacLaine, Shirley	201
Malden, Karl	181n
Murphy, George	161, 233-8
Martin, Tony	195
Massey, Raymond	57, 85
Matter of Life and Death, A	57
Mature, Victor	158n
Mayer, Louis B.	12, 15-18, 71, 102, 104, 122n, 154
-resignation from MGM	18
Mayo, Virginia	xix, 122-3
McCambridge, Mercedes	66-7
McLintock!	171
Meighan, Tommy	33

Méliès, Georges	9
Menjou, Adolphe	33, 35-6
Merrill, Gary	114n
Method, The	109-10
-see also, acting	
MGM	9, 10, 13, 15, 210, 214, 237, 275, 280
Milland, Ray	79
Miller, Ann	ix, 199, 200-1
Mitchum, Robert	xxii, 166
Moguls, the	6, 12-13, 71-2, 101-4, 217n, 281-2
Motion Picture Patents Company (MPPC)	
-see also, Edison Trust	
Monroe, Marilyn	62, 118, 145, 229
Montalban, Ricardo	206-7
Morley, Sheridon	83n
Motion Picture Alliance (MPA)	244
movies as an art	109n
Musicals	191-203
-definition of,	191n
Music Corporation of America (MCA)	241n
National Rifle Association	67, 252-3
Night of the 200 Stars	viii-xiii
Nickelodeons	2
Niven, David,	49-61
-autobiography	49-50, 60-1, 67n
-on Errol Flynn	127
-on Lana Turner	161n
Noir, see film noir	
Novak, Kim	208-9
Novarro, Ramon	176n

O

Oberon, Merle	51, 54-5
O'Brien, Pat	102-3, 241
Ocean's 11	208n
O'Connor, Donald	112, 200
Odets, Clifford	218
O'Hara, Maureen	
-autobiography	81.182n
-on John Ford	182
On the Town	ix, 193
Outlaw, The	22
On the Waterfront	218n
Office of Strategic Services (OSS)	264

P

PACs	252n
Palmer, Lilli	92
Paramount Studios	8, 10, 11, 18, 214
Parks, Larry	228, 229
Parrish, Robert	xxi, 7
Pascall, Gabriel	167n
Pathé	1, 25, 33, 35, 45
Peyton Place	162
Pickford, Mary	32, 37, 40-1
-autobiography	41
Pillow Talk	109
Poitier, Sidney	210-11
Powell, Dick	59n, 186
-see also, Four Star Television	
Powell. Eleanor	201

◄ 324

Powell, Jane	200
Power, Tyrone	163, 183
Preminger, Otto	148, 149n
Previews	xviii-xix
Price, Vincent	148n

Q

Quinn, Anthony	xx, ix, 4, 126, 172-176, 178, 206, 207n
-autobiographies	177

R

Raft, George	76n, 113, 207n
Rathbone, Basil	84, 126, 134
Rat Pack, The	208n
Reagan, Ronald	67, 233-4, 23, 239-248
-and Westerns	244
-autobiographies	247, 244, 280-1
-HUAC	221-2
Red River	181
References-Books by Actors	297-312
References-General	287-295
Republic Studios	27, 260
Reynolds, Debbie	111-12
RKO (Radio-Keith-Orpheum Pictures)	10, 21-2, 214
Robinson, Edward, G.	110, 188, 222-7
Rogers, Ginger	ix, x, 21-2, 112
-autobiography	197-8
Rogers, Roy	192-3
Rogers St Johns, Adela	2-3, 216n
Romero, Cesar	58n, 208n

Rooney, Mickey	108, 161, 202-4
Russell, Gail	186
Russell, Jane	22

S

Sakall, S.Z.	77n, 78
Salome, Where She Danced	169
Samson and Delilah	158
Sanders, George	67, 86 et seq, 120
Santa Fe Trail	241
Schary, Dore	18, 230
Schell, Maria	82-3
Schell, Maximilian	83n, 98
Schenck, Joseph	19, 24
Schenck, Nicholas	18, 19, 112
Schwarzenegger, Arnold	213n
Scott, Lizabeth	vii-xii, 250n, 184
Screen Actors Guild (SAG)	64n, 215, 231, 237, 252
-and Charlton Heston	247
-and Ronald Reagan	243
Screenwriters, see writers, screen	
Screen Writers Guild (SWG)	215, 232
Selig, William	8n
Selznick, David O.	12, 17n, 92, 110-1, 132
-his brother, Myron	117
Sennett, Max	37, 197
Shaw, Artie	163
Sheffield, Johnny	xn
silent films	32-3
Sinatra, Frank	206n, 250n
Singin' in the Rain	194

Smith, C. Aubrey	85-6
Spartacus	208
Squaw Man, The	4, 6
Stanlislavski, Constantin	109-10n, 218
star-contracts	104-5
star-military service	243
star-popularity	161n
star-rivalries	101-2
Sternberg, Joseph von	94-6
Stompanato, Johnny, see Turner, Lana	
Strasberg, Lee	82, 109-10, 218n
Strode, Woody	178, 207-8
stuntmen and women	68, 108, 179-180
Suddenly	259
Swanson, Gloria	201
Sweet Charity (1968)	199

T

Talent agencies	117-120
Tarzan films	x, 163, 268n
Temple, Shirley	201-2
Ten Commandments, The	4, 250
Thalberg, Irvine	12, 53
Thomas, Parnell	225, 227
Tierney, Gene	63, 66n, 146-154, 156n
-autobiography	152-3
-mental problems	152-4
Tormé, Mel	195
Tracy, Spencer	62-3n, 65
Trubshaw, Michael	52-3
Trumbo, Dalton	225, 227, 231-2

Turner, Lana	160-5
-discovery of,	61
-marriages	163-4
-Stompanato relationship	164
Twentieth Century Fox, see Zanuck, Darryl	

U

Unions in Hollywood	214 et seq
United Artists	23-4, 37, 111n
Universal Studios	2, 10, 22-3
Ustinov, Peter	56n, 170

V

Valentino, Rudolph	176n
Vaughn, Robert	231, 284
Veidt, Conrad	73n

W

Wagner, Robert	ix, 108, 121, 173n, 284
Waldorf Declaration	230
Wallich, Eli	206n
Wallis, Hal	250
Walsh, Raoul	19, 68n, 108-9
Warner Brothers	10, 19, 21
Warner, Jack---	21, 113-6, 133
Wasserman, Lew	117-8, 119, 120, 241n, 24
Wayne, John	108, 171, 182
Webb, Clifton	148, 187-8
Webb, Jack	107

Wee Willie Winkie	202
Weissmuller, Johnny	xv, 268n
Westerns	178-183
-singing	192-3
Wilcoxon, Henry	7, 182n
Wilder, Billy	118
Wilde, Cornel	149n, 250n
Wiles, Buster	68
Williams, Esther	119n
Winters, Shelley	186n
Witness for the Prosecution	97
women writers	216
Wood, Natalie	173
Words and Music	201
Writers, screen	216
-see also, women writers	
Wyler, William	251
Wyman, Jane	67. 242, 244

XYZ

Young, Loretta	19, 53, 122n
Zanuck, Darryl F.	19, 147, 148, 150, 282
Ziegfeld Girl	162
Zorba the Greek	ix, 175
Zukor, Adolphe	11, 18, 19, 40

CPSIA information can be obtained at www.ICGtesting.com
Printed in the USA
BVOW011147110512

290011BV00005B/7/P